Teaching Social Studies in Elementary Schools
A Social Constructivist Approach

Susan E. Gibson

University of Alberta

NELSON / EDUCATION

NELSON / EDUCATION

Teaching Social Studies in Elementary Schools:
A Social Constructivist Approach

by Susan E. Gibson

Associate Vice President, Editorial Director:
Evelyn Veitch

Editor-in-Chief, Higher Education:
Anne Williams

Executive Editor:
Cara Yarzab

Senior Marketing Manager:
Dave Ward

Developmental Editor:
Sandy Matos

Photo Researcher and Permissions Coordinator:
Sandra Mark

Content Production Manager:
Sabrina Mansour

Senior Content Production Manager:
Natalia Denesiuk Harris

Production Service:
ICC Macmillan Inc.

Copy Editors:
Erin Moore
Tara Tovell

Proofreader:
Tami Taliaferro

Indexer:
Dave Luljak

Manufacturing Coordinator:
Loretta Lee

Design Director:
Ken Phipps

Managing Designer:
Katherine Strain

Interior Design:
Peter Papayanakis

Cover Design:
Jarrell Breckon
Ken Phipps

Cover Images:
Boy reading: WizData, inc./
Shutterstock
Child and teacher: © iStockphoto
.com/marmion
Children walking: Jose Fuente/
Shutterstock
Boy drawing: Dragan Trifunovic/
Shutterstock
Tibetan child: Elena Yakusheva/
Shutterstock

Compositor:
ICC Macmillan Inc.

Printer:
Webcom

Library and Archives Canada Cataloguing in Publication Data

Gibson, Susan Elaine, 1953–
   Teaching social studies in elementary schools : a social constructivist approach / Susan E. Gibson.

Includes bibliographical references and index.
ISBN 978-0-17-610438-2

   1. Social sciences—Study and teaching (Elementary).
2. Constructivism (Education).
I. Title.

LB1584.G43 2009   372.83′044
C2007-907012-4

ISBN-13: 978-0-17-610438-2
ISBN-10: 0-17-610438-0

Thank you to my family, my husband Patrick and my daughter Holly for their unfailing patience and support and to my teacher daughter, Amber, for her enthusiasm and her creative ideas.

BRIEF CONTENTS

CONTENTS

PART TWO: HOW DO YOU SELECT AND ORGANIZE THE CONTENT OF YOUR SOCIAL STUDIES PROGRAM?   78

PART THREE: HOW DO YOU LOCATE AND SELECT RESOURCES TO ASSIST IN TEACHING SOCIAL STUDIES CONTENT? 134

CHAPTER 7   What Factors Might Influence Your Selection of Resources for Your Social Studies Program? 137

CHAPTER 8   Why Use Children's Literature in Social Studies? 157

CHAPTER 9   How Can Electronic Resources Be Used for Information Gathering in Social Studies?   173

PART FOUR: WHAT ACTIVITIES WOULD HELP YOU TO MEET THE GOALS OF YOUR SOCIAL STUDIES PROGRAM?   194

CHAPTER 10   What Approach to Teaching Would Best Meet Your Goals for Your Social Studies Program?   197

CHAPTER 11   How Can Learning Activities Help You to Meet Your Goals for Your Social Studies Program?   218

CHAPTER 12   How Can Online Learning Activities Be Used to Develop Students' Higher-Level Skills in Your Social Studies Program?   238

PREFACE

Mapping the Planning Journey

A glance into Mr. Wilson's Grade 2 classroom in Manitoba shows the children seated on the floor in front of a large screen engaging in a discussion using videoconferencing with a marine biologist from Vancouver about the endangerment of Canadian polar bears due to the melting of the ice cap from global warming. While engaging in research on communities in Canada's Arctic, the children had come across information on the problems that polar bears are encountering and they wanted to talk to someone who could help them to understand the problem as well as look for ways to help to address it. Mr. Wilson had arranged the videoconference with an expert from the University of British Columbia.

The children you will be engaging with as social studies teachers face a very different future than the one you are experiencing as an adult. John Bransford, Ann Brown, and Rodney Cocking of the National Research Council claim in their book, *How People Learn* (2000), that the work of the future will be increasingly challenging and will require important skills such as the ability to frame problems; to find, integrate, and synthesize information; to create new solutions; to work cooperatively with others; and to learn on one's own. They state, "If teachers are to prepare an ever more diverse group of students for much more challenging work, they [the teachers] will need substantially more knowledge and radically different skills than most now have and most schools of education now develop" (p. 136). One aspect of this important new knowledge that you will need as a beginning Canadian teacher is an understanding of what is now known about how children learn based on the latest brain research. A second aspect of the new knowledge that you will need is an understanding of how that knowledge about children's learning applies in the classroom.

The latest brain research tells us a great deal about how the brain functions and points to constructivism as a theory about learning that stresses the important role of learners in making their own meaning through active engagement with others; much like the children in Mr. Wilson's class are doing. Constructivism has recently become the philosophical foundation upon which social studies curricula across Canada has been built as well as becoming a more common place term in Canadian teacher preparation programs. Unfortunately, a comment that I frequently hear from teacher candidates is that they are lectured to a lot about constructivism in their teacher preparation course work, but they never actually get to experience constructivism in action. This concern is an example of what is often perceived to be a theory to practice gap between teacher preparation programs and schools.

It has long been acknowledged that teachers tend to teach as they are taught, not as they are told to teach. Thus, there is an urgent need for modelling how to apply constructivist learning principles in the classrooms. This book is designed to engage you in activities that will lead you to a better understanding of social constructivism as well as encouraging a commitment to the implementation of constructivist principles in your future classrooms. I also anticipate that having experienced constructivism in action will empower you to go out to your schools seeing yourself as agents of change as you work with colleagues who are unfamiliar with these transformative ways of thinking about teaching and learning.

The Organization of the Text

The material in this book has been designed with four basic beliefs about learning based on social constructivism in mind. These principles are at the heart of my philosophy of education. I begin with the premise that we all come to this learning experience with different backgrounds, experience, and knowledge and that learning new knowledge is a process of building on those experiences and revising that prior knowledge. Second, I believe that learning needs to be relevant and take place in a context that is meaningful to the learner. Third, I believe that learning is collaborative and that meaning is made through active engagement as we explain our ideas to others, as we listen to others' ideas, and as we discuss those ideas together. Finally, I believe that time and space for thoughtful, personal reflection is necessary to ensure meaningful learning and growth.

If I were to use a metaphor to represent my philosophy of education based on these principles, I would use an architectural design model with the principles as my four foundational cornerstones.

Throughout this book you will find opportunities to engage with the material in ways that support these four learning principles. The **Looking Back** activities are intended to challenge you to examine the beliefs and ideas that you bring to this learning experience based on your previous experiences with social studies. The **Active Engagement** activities provide you with

My Four Foundations of Learning

Collaborative

Experiential

Reflective

Meaningful

opportunities to interact with the ideas being discussed and to collaborate with other learners. To make your learning personally meaningful and relevant to you as a future teacher, regular **Classroom Application** examples have been included to demonstrate how you might use what you are learning about in the elementary classroom. Finally, you will need to be prepared to take a critically reflective stance as you engage with these pages in order to question your personal assumptions. It is important that you come to understand why you see the world the way you do, to understand that the perspectives you bring to the learning experience can be limiting, and to come to realize that in order to transform your learning you may need to make a shift in your views or adopt a new idea (Mezirow, 2000). Accordingly, regular **Reflection Points** have been interspersed throughout the text to assist you in becoming more critically aware of your own worldview.

Inquiring Into Social Studies Teaching and Learning

This book, intended for primary and junior teacher candidates, has been designed using a social constructivist oriented, inquiry-based learning model. The inquiry-based approach to learning is an instructional model that exemplifies the four basic learning principles identified as key organizers for the experiences in this book. This model promotes active engagement with learning, situates learning in the examination of real-life questions and concerns of relevance to the learners; encourages learners to make choices about how and what they learn; and urges learners to collaborate. It can also provide a more structured method to assist in the building of thinking and problem-solving skills.

The content of this book has been organized around five key inquiry questions related to teaching and learning social studies. All five of the questions deal with a specific aspect of planning your social studies program. Each of the five inquiry questions is addressed in a separate section. The key questions as reflected in the part titles are:

Part One: Why is it important to set goals for your social studies program?

Part Two: How do you select and organize the content of your social studies program?

Part Three: How do you locate and select resources to assist in teaching social studies content?

Part Four: What activities would help you to meet the goals of your social studies program?

Part Five: How should children's learning in social studies be assessed?

All five parts are broken down into chapters; the chapter titles are sub-questions related to the key inquiry question under investigation.

These questions were selected to actively engage you in inquiry about teaching and learning social studies as a way of demonstrating the benefits for you of this approach to learning. Through the readings and activities provided, you will have the opportunity to explore these questions and to reflect on what the investigation of these questions causes you to think about your roles and responsibilities as a social studies teacher. Once you have examined all of the inquiry questions, you should be in a better position to design an effective social studies program for your future classroom.

To assist you further in your investigation of the inquiry questions, there are also frequent **Technology Links** that provide further reading in specific areas using online sources as well as suggestions for how to integrate technology effectively into social studies.

Chapter Overview

In Part One, we begin our look at the planning process by investigating the key inquiry question: Why is it important to set goals for your social studies program? In Chapter 1 we spend some time looking at the purpose for establishing learning goals and how to go about setting goals. Goals take several forms including your own personal professional growth targets, the curricular goals, and the goals for student growth (learning outcomes). This is an important starting point for you as a beginning teacher because the first task before you when you start your new teaching job will be to decide on what you hope to accomplish in your teaching over the upcoming year. In Chapter 2, I model goal setting for you by explaining what I am hoping to accomplish (my goals) by taking a social constructivist approach to this book. Here there is also a more in-depth exploration of social constructivism as a theory about learning.

Chapter 3 takes a close up look at what social studies is all about and why it is taught in elementary schools, as influences on your goal setting. A number of differing perspectives on social studies is provided including those of teachers, children, other teacher candidates, and those expressed in curriculum guides. Chapter 4 examines in detail the role of citizenship education in social studies. While educating citizens is the generally agreed upon definitive goal of social studies, decisions have to be made about what view of the good citizen is to be adopted and how best to teach it to students. Seven different ways of thinking about social studies as citizenship education are presented; each with its own inherent beliefs about what is important knowledge and how it is best learned, and the role of the teacher and the students in that learning. Each view suggests a different implicit curriculum—the values, roles, and self-concepts children learn inadvertently from their teacher. You are encouraged to examine the significant differences among these views in order to identify which view best fits with your beliefs about teaching, learning, and social studies. This should help you to begin to think about what your own priorities for student growth should be and to develop your teaching goals accordingly.

Part Two turns to differing views of what should be taught in social studies. You will examine how to go about selecting and organizing the content to be taught in your social studies program. Chapter 5 looks at the curriculum as an influence in your content selection process. Chapter 6 examines other influences on your decision making including your goals, interests, and past experiences, the children's interests and abilities, the context in which you are teaching, and the available resources.

Part Three asks, "How do you locate and select resources to assist in teaching social studies content?" Chapter 7 engages you in examining different approaches to resource selection based on your goals and your students' needs and interests. Chapter 8 focuses on the selection and use of children's literature, including fiction, nonfiction, and poetry, as resources in your social studies program. Chapter 9 examines the variety of computer-based resources, both software and web-based, for developing students' information location and application.

Part Four focuses on decisions about how to teach social studies. Chapter 10 presents three possible alternative approaches to organizing activities for instruction, including teacher directed, shared direction, and student directed. Chapter 11 examines a variety of learning activities to assist in developing students' research skills, higher level thinking, collaborative and cooperation skills, and participation skills. Chapter 12 investigates the potential of computer technologies as pedagogical tools for enhancing learning in social studies.

Part Five questions how to assess children's growth and learning in social studies. Here too differing views on the purposes of assessment are presented and a variety of assessment tools is examined.

Finally, in the Closure an attempt is made to model how all of the five areas of inquiry in the book including goal setting, content choices, resource alternatives, activities selection, and assessment approaches can be pulled together in order to plan an effective social studies program. An example of an instructional plan representing one possible type of organizing structure is provided to help you plan a format that might work best for you.

Throughout the text, you are encouraged to explore multiple viewpoints on each of the five key inquiry questions in order to construct and clarify your own personal views on and answers to each question. A central reason for using this approach is to help you to become a better decision-maker about priorities of student learning and growth, and then use those high priority goals to choose content, resources, activities, and assessment strategies. Although assessment is addressed last in the text, this does not mean that it is the last thing that you need to think about in planning your program. In fact, some experts suggest that beginning your planning by thinking about where you want to end up and looking back from that end point is a powerful way to plan (Wiggins & McTighe, 2005).

While the emphasis in these pages is on the teaching and learning of social studies as a school subject, it is acknowledged that as an elementary school generalist you will be teaching a number of different subject areas. My hope is that you will feel better prepared to make important planning and teaching decisions about both social studies specifically and about your overall program as a generalist after completing this part of the learning-to-teach journey.

Instructor's Manual

The Instructor's Manual has been prepared by Susan E. Gibson. The Instructor's Manual is a chapter-by-chapter summary of the main textbook. Features include chapter outlines, content overviews, activity ideas, a glossary, additional online and print resources, and reflective/review questions. A list of websites will be included as well for both student teachers and elementary students to help them start to integrate technology.

Website

The textbook has a companion website that includes weblinks and online references referred within the chapters. Each chapter within the book discusses or introduces websites that students can link to from the book's main website. Wherever the "WWW" icon appears in the chapters, the reader can find the related websites, online articles, templates, and examples of social studies presented in the book. The site is organized by chapter so that each reference is easy to find and just a click away.

About the Author

Susan Gibson has been working in the area of social studies since she began her career in education in 1976. After spending 11 years teaching both elementary and middle school in Ontario and Alberta, she made the transition to pre-service education. Since then she has been looking for ways to help teacher candidates develop a passion for social studies and a desire to engage young children in meaningful social studies experiences. This book reflects the findings from her years of research into what experiences pre-service teachers identify as particularly powerful for them in learning to understand and teach social studies. Dr. Gibson is currently a professor in the Department of Elementary Education at the University of Alberta in Edmonton, Alberta.

Acknowledgements

Over my 30 years in education, there have been countless teachers, children, pre-service teachers, and colleagues who have inspired me about the possibilities for making social studies teaching and learning exciting and meaningful. Their stories are reflected in the numerous examples provided throughout this book. I would like to acknowledge specifically Dr. Brenda Basiga and Ms. Catherine Coyne who are both practicing social studies classroom teachers. Thank you also to the reviewers of the manuscript who provided valuable feedback during the writing process and to Sandy Matos, Tara Tovell, and Sabrina Mansour for their constant and unfailing encouragement during the editing process.

Special thanks are given to the reviewers of this text who reviewed this text from its initial proposal through the manuscript revisions. They include:

Jon G. Bradley, McGill University

Ottilia Chareka, St. Francis Xavier University

Elspeth Deir, Queens University

Kristen Ferguson, Nipissing University

Larry Glassford, University of Windsor

Marianne Larsen, The University of Western Ontario

John Meyers, OISE/University of Toronto

Amy von Heyking, Ph.D., University of Alberta

Teaching Social Studies in Elementary Schools
A Social Constructivist Approach

Part One

Goals

Why Is It Important to Set Goals for Your Social Studies Program?

Part One of our investigation into planning your social studies program addresses the question of why goal setting is an important initial step in thinking about teaching. As a teacher, you will need to have a "big picture" of what you hope to accomplish over the span of your social studies program, including your own professional goals, the curricular goals, and what you hope your students will know, be able to do, and feel by the end of your program (learning goals), before thinking about the *what* (content) and *how* (activities and resources) that will make up your program.

In Chapter 1, we begin our look at goal setting by examining some of the concerns that have been raised about the teaching of social studies and how goal setting may help to address those concerns. Here, you are introduced to the idea of the teacher as reflective practitioner and you are encouraged to begin engaging in reflection on possible goals for your future social studies program.

Chapter 2 provides you with a model of how to begin goal setting by showing how constructivist learning theory informed the approach taken to this book. The key principles of social constructivism are examined more deeply, as are the approach's implications for social studies teachers. You are encouraged to think about how you can use these principles as a social studies teacher to guide your decision making about content selection, resources, activities, and assessment as you progress through the remaining chapters of the book.

In Chapter 3, we begin the close-up investigation of what social studies is and why we teach it, as a first step in thinking about your goals. You are provided with a number of differing perspectives on social studies, including those of teachers, children, other student teachers, and those expressed in curriculum guides. Then, in Chapter 4, we examine in detail the role of citizenship education in social studies. While citizenship education is the generally agreed-upon goal of social studies, the question of whose view of how to educate citizens is most appropriate remains. Seven different ways of thinking about social studies as citizenship education are presented, each with its own beliefs about what is important knowledge and how it is best learned, and what the roles of the teacher and the students are in that learning. Each orientation toward citizenship education carries with it a different hidden curriculum—or the values, roles, and self-concepts children learn as a result of the teaching methods used by their teacher. You are encouraged to examine the significant differences among these orientations in order to identify which one best fits with your beliefs about teaching, learning, and social studies. Such reflection should help you to think further about your priorities for student learning as well as your professional goals.

Chapter 1

Why Is Goal Setting Important?

"I really like social studies cause it's fun and interesting. It's my favourite subject. I like learning about other people and countries. My class has penpals that my teacher got us. Mine's from Paris, France. I like talking to her about what she likes to do and her school and her family. My favourite thing in social studies is doing research projects."

(Sylvie, Grade 4 student)

Here is Sylvie corresponding with her epal.

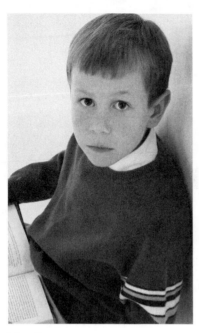

Meet Casey.

"Social studies is so boring. Why do I have to learn about dead people and dates and explorers and stuff like that? All we ever do is read stuff in the textbook and do worksheets. I don't like writing lots of notes either."

(Casey, Grade 4 student)

Exposing a Potential Problem with Social Studies

Nearly 40 years ago, A. B. Hodgetts' in his work *What Culture? What Heritage?* reported that social studies classrooms were drab places that were dominated by chalk and talk, text recitation, and the lecture method. In the mid-1980s, Mark Schug, Robert Todd, and R. Beery (1984) claimed that students were less than positive about their social studies experiences because they were being taught in an uninteresting way and the content had very little relevance to their lives. In his work, Kieran Egan (1991) reported that children did not seem to like social studies, nor did they retain what they experienced.

Even though these studies are decades old, many students' today report having similar experiences with social studies, as reflected in Casey's comment at the beginning of the chapter. As recently as 2005, Yali Zhao and John Hoge conducted a study entitled "What Elementary Students and Teachers Say about Social Studies." They interviewed 300 children from kindergarten to Grade 5 and found that, "Most children who do not like social studies say 'it is boring and useless,' 'it's reading the textbook' and 'it doesn't apply'" (p. 3). Stephen Thornton (2005) added that although the required social studies curriculum is taught and ostensibly learned, many students quickly forget the material and their "encounters with it leave many of them cold" (p. 3). Unfortunately, not only do a lot of students appear not to like or retain what they learn in social studies, but a provincial assessment of social studies in British Columbia in 1996 found that they are also leaving school without important life skills and the knowledge necessary for making informed decisions about public and civic affairs (Bognar, Cassidy, & Clarke, 1997). Alan Sears (1996) concludes that part of the problem is a mismatch between what is reflected in the official curriculum and the way in which it is being represented in the classroom.

While the findings of these studies paint a rather bleak picture of social studies, my intention is not to discourage you as a beginning teacher but rather to challenge you to look for ways to make social studies an exciting, positive experience for both you and your students. It would be wonderful if all children felt the way that Sylvie, the student in the opening example, does about her social studies experiences.

This chapter begins with the premise that there is room for improvement in the way that social studies is currently being conceptualized and taught in many classrooms. I know that you would want your students to recognize that social studies is an important subject for them to learn, both for its present and future benefits, and that you would want them to enjoy, see value in, and remember their experiences with social studies. But you are probably wondering how to go about making learning in social studies more interesting and meaningful for your students.

REFLECTION POINT

John Chiodo and Jeffrey Byford's study (2004) of students' social studies experiences found that active involvement, students' perceived utilitarian value of what was being learned, and teacher's enthusiasm all affected students' views of social studies. As well, Ava McCall's (2006) investigation of exemplary elementary social studies teachers found that they all articulated clear goals and had a strong sense of purpose; they actively involved students and challenged their thinking; they taught content in a way that was meaningful to students—i.e., by emphasizing local connections and things of relevance to their lives and by focusing on current events; they integrated social studies with other subjects, especially language arts through the use of children's literature; and they engaged in ongoing professional development to improve their teaching regardless of how many years they had been teaching.

What do you think of the students' claim that teacher enthusiasm made a difference in how much they liked social studies? If making learning in social studies more interesting and meaningful for your students is one of your goals, how can these two research studies help you to think about how to do that?

You are about to embark on a journey to try to find out how to think about social studies teaching and learning so that your students will value it as a subject and be motivated to want to learn it. As a part of this journey of discovery, you will need to take a good hard look at what it is that you want your students to take away from their social studies experiences in school and decide on how best to ensure that you are accomplishing those goals.

Encouraging Reflective Practice

LOOKING BACK

What does the term "reflective practice" mean to you? What experience have you had with reflection? How helpful was that experience for you in clarifying your thinking about what you were learning? What could have made that reflective experience a more effective learning strategy for you?

The approach that has been taken in these pages is based on a model of teacher professional development that promotes reflective practice. Reflective practice is practice that is based on the understanding that we all have personal beliefs about teaching and learning that act as powerful filters through which everything we experience as teachers is sifted, whether we are aware of it or not. These beliefs influence our decision making about what we teach, how we teach it, and how we determine if our students have learned it. Our beliefs also influence what our students take away from the learning experience.

Unexamined beliefs can result in an implicit or hidden curriculum occurring, in which your teaching does not match your beliefs. Eliot Eisner (1979), John Goodlad (1984), and Philip Jackson (1968) have been instrumental in defining the term "hidden" or "implicit curriculum." According to these experts, this latent curriculum includes things such as the beliefs, attitudes, values, and philosophies that are evident both in the way a teacher manages the learning environment and in the teacher's expectations and interpretations of behaviour, as well as in the messages that textbooks and other materials convey. The problem occurs when the hidden curriculum does not match the overt curriculum.

CLASSROOM APPLICATION

It is the first week of school in Ms. Stephenson's Grade 3 class. Ms. Stephenson has spent much of the week setting up the rules for the classroom. A list of behaviours that are not allowed in the classroom has been posted on the front bulletin board. One example of a rule is no talking without raising your hand. Another is no disturbing other people in the classroom. A third is no leaving the classroom without her permission. There are 10 rules altogether. Ms. Stephenson has reviewed the rules with the class and explained the consequences for breaking them. The children have been told that they will have to stay in at recess and do school work if bad behaviour persists. In social studies, Ms. Stephenson is starting a new unit on government, democracy, and human rights. What hidden curriculum is at work in this classroom? Does the way that the social studies classroom is managed reflect basic democratic principles? How might you go about setting up your classroom in a way that offers the children a more democratic experience to ensure a better fit between the overt curriculum and the hidden curriculum?

The hidden curriculum can have a powerful effect on students' self-concepts, and on the roles and degree of responsibility they learn to take in their schooling. Eisner contends that these messages inherent in the hidden curriculum "are profoundly more powerful and longer lasting than what is intentionally taught or what the explicit [what is overtly communicated] curriculum of the school publicly provides" (1979, p. 213). Allowing unexamined beliefs to shape social studies teaching can result in instruction failing to affect students in desired ways.

REFLECTION POINT

Over 20 years ago, J. Davis in *Planning a Social Studies Program* claimed that classroom management was at the heart of the hidden curriculum: "The culture and organization of schools . . . focus much of the energy of teachers and administrators on matters of management and control rather than on teaching and learning of social studies—particularly the teaching and learning of higher-level thinking skills, participation skills and democratic values" (1983, p. 11). Davis suggested that because the perception of control was so important to teachers—as it was believed to garner the respect of colleagues, administration, and parents—they chose to use a limited range of activities in the social studies classroom to ensure that control would be maintained. Do you agree with Davis's views on the hidden curriculum? Was this true for you in your schooling experiences? What roles, norms, values, and self-concepts might students learn if they experienced schooling like this 200 days a year? What kind of citizen qualities would be promoted by this hidden curriculum? Would you say that this emphasis on a controlled learning environment is still a part of the hidden curriculum in the classrooms of today? If yes, why might that be so? What other external factors besides garnering the respect of peers and administrators might be at work—i.e., sociopolitical context; the accountability movement in education, ministry, and school board directives, provincial achievement exams, etc.? How might you be able to find out what external forces are influencing your teaching and your students' learning?

Examining the notion of a hidden curriculum at work in the classroom is an important reminder to you as a beginning teacher to strive to align what you teach with how you teach it. One way to uncover the implicit curriculum at work is to engage in regular and ongoing reflection on your teaching.

Defining Reflection

In *How We Think*, John Dewey (1933) wrote, "Reflective thinking is active, persistent and careful consideration of any belief or practice in the light of the grounds that support it and the further consequences to which it leads" (p. 4). John Barell (1991) in *Teaching for Thoughtfulness* added a sense of purpose to the exercise by explaining that through reflectiveness we should be attempting to make a difficult situation more meaningful as we search for clarity and understanding. Critical to this process, according to Jerome Bruner (1986) in *Actual Minds, Possible Worlds*, is taking a step back from what you know in order to think about that knowledge. By reflecting back on prior learning, we can best determine whether what we have learned is justified under present circumstances. Through reflection we can also assess our actions and our thinking to help us to plan for the future. Ultimately, by becoming more critically aware of the ideas we have gained from our prior learning, and how those ideas are influencing and in some cases constraining the way we are experiencing our world in the present, we can experience perspective transformation in which we change our perceptions, understandings, and feelings and develop and act on new understandings (Mezirow, 1990).

Becoming a Reflective Practitioner

Thoughtful, personal reflection is necessary to help teachers make sense of both their thinking and actions as professionals and to ensure continued learning and growth (Adler, 1994). Social studies teaching that is based on reflective practice acknowledges the teacher as the facilitator of the classroom who is responsible for making critical decisions about all aspects of teaching on an ongoing basis. To ensure that these decisions are sound, a reflective practice stance helps social studies teachers to stay aware of what beliefs, ideas, and feelings are influencing their thinking and actions. Learning about teaching thus is envisioned as an ongoing and never-ending investigation into personal professional growth and improving practice.

CLASSROOM APPLICATION

Here are Grade 1 teacher Jean Watson's thoughts on reflection: "What never ceases to surprise me is how much I can learn by stopping at regular points in my teaching to think about how things are going. I have made it my mission to write a Thought for the Day at the end of each day plan where I write about something that stood out for me over the course of the day. I look back over what I've written at the end of the week and then use those ideas to help me to think about where to go next in my units." How might you ensure that you take time for regular reflection on your teaching?

There is no such thing as a "recipe book" of routines and practices that can be transferred from teacher to teacher and from classroom to classroom. Rather, teaching is recognized as a very individualized endeavour. As well, what works for a teacher with one group of children in one year may not prove as successful for the same teacher in subsequent years. While the official curriculum will direct much of the decision making in the classroom, there is still room for your individual interpretation as the teacher and for putting your own individual stamp on what happens—particularly with regard to how the official curriculum is put into practice in your classroom. As a result, having a firm foundation in educational philosophy and engaging in ongoing reflection on how your belief system is guiding your classroom decision making is imperative.

While these beliefs about learning apply to all learners no matter what their age, they have particular significance for you as you learn about becoming a social studies teacher. It is paramount that you take frequent opportunities to investigate your own personal beliefs about teaching and learning in order to always be consciously aware of how they are influencing your thinking about teaching. You are encouraged to take the opportunity as often as possible to make your learning about social studies as personally meaningful for your future practice as you can.

Accordingly, the experiences provided in this book are meant to encourage you to adopt a reflective disposition as you begin to uncover and reflect on your current beliefs about teaching and learning. As part of this reflection, you will need to think about how your beliefs have been shaped by your experiences prior to entering your education program, especially in relation to what those experiences have caused you to believe and value about your roles and responsibilities as an educator. You will need to reflect on who you are as a person and the beliefs and assumptions that you bring to your teaching based on your cultural knowledge, attitudes, and experiences. According to Young Pai, "our goals, what we teach, how we relate to children and each other are rooted in the norms of our culture" (cited in Gay, 2000, p. 23).

As you read this text, be prepared to be both critically reflective and active in searching for understanding about what it means to teach social studies.

ACTIVE ENGAGEMENT

Donald Murray states, "Writing is the most disciplined form of thinking—a way of processing and remembering information and making meaning. It is thinking on paper" (cited in L. Robb, 2003, p. 59). Try keeping a reflective journal in which you record your thoughts as you participate in the **Looking Back, Active Engagement, Classroom Application,** and **Reflection Point** activities throughout this book. Do frequent check-backs to see how your thinking is becoming clearer or changing. Pay particular attention to thinking about your own thinking (metacognition) as you begin to uncover and reflect on your current views on teaching and learning: how have these views been shaped by your experiences prior to entering your education programs and by your education courses and experiences to date, and what have they caused you to believe and value about your roles and responsibilities as a beginning teacher? Your

(Continued)

responses to these questions can help you to develop and continue to refine your personal philosophy of education. As you engage in this "looking back," also consider questions such as

- How does this fit with what I already know?
- What has influenced me to believe what I do?
- Are there inconsistencies in my thinking?
- What else do I need to know and do to develop my understanding?
- How is my thinking changing?
- How do I feel about these changes?
- Why is this change in my thinking important?

REFLECTION POINT

What do you hope to accomplish in your social studies program? How will you accomplish it? How can your social studies program be designed to help you to accomplish what you want?

Taking time to pause and use new knowledge through activities like journal writing is important for learning.

Children as Reflective Learners

Critical reflection is also an important practice for the children in your classroom to engage in as it places high priority on growth in the independence, responsibility, ownership, and self-direction of learners. Immersing learners at the outset in setting their own personal growth goals and checking back to see how what they are learning relates to those goals is one way to engage them in critical reflection. Such reflection helps to establish links between previous knowledge and new knowledge; as thinking is monitored, connections between what used to be known and believed and what is now known are noticed. Not only does making these connections help to create meaning, but learners also come to better understand the processes involved in learning as they pay attention to these connections. Thus, taking frequent opportunities throughout social studies learning experiences to uncover these beliefs and critically examine their influence on how the new learning is being understood is an important step for learners as it can lead to clarification and transformation of thinking. Carol Rodgers notes, "Thinking, particularly reflective thinking or inquiry, is essential to both teachers' and students' learning" (2002, p. 842). She would argue that it is important that you engage your students in some form of reflective writing on a regular basis.

CLASSROOM APPLICATION

One example of a reflective activity is learning logs in which students of all ages can capture their thoughts on their learning experiences. Miss Boyle's Grade 1 class starts the year off by drawing their reflections in their logs and then orally sharing the meaning behind their pictures with her and the class. By the end of Grade 1, the children's entries have progressed to drawing accompanied by some explanatory text, with the amount of text increasing as the child's skills and abilities develop. Miss Tanner also uses learning logs with her Grade 4 class. To help to guide her students' reflections, she asks them to respond to questions such as, What did you do in social studies class today?, What did you find most interesting?, What did you learn that was new?, What confused you?, and "What questions do you still have? Mr. Barker has his Grade 6 class provide written reflections in their logs using the following sentence starters:

- One thing I learned in social studies today was . . .
- I changed my thinking about . . .
- I was surprised that . . .
- I think that . . .
- I wonder . . .
- I predict . . .
- Something I found interesting was . . .
- I still want to know . . .

W | W **Technology Connection** A reflective tool that is gaining in popularity in elementary schools is blogging. Web logs or "blogs"—are online journals that can be either private or public and that can be used for all ages. Ms. Daniel, a Grade 4 teacher, uses her blog to allow her students to share their social studies investigations about Alberta's lands and peoples with each other and with outside experts such as a provincial conservation officer. (For a link to the blog, please visit the book's companion website.)

For younger children, there are blogs that allow for pictorial reflections as well as text-based ones. Links to educational blogging sites are provided on the book's companion website.

The Importance of Goal Setting to the Beginning Teacher

ACTIVE ENGAGEMENT

In small groups, think back on your experiences with social studies from primary school through high school. What were your classes like? What kinds of things did your best social studies teachers do? What activities in social studies do you remember as the

(Continued)

ones from which you learned the most or were the most fun or the most exciting? What was missing in your social studies experiences? Based on both positive role models and mediocre ones, what characteristics of an excellent teacher come to mind? Share your experiences with a few people in a group. As a group, synthesize your common shared experiences on chart paper and then try to come up with a group representation of what effective social studies learning experiences are all about. Try depicting these recollections in either narrative, poetic, pictorial, or brainstorm web format. When finished, reflect on what this exercise might tell you about what you consider to be important goals for your teaching of social studies and how your goals compare to those of your peers. Based on what you believe makes excellent teaching, list what some of your potential goal priorities as a teacher might be. What does this tell you about the kinds of student growth that you value? How can you use what you have created in this activity to begin setting some professional growth goals for yourself as a social studies teacher?

I begin with the assumption that you want to become an excellent social studies teacher. In order to tell whether you are becoming an excellent teacher, you have to ask that age-old question, "Did that activity today work?" When teachers ask that question, they often think about the short-term effects of how students responded to the activity—i.e., did students enjoy it, show enthusiasm while doing the activity, stay on task rather than wander off task, behave appropriately rather than intentionally disrupt the activity? For you as a beginning teacher, these short-term effects will be important. In addition to these immediate, easily observable effects, a second criterion needs to be used to determine what works. Teachers need to ask what kind of growth results from the whole collection of activities planned. To determine whether you are becoming an excellent teacher, you need to be clear about what kinds of student growth are most important to you, and then assess the success of the set of activities you've planned in helping your students to reach these learning outcomes. Curriculum documents can help to determine what growth to look for.

Another equally important part of becoming an excellent social studies teacher is developing a clear conception of the curricular goals along with your own professional goal priorities, and consistently planning activities that are likely to promote the kinds of learner growth valued most highly and to ensure student success.

CLASSROOM APPLICATION

Miss Johnson, a beginning elementary social studies teacher, had this to say about her goals for her social studies program: "My goals for my social studies program lie in the success of my students. Foremost I want to ensure that the program meets the needs of my students. While I want my program to achieve the outcomes of the curriculum

14   PART ONE   Why Is It Important to Set Goals for Your Social Studies Program?

NEL

I need to ensure that it is active and engaging for my students. I believe that my students need to become independent thinkers who can understand the world around them and I want to maintain an authentic, real world focus in our studies. I also want my students to see themselves in what they are learning about in social studies. To me social studies is both a window and a mirror for my students." What does Miss Johnson believe about learning? How might her beliefs help her to plan an effective social studies program?

So far, we have seen that planning an effective social studies program begins with the clarification of goals. These goals are important for guiding all decisions about curriculum, planning, instruction, and assessment that you will make as a teacher. Without clear goals, such decision making can appear disjointed and directionless. According to John Dewey (1933), "There is no surer road to educational problems than teachers who do not understand the purposes of their actions" (p. 45). Therefore, the choice is not *whether* teachers will make decisions about goals, but *how* they will make them.

REFLECTION POINT

Imagine that you are at the end of your teaching career and your former social studies students are writing tributes to you. What would you hope that some of those tributes would say? How does this exercise help you to think about your own professional growth goals for your teaching of social studies?

Teachers' professional growth goals, or what they hope to accomplish through their teaching, can be distinguished from curricular goals and learning goals. In social studies curriculum documents, learner goals are often written as expectations or outcomes. These learner goals include students' knowledge, skills, attitudes, and dispositions to be developed as a result of their learning experiences. Usually these outcomes are so abundant that teachers need to read curriculum guides critically and interpretively. They find themselves placing more emphasis on certain expectations and giving less attention to other goal statements they believe are not as important. Since the amount of instructional time for social studies is limited (usually to about 10 percent of the total number of instructional hours available for all subjects over a school year), goal priority setting is critical. Teachers will not all agree on which curricular goals are highest priority. Some will see teaching Canada's history and geography as their major goal; others will see the development of decision-making skills as their paramount task; and still others will want to develop their students' understanding about their world and the issues that affect it on a global scale.

The way you answer the questions What is worth doing? and What works? will help you to decide on your own highest priority goals for teaching social studies. Your answer to these questions will also play a key role in what kind of student growth you look for when deciding whether what you are doing is working. Effective teachers consciously make decisions about priorities regarding student growth, and then use their highest priority goals to choose content, materials, activities, and assessment strategies that best contribute to the attainment of those goals.

How Your Beliefs about Teaching and Learning Shape Your Goals

Central to the selection of your goals for your social studies program are the beliefs that you have about teaching, learning, the nature of knowledge, and how one acquires that knowledge. To ensure that you have ample opportunity to examine and clarify your thoughts and to envision what you might want to change about your current thinking, the focus throughout this book will be on helping you to clarify your goals for your social studies program and then using these goals to assist you in selecting content, resources, activities, and assessment strategies to reach your goals.

REFLECTION POINT

Here are some important foundational questions that can help to bring your beliefs about teaching and learning to the surface so that you can decide if there is anything about your views that you might want to change. Take a moment to respond to each of the following questions, and then reflect on why you responded the way you did (i.e., because of life experiences, race, ethnicity, political beliefs, socioeconomic status, etc.) and on what your responses tell you about the assumptions, norms, beliefs, and expectations you are bringing to your teaching:

- What is learning?
- How does learning happen?
- Does everyone learn the same way?
- What can be done to facilitate learning?
- What are your students' roles in their learning?
- What is your role as the teacher in that learning?

What do your responses to these questions tell you about potential goals for your social studies program? Do you have any new insights about yourself as a beginning teacher as a result of this exercise? How might you use your new understanding to guide your decision making about your social studies program?

ACTIVE ENGAGEMENT

Now that you have examined some of your core beliefs about teaching and learning, how would you respond to each of the statements in Table 1.1 in terms of your current thinking about your goals for teaching social studies?

TABLE 1.1 ■ **Determining Your Social Studies Goals**

MY SOCIAL STUDIES GOALS	STRONGLY DISAGREE	DISAGREE	UNSURE	AGREE	STRONGLY AGREE
Social studies should assist the learner in the search for "self."					
Social studies should focus on issues of globalization.					
Students should learn the basic obligations and responsibilities of good citizenship from their social studies teachers.					
Learning facts and concepts should be the primary objective of a good social studies program.					
Actively involving children in community projects is the best way to learn about being a good citizen.					
Social studies ought to be concerned primarily with history and geography.					
Elementary-age children can understand how to bring about change.					
Developing attitudes is the least important aspect of social studies.					

(Continued)

MY SOCIAL STUDIES GOALS	STRONGLY DISAGREE	DISAGREE	UNSURE	AGREE	STRONGLY AGREE
The most important resource for classroom learning is a good textbook.					
Building an active citizen self-concept requires doing something about the problems and issues studied.					
Learning to become a thoughtful problem solver and decision maker is an important part of social studies.					
Social studies should teach students to take pride in their cultural and ethnic heritage.					
Map skills are probably the most important skills in the social studies curriculum.					
It is most important that students investigate to find answers to their own questions in social studies.					
Students need to develop the ability to question their own cultural conditioning.					
Social studies teachers should use reflection to help students clarify their thinking about issues that concern them.					
Students should learn about cultural universals* in social studies.					
Students should learn methods of inquiry and analytical skills.					

*Cultural universals are those things that are common to a group of people and that are passed on to succeeding generations—i.e., family roles, belief systems, communication, education, food and clothing preferences, etc.

Exercises such as the one in Table 1.1 are intended to help you to reflect on your goals, which in turn will assist in the framing of your future social studies program. These goals are shaped by your educational philosophy; indeed everything that you do as a social studies teacher will be based on your educational philosophy, whether you are aware of it or not. This philosophy reflects your assumptions and beliefs about how your students learn and the roles to be played in that learning by you as the teacher and by your students. Differing educational philosophies result in varying educational practices. These differences will be examined in Chapter 2.

ACTIVE ENGAGEMENT

To get some practice in goal setting, try identifying several goals you wish to achieve in your social studies curriculum and instruction course. These goals should be focused on the development of understanding, not on accomplishing specific tasks, i.e., one of your goals as a teacher candidate might be to develop a clearer understanding of what social studies is all about; another one might be to increase your background knowledge of Canadian history, particularly as it pertains to the content outlined in your province's/territory's curriculum document for social studies. Once you have articulated a few goals, try breaking them down into smaller, more specific action steps that will help you to move toward achieving them. Turn to a partner and share your goals and your action plan. Discuss how to determine if your goals are guiding your learning throughout the course. Decide on frequent checkpoints throughout your learning journey and take the time to ask yourself whether you are moving in the right direction toward your goals. Rethink your plan if you aren't happy with your progress.

Not only will you need to set goals for your own professional development as a teacher; you will also need to be clear about curricular goals and student learning goals. You will need to ask yourself what you hope to see your students accomplish as a result of their social studies experiences. Sharing these goals with your students can help them to see the purpose behind what you are asking them to do. One strategy for sharing your goals for your students is to post them somewhere in the classroom and take the time to explain them to the class. This process not only models goal setting for students but also helps them to see why they are doing what they are doing. Engaging children in goal setting for their social studies learning experiences can help to increase their active involvement in the learning, can boost their motivation to want to learn, and can give them a greater sense of control over and responsibility for their own learning.

Mrs. Shelley, a Grade 5 teacher, believes that personal goal setting is a powerful beginning point for any new learning for her students because it can help them to better understand what they hope to accomplish and decide what they need to do to reach their learning goals. One way that Mrs. Shelley engages children in goal setting is by using a graphic organizer called the KWHL (Know, Wonder, How, Learned) technique (Ogle, 1986). At the beginning of her social studies unit on Canada's geographic regions, she has her students fill in the first three columns of a chart like the one provided here:

TABLE 1.2 ■ Example of KWHL Graphic Organizer for a Study on Canada's Geographic Regions

KNOW	WONDER	HOW	LEARNED
What do I think I already know about Canada's geographic regions?	What would I like to find out about the geographic regions of Canada?	How and where can I find answers to my questions?	What did I learn about Canada's geography? How did I learn it? What could I do differently next time to learn more?
Canada is very big. Canada has mountains in the west. The prairies are flat. Canada has 10 provinces. The north is called territories. Canada has lots of lakes. Canada is mostly covered with trees. People in the Maritimes eat lots of fish.	Is Canada the biggest country in the world? How long would it take to drive from one side of Canada to the other? Are Canada's mountains the biggest? How cold does it get in the Arctic? Where do most of the people in Canada live? Why?	Read books. Go on the Internet. Ask people from different parts of Canada. Look at maps.	

Once the study of the topic is finished, the children are encouraged to assess their overall learning by filling in the fourth column and cross-checking their responses with those in the first three columns to see if they have changed any of their initial ideas. The questions in the "Learned" column also help the children to begin to think about the learning strategies they used and how effective they were for helping them to grow as learners.

Chapter Summary

This chapter began with the premise that something isn't working in social studies, especially regarding students' perceptions of its value and its likeability. I argued that part of the problem can be traced to a lack of clear purpose and direction on the part of many social studies teachers. Accordingly, the chapter encouraged you to take on a reflective disposition as you learn about becoming a social studies teacher in order that you are continuously investigating and clarifying what you believe about teaching and learning, and about how those beliefs are shaping your thinking and decision making.

Goal setting was identified here as the first step in planning an effective social studies program. These goals include both your own professional goals as a beginning teacher as well as the goals that you have for your students' learning. Since your goals are shaped by your beliefs, ongoing reflection is important to being able to clearly articulate both those goals and the educational philosophy upon which they are based. Being aware of your underlying educational philosophy and its role in shaping your teaching can help to ensure that your students do not experience the effects of a hidden curriculum. By way of example, in the next chapter I present my educational philosophy and the beliefs that I have about how people learn, based on the theory of social constructivism.

Chapter 2

Why Social Constructivism as a Theoretical Framework?

The first thing that strikes one when walking into Mr. Bali's Grade 6 classroom is the level of busyness. The children's desks are grouped in clusters of four. One cluster of children is talking and recording ideas on chart paper. Another is on the floor painting a mural. Another is assembled around a computer working on a PowerPoint presentation. A group sitting on a couch in the "Reading Corner" is pasting newspaper articles in a scrapbook. Mr. Bali is talking with another group gathered around a papier mâché model. There is also a group making a poster using photographs from the Internet and magazines. The classroom walls have a variety of students' work on display. A large pocket chart shows the names of the students who have been grouped together. Hung beside this chart is a poster labelled "How to make the most out of working together." At the back of the classroom a bulletin board bears the title "Our Social Studies Investigation." In the middle of this bulletin board is written the question "What are some of the current global issues affecting Canada's international relations?" The students have written words such as "pollution," "climate change," "poverty," "disease," and "war" on strips of paper in a web pattern around the question. On the front board, Mr. Bali has written, "Should Canada take a more active role in addressing global warming? Be prepared to present and defend your group's ideas." This is the issue that each group is investigating.

What does this classroom snapshot tell you about Mr. Bali's educational philosophy? Compare/contrast your schooling with what the children in Mr. Bali's class are experiencing. What might be some of the benefits and concerns that you would have with teaching in this way?

As you read in the previous chapter, all teaching is rooted in educational philosophy. An educational philosophy explains a teacher's beliefs about what constitutes learning, how learning happens, what can be done to support learning, and the teacher's and students' roles in that learning. In this way, educational philosophy is rooted in learning theory.

Different educational philosophies suggest different starting points for planning a social studies program. These theories about learning can be used to help you in thinking about your educational philosophy. Here we will examine two competing theories about the nature of knowledge and how people acquire it—a transmissionist approach to learning and a constructivist approach to learning.

A Transmissionist View of Learning

One educational philosophy that has dominated social studies education in the past is based on a view of learning known as knowledge transmission. Knowledge transmission begins with the underlying assumption that reality is objective and that it exists in the world independent of the individual. Transmissionists hold the belief that there is a fixed, reproducible body of knowledge and enduring understandings about the world that all people need to know. Learning is believed to be the passive transmission of that information from a more knowledgeable individual to one who is less knowledgeable. Teachers know what this specialized knowledge is and their job is to transfer it to their students. In teaching this specialized knowledge, the teacher's role is to break the information to be received by the students down into small, easily remembered bits. One step builds on the next in an organized progression as these bits are taught in a hierarchical and sequential order, from part to whole, through a series of lessons. Simple facts precede more complex facts, and the learning of facts precedes thinking about them. The students are told about the reality of the world and they are expected to take in, accept, and remember what they are told. Since all of the students in a class are exposed to the same learning sequence, it is expected that they are all "on the same page" at all times and that they should be able to produce the same results. Assessment of students' learning often involves accurately recalling the transmitted information on a test.

CLASSROOM APPLICATION

Students in Madame Giroux's Grade 5 social studies class are learning about the events that led up to Confederation. They are directed to read a passage from their social studies textbook and then fill in a timeline showing the dates and descriptions of those events in chronological order. A matching test requiring them to connect the date in column A to the correct event in column B is used to check what they have learned. What does an activity like this suggest about how people learn? What might be the benefits and drawbacks to using such an approach to learning?

Transmissionism has been associated with B. F. Skinner, an American psychologist, and his behaviorist theory of learning. Skinner was interested in the measurable aspects of how people learn, or their behavioural outcomes. According to the behaviourist view, learning involves changing behaviour by external control through both positive and negative reinforcement. If the student is exposed to new learning and then is rewarded through praise, a good grade, or some other form of reward (e.g., stickers) then the student will retain what has been transmitted. If the student receives negative reinforcement then he or she will be more motivated to want to do better the next time. Learning, therefore, is a sequence of stimulus (any teaching event—e.g., a lecture, a video, etc.) followed by reinforcement.

LOOKING BACK

Meet Jasmine, a student teacher, who had this to say about her memories of social studies in elementary school: "I can remember that we studied about explorers but all that comes back to me is writing down copious notes that my teacher had written on the blackboard. When we came into the classroom the maps were pulled down over the notes to make sure that we didn't start writing until she gave us the okay. I still have my notebook from Grade 5. There are pages and pages, written in beautiful penmanship I might add, about the voyages of Jacques Cartier, John Cabot, the Vikings and Christopher Columbus. The odd time we also got to colour maps that showed the routes those explorers took on their voyages, then we glued the maps into our notes. Our notebooks were collected by the teacher and marked for neatness and organization. I always got a gold star on mine. I remember having to memorize all of that information about the explorers for tests but I can't recall any of it today."

Did you ever experience this type of social studies learning in your schooling? If yes, describe your experiences. How did you feel about learning in this fashion? What hidden curriculum was at work in Jasmine's classroom?

Technology Connection For more information on the behaviourist theory of learning, follow the links on the book's companion website to relevant pages on the Funderstanding (http://www.funderstanding.com) and Learning and Teaching (http://www.learningandteaching.info) websites.

A Constructivist View of Learning

Another educational philosophy, the constructivist view of learning, is based on the belief that learners cannot simply receive objective pieces of knowledge from others because reality is subjective and exists only inside people's heads. Each individual constructs his or her own understanding of his or her unique world. Since learners construct their own reality, or at least interpret it based upon their experiences, what they know does not exist prior to their creation of it and it cannot be transmitted to them from a more knowledgeable person. From this view, learning is a process that involves the interaction of past experience, personal intentions, and new experience. People construct their knowledge and understanding through active engagement that includes investigating, questioning, reflecting, and collaborating. What is constructed varies for everyone; no two people interpret things exactly the same way. Influences such as life experiences, group affiliations, gender, cultural identities, values, and beliefs act as lenses through which people interpret their worlds. Teaching is a process of supporting that knowledge construction rather than transmitting the teacher's own knowledge. The teacher acts as a guide by building on what children bring to the learning experience (a process called *scaffolding*) and supporting their new learning. The motivation to learn is internal to the learners and is influenced by how relevant and meaningful what is being learned is to their lives.

REFLECTION POINT

What do you think of the belief that we all see the world differently from others? What implications does such a view have for the teaching of social studies?

Differing Views of Constructivism

As I noted in the Preface, I have found support for my beliefs about teaching and learning in constructivist learning theory and accordingly I have designed this book using a constructivist view on learning. However, while all constructivists agree that the knower creates knowledge, not all agree on how that knowledge is constructed. There are different interpretations of constructivism, and I briefly examine two of these perspectives here: cognitive constructivism and social constructivism. (This is not meant to be an exhaustive review of either of these interpretations, so I have provided links to websites for further reading if you are interested or need more information.)

TABLE 2.1 ■ Summary Chart Comparing Two Learning Theories

LEARNING THEORY	TRANSMISSIONIST VIEW	CONSTRUCTIVIST VIEW
What is learning?	Learning is assimilating objective reality. Learning is about taking in an externally controlled body of content. Learning is fact oriented. Learning is about getting the right answer. Learning is about gaining transmitted knowledge.	Learning is about making sense of one's world. Learning is a process. Learning is divergent. Learning is interpretation oriented. There are many answers, but there is a best choice. Learning involves changing the understandings that learners construct.
How does learning happen?	Learning happens by changing external, observable behaviours. Listen, read, recite, test, recall Reward Positive and negative reinforcement Extrinsic motivation	Learning is about cognitive change. Learning happens by active engagement in problem solving and critically examining evidence. Collaboration Interaction Intrinsic motivation
Does everyone learn the same way?	Yes Knowledge is fixed, objective, universal, and independent of the knower. Everyone needs to get the correct answer.	No Knowledge is individually constructed. Life experience and context are influential. Learners have differing learning styles and display multiple intelligences.
What can be done to facilitate learning?	Teacher instruction Teacher use of positive and negative reinforcement Teacher dissemination of information incrementally Elimination of wrong thinking Testing of recall	Create learning contexts that encourage active learner involvement and ownership of learning. Recognize learner's misconceptions as important windows into their thinking. Encourage reflection. Challenge higher-level thinking. Engage learners in problem solving activities. Provide multiple sources of information.
What is the role of the teacher in the learning?	Teacher as centre of learning Learning is teacher–dependent. Teacher as generator of important knowledge Teacher as presenter of information Teacher transfers knowledge.	Teacher as guide and facilitator of learning Values student initiative Encourages student empowerment Acknowledges student's ideas and prior knowledge Scaffolds
What is the role of the learner?	Dependent on teacher Passive Externally motivated Listen, read, answer questions	Independent risk takers Active Internally motivated Reflect Collaborate

In the previous chapter, you were challenged to think about a set of questions that could be used to uncover your beliefs about teaching and learning as a way to begin the goal setting process. Those same questions have been used here to exemplify the differences in thinking from a transmissionist perspective and a constructivist perspective on learning.

With a peer, discuss the summary chart on the two theories of learning (Table 2.1). How does the chart help you to understand the differences between the two theories about learning? Which one appeals to you more? Why? Do you and your partner agree? How can these theories help to inform your thinking about your educational philosophy? How might the educational philosophy that you choose help to shape your goals for your social studies program?

Cognitive Constructivism

Cognitive constructivism focuses on the individual as meaning maker. This view of constructivism is based on the psychological view that the individual constructs knowledge through interactions with his or her environment. The work of Jean Piaget and his cognitive developmental theory has informed this view of constructivism. According to Piaget, cognition is a biological process. All children go through the same logical progression of age-related stages in their development of thinking and conceptualizing, from the more concrete to the abstract, regardless of the content or knowledge domain in which the thinking occurs. Maturation is the key to all learning; certain things cannot be understood or learned until the child is at the developmental level at which she or he is ready to learn them. All children reason differently at different stages of their development. Piaget identified these stages as sensorimotor (birth to 2 years old), preoperational (ages 2 to 7), concrete operational (ages 7 to 11), and formal operational (12 to adult).

Central to cognitive constructivism is the belief that children, depending on their maturity level, construct their own knowledge schemes that they use when dealing with their world. As they engage with and make sense of their environment, they go through two processes. One learning process is assimilation, in which what is learned is added to what is already known. The other process is accommodation, in which previously understood schemata are changed in order to fit the new ideas. Some form of dissonance between what was originally believed and what is being experienced has to be felt in order for accommodation to occur (Singer & Revenson, 1996).

 Technology Connection For more information on Jean Piaget's cognitive developmental theory and on cognitive constructivism, visit the book's companion website, where links are provided to pages on the following websites:

- Funderstanding: http://www.funderstanding.com
- Theory into Practice database: http://tip.psychology.org
- The Psi Cafe: http://www.psy.pdx.edu/PsiCafe

Ryan, a teacher candidate, was asked to think back on his experiences with social studies and use those memories to help him envision his future social studies classroom. Here is what he said: "My experience with social studies for the most part was a chore. A lot of my teachers just gave facts to memorize and we were required to list off a bunch of stuff. I really disliked teachers who stressed reading and rote memorization. I always found social studies too broad and too focused on learning mere information, particularly dates of historical events. I want kids to look forward to coming to class. I want social studies to be interesting for them and for it to have meaning. I want to be sure to ask them their opinions and really listen and to encourage them to not be afraid to ask questions and participate in class. I want my students to be actively involved rather than just receive knowledge. I want to help my students to see that there are always other ways of looking at things. I want to teach them to inquire critically, to talk about what they are thinking, to apply their opinions, and to take a chance. I want my students to know that their opinion matters. I want to have a lot of discussion, especially students talking to each other and asking a lot of questions to try to better understand what they are learning about. I want to keep an open atmosphere in my classroom to encourage discussion and the airing of opinions. I want to give them a sense of pride."

What do Ryan's statements tell you about some of his goals for his social studies program? What learning theory would appear to offer support for his ideas? Create your own wish list for your future social studies program.

Social Constructivism

The social constructivist model of learning begins with the assumption that all knowledge is social in nature. While cognitive constructivism focuses on the individual making meaning based on his or her interactions with the natural world, social constructivism sees the social world of learners as playing an intricate role in how they make sense of their world. Reality is negotiated through social consensus. For knowledge to be seen as being truthful and useful, it has to fit with that consensus. Learning therefore occurs in a context of social interactions leading to understanding.

One theorist who has been associated most often with social constructivism is Lev Vygotsky and his social development theory. Vygotsky (1978) argued that children can learn and understand new things and attain more advanced levels of cognitive and skill development no matter what their age as a result of social interaction. Interacting with others is critical to children's learning and cognitive growth because making meaning involves explaining and interpreting ideas for others, negotiating with others' ideas, listening to and sometimes adopting others' views, and at times having to resolve conflicts between contrasting ideas. All learners bring prior knowledge and experience to these interactions. Meaning is continuously being negotiated and modified, and knowledge is being created by everyone involved in these interactions. Language plays a key role in cognitive development as the child engages in problem solving, discussion, and negotiation with others.

Teachers facilitate the development of cognition in their students by scaffolding or supporting children's movement through higher level functioning, a phenomenon Vygotsky referred to as the zone of proximal development (ZPD). The ZPD is the gap between what the child understands about a particular skill or content area and what the teacher is trying to teach. Initially, the teacher plays a more prominent role in directing the child's learning using scaffolding to support and guide the child's development so that the gap between the current level of skill or understanding and the desired level is narrowed. But eventually the responsibility for the learning shifts to the child and the teacher is able to provide less guidance.

While Piaget believed that all children follow a similar pattern of stages in their cognitive development, Vygotsky saw the development of intellectual abilities as being more specific to the culture in which the child was raised. Members of a cultural group share a common language, customs, values, and beliefs and these can determine what is experienced, how those experiences are interpreted, and how they are communicated to others. Thus, children acquire both knowledge (what they come to know and think) and the tools for acquiring that knowledge (the strategies they use to learn) from their interactions with their others and their surroundings (i.e., group affiliations, cultural identity, interactions with parents, siblings, and friends; their neighbourhood, nationality, the media and popular culture, etc.).

REFLECTION POINT

The point has been made here that a child's cultural background has a significant impact on his or her development. However, Gay (2000) claims that most teachers have on what she refers to as "cultural blinders" (p. 71). What do you think she means? Would you agree with her claim? How does this conflict with what Vygotsky says about the powerful influence of a child's cultural background on his or her learning? What might you do to address this concern in your teaching?

 Technology Connection Read more about Vygotsky's social development theory and social constructivism on the book's companion website, where links are provided to relevant pages on the following websites:

- The Theory into Practice Database: http://tip.psychology.org
- Funderstanding: http://www.funderstanding.com
- The Psi Cafe: http://www.psy.pdx.edu/PsiCafe
- Southwest Educational Development Laboratory: http://www.sedl.org
- Thirteen/Ed Online: http://www.thirteen.org/edonline

When asked to describe her teaching philosophy, here is what Grade 1 teacher Ms. Wong says: "As an early childhood educator, I strongly believe that children learn more effectively when I teach the whole child. Children are naturally curious, active learners who have individual interests, abilities and needs. The learning environment must be a fun and stimulating place where children feel safe and respected. It is crucial to keep in mind the many different learning styles of children (e.g., auditory learners, tactile learners, visual learners). My classroom is full of complex children with many differences and diversity. These children come to my classroom with different knowledge, life experiences and backgrounds that generates a range of attitudes towards learning. I am constantly remembering that when I am planning my lessons."

Ms. Wong takes her class on fieldtrips out into the community on a regular basis.

What does Ms. Wong's educational philosophy statement tell you about what she believes regarding teaching and learning? Which learning theory might have guided her philosophy? What information does her philosophy statement give you? How can Ms. Wong's philosophy statement help you in thinking about how to describe your own philosophy?

The Principles of Social Constructivism

Social constructivism is not a theory about teaching, but much has been written about the ways in which its core beliefs about how people learn can be used to guide and support teaching. Here, I have synthesized what the literature says about learning based on social constructivism into five principles. As shown in Figure 2.1, these principles include incorporating prior learning, supporting individual knowledge construction, actively engaging learners, recognizing the importance of social context, and encouraging reflection on learning. A statement about what each principle means and its implications for you as a teacher, as well as an example of how to use the principle to guide your classroom practice in social studies, has been included.

FIGURE 2.1 ■ Principles of Social Constructivism

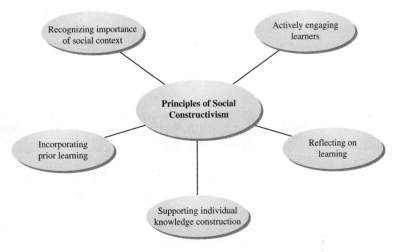

Principle #1: Incorporating Prior Learning. One of the central ideas of social constructivism is that learning is a building process that begins with a foundation of prior learning. Learners come to any new learning situation with varying amounts of prior knowledge that is culturally based. They have already developed schemata or mental maps to organize and represent what they know and have made what seem to them to be logical and meaningful links amongst these pieces of stored knowledge. These ideas are held on to until they are modified or replaced by more satisfactory explanations.

In order to design meaningful learning experiences, teachers must be aware of the range of the initial ideas that students have constructed and how these ideas might support or interfere with what is being experienced in the classroom. Thus, constructivist teachers begin any new learning experience by first trying to determine what the child is bringing to the learning experience and the degree of his or her prior knowledge on a topic and then adapting their teaching to address students' beliefs and ideas.

Constructivist Teaching Tip:

A social studies teacher who bases his or her teaching on constructivist learning principles begins with what a child already knows about a topic or concept.

Teachers can use a variety of strategies to elicit students' prior knowledge. These strategies can also be used to develop students' literacy skills. Earlier, we looked at the Know-Wonder-How-Learn chart. Some other strategies include brainstorming, class discussions, Venn diagrams and concept maps. (See http://www.graphic.org for examples of these and other graphic organizers). The concept map is a visual thinking technique that requires students to identify a central idea and then brainstorm related ideas and show the connections between each of the brainstormed ideas and the central one. The teacher is able to get a sense of students' initial understanding of a concept by seeing what the learners feel they know about a particular concept or topic, how they are arranging their ideas, and what connections they perceive between their ideas.

Figure 2.2 shows a concept map that Jason did for his Grade 5 teacher at the beginning of a unit on Canada's geography and people. He was asked to include at least eight things that he knew about Canada.

What does Jason's concept map tell you about his knowledge of Canada? What might be the next step that you would take with Jason to help him to address his inaccurate understandings?

FIGURE 2.2 ■ Concept Web: Jason's Web about Canada

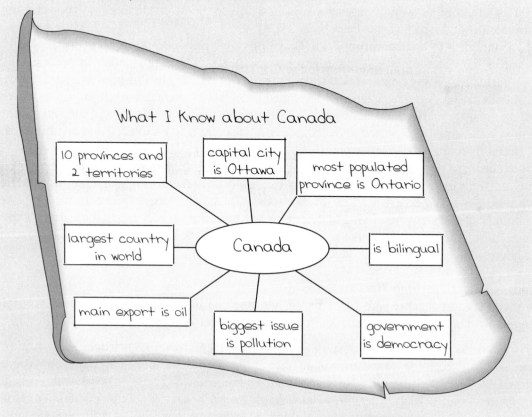

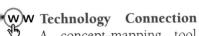 **Technology Connection** A concept-mapping tool commonly used for kindergarten to Grade 5 classes is the visual learning software program Kidspiration (see Figure 2.3). For a demonstration of how the software can be used in social studies, visit the book's companion website and follow the link to the Kidspiration website, where you can try out a free trial version of the Kidspiration software.

Older students can use a more advanced version of the software called Inspiration. This version will provide several social studies examples, particularly the Inspired Sites

FIGURE 2.3 ■ Kidspiration Web on Transportation

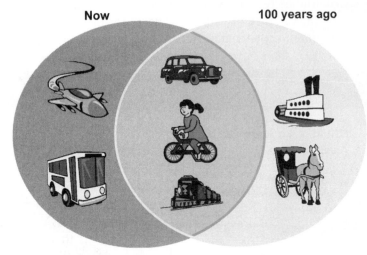

section that provides examples of how teachers have used this tool to uncover students' thinking.

Principle #2: Supporting Knowledge Construction. Learning is a process that children actively engage in as they attempt to make meaning by developing mental models to help make sense of their experiences. The brain's key function is to sort out all of the experiences that learners are exposed to in their environment and to try to make sense out of them by comparing them to previously stored knowledge. The brain innately seeks meaning through seeing patterns and linking new knowledge to what is known (Caine & Caine, 2005). As they learn, students select from the available information and construct their own personal meaning by placing the new information and experiences in the context of what they already know. All learners internally control their own learning; no two children learn in exactly the same way, as factors such as nationality, race, gender, and religion, as well as the media and popular culture, all influence their ideas. Students acquire different knowledge from the same experience and they apply their understanding in different ways, often without being aware of the process.

Understanding and nurturing the learning of students is the primary task of constructivist teachers (Brooks & Brooks, 1999). They use students' ideas as a way to better understand the students' reasoning. They plan activities that make use of the learners' background knowledge and encourage learners to add to that knowledge by providing learning environments that shift thinking to more sophisticated levels of understandings and require students to apply the new information creatively. Constructivist teachers also seek out inconsistencies between learners' current understandings and the new experiences before them. These inconsistencies can be used as a starting point in designing experiences that help children to develop more accurate understandings. Ongoing activities that reveal the ways in which learners' mind maps are changing are important to help the teacher in this scaffolding process.

Constructivist Teaching Tip:

A social studies teacher whose practice is based on constructivist learning principles recognizes the importance of helping students to link new ideas to what is already known and of building on and challenging the accuracy of the child's prior understandings.

CLASSROOM APPLICATION

FIGURE 2.4 ■ Carmen's Map of Alberta

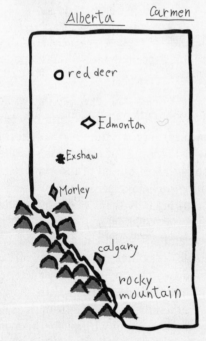

What information would this map give Miss Chambray about Carmen's knowledge?

Before beginning a unit on how Alberta's geography affects where people choose to live in the province, Miss Chambray wanted to find out what her students already knew about the subject. For an introductory activity she asked her class to draw a map of Alberta and then indicate at least five things that they knew about the province on their maps (i.e., capital city, other urban areas, main natural resources, landforms, waterways). Figure 2.4 shows Carmen's map.

Principle #3: Actively Engaging Learners. Since people are constantly trying to make sense of their worlds, constructivism acknowledges the importance of learners taking an active role in their learning. Active engagement in exploring relevant problems and issues can not only help learners to connect new learning with their previously known information and to restructure information in ways that make sense to them; it can also challenge them to use the new information being gathered in meaningful ways. When students are encouraged to view problems and issues from different positions and to identify multiple viewpoints on any given issue, their learning experiences are particularly powerful. Investigating a particular position and then representing that viewpoint to others can help students to see potential flaws in their own prior ideas.

Rather than "teaching" the student in the sense of presenting or even assigning information, the goal of the constructivist teacher is to support the students' learning. Thus, the constructivist teacher takes the role of a facilitator helping students to develop thinking and reasoning skills and a deeper understanding of the ideas being examined as well as encouraging them to become independent learners. In view of the fact that learning occurs best when what is being learned is relevant for the learner, constructivist teachers engage children in meaningful inquiry about subjects that are of interest to the children and are in some way connected to their lives outside the classroom.

Constructivist Teaching Tip:
A social studies teacher whose practice is based on constructivist learning principles actively engages children in multiple, meaningful, interactive, and challenging experiences that assist them in uncovering, building on, and making connections between initial ideas and new information.

Principle #4: Recognizing the Importance of Social Context. A fourth key idea of constructivism is that learning is interpersonal. Learning does not take place in a vacuum but rather through social interaction with others, including teachers, peers, and outside experts. Learning requires the opportunity to discuss and compare one's understanding of an idea with others. Making meaning is a dialogic process involving persons in conversation; thus, individuals' understandings are constructed through engagement in talk about problems and tasks. Knowledge is created as learners test the fit or usefulness of their conceptual understandings in interaction with others and in contexts in which the knowledge is applied. Listening to the views of others provides the opportunity to build understandings from multiple perspectives. Social interaction also contributes to the motivation to learn and the development of interpersonal skills.

Active engagement is necessary for meaning making.

CHAPTER 2　Why Social Constructivism as a Theoretical Framework?

FIGURE 2.5 ■ **The Collaborative Learning Experience of Constructivism**

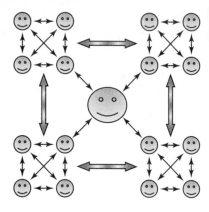

Constructivist teachers capitalize on the fact that social interaction is integral to learning by using processes that encourage students to work together in groups, to participate in real-life collaborative projects, and to engage in conversation. In order to stretch students' initial conceptualizations, constructivist teachers encourage learners to articulate and discuss their ideas with others. In this regard, discussion and debate are two strategies that can be particularly powerful. Oral classroom exchanges become more of a three-way process that includes questions directed from students to the teacher and to each other (as illustrated in Figure 2.5) rather than the more traditional one-way process in which questions are posed only by the teacher. Careful monitoring of these collaborations by the teacher can reveal the ways in which individual students' ideas and understandings are being confirmed, clarified, and/or reshaped through these experiences.

Constructivist Teaching Tip:

A social studies teacher whose practice is based on constructivist learning principles provides ample opportunity for a variety of collaborative learning experiences both amongst the learners in the classroom as well as with others beyond the classroom and school walls.

Principle #5: Reflecting on Learning. The fifth principle of social constructivism is that learning is intrapersonal: it needs to be individually processed and internalized to truly have meaning. Students need to be provided with ample opportunities throughout the learning process to reflect on their ideas, in terms of both what they initially believed about a particular topic, concept, issue, or problem and how the learning experiences they have been engaged in have shaped both their beliefs and their prior understanding. Sometimes the learning experiences result in the students changing their view of the world in very significant ways, but learning does not always require a change of view. New information can simply add to or elaborate on the students' initial schemata in ways that help to deepen their understanding.

While the brain naturally searches for meaning, research has indicated that the brain cannot pay attention to new stimuli and successfully process meaning at the same time. Thus, periods of purposeful processing time and reflective pauses are important to facilitate meaningful learning (Caine & Caine, 2005). Reflection time is also important for helping students understand how and why they learn. It gives students opportunities to talk and write about what their learning means to them, how they care about it, and how it is connected to their lives and other knowledge that they have.

Constructivist teachers provide students with ample time for reflection, beginning with the initial stages of learning when students are encouraged to examine their prior ideas and beliefs and culminating with a look back at those ideas at the end of the learning segment. In this way, the constructivist teacher is helping students to take responsibility for their own learning as well as develop the life skill of learning how to learn. Opportunities for frequent reflection on what the learner is experiencing assists in personal sense making, as does ongoing interactive feedback that is both teacher-generated and self-generated. Frequent and ongoing feedback from the teacher that focuses on students' use of knowledge can help to advance the meaning making process.

Constructivist Teaching Tip:

A social studies teacher whose practice is based on constructivist learning principles encourages and provides students with ample personal reflection and processing time to aid in their construction of meaning.

One example of a reflection-feedback tool, discussed in Chapter 1, is journal writing. Another similar tool is the learning log. Using a log, learners can be encouraged to pause at the end of a lesson or day to look back and reflect on their learning experiences. A small, lined notebook is good for recording reflections as it keeps all of the learner's entries in one place and can be used as an ongoing record of the child's development and self-assessment over the school year. Learners can be encouraged to look back at earlier entries throughout the year and to reflect on their growth and on changes in their thinking. Reflections can be formally structured—i.e., written in response to specific questions assigned by the teacher— or can take the form of unstructured, free writing about anything of particular interest to the children.

Younger children can use a notebook with pages half lined and half blank to draw a picture of what they did in class that day and what they learned, as well as how they felt about that learning, and a few words of text could accompany the picture. Older children can write more detailed descriptions of their learning experiences, including what they found most interesting and why, and what questions they still have; they should also include some comment on their learning. They can be encouraged to think about questions such as, How much effort did I put into my work today?, Did I stay on task?, What would I do differently the next time?, and How can I continue to improve? The children can share their entries with other learners and ask questions of each other. These logs can be used as an ongoing assessment tool that both acts as a guide for the teacher regarding the students' interest in learning and their motivation to learn what is being taught and provides a way of monitoring students' effort and assessing their progress.

CLASSROOM APPLICATION

Figures 2.6 and 2.7 present samples of excerpts from two different Grade 2 students' learning logs that show their reflections about their field trip to a farm. Compare and contrast the information provided about these two students in their learning log entries.

(Continued)

FIGURE 2.6 ■ **Sample #1**
Excerpt from Learning Log

Monday, April 15, 2005

On a Farm you have to feed your pets.

The way they get to school is they get bussed.

When you live on a farm your nabbers are far away.

FIGURE 2.7 ■ **Sample #2**
Excerpt from Learning Log

All About Denise

Denise lives on the farm. She has cows and barn cats.

REFLECTION POINT

What experiences have you had with the theory of constructivism so far in your teacher education program? What do you know about constructivism based on that experience? How do the ideas about constructivism presented here fit with what you had previously learned about the theory? Is there anything missing that you feel would be important to add? Has your mental map about constructivism been changed in any way?

ACTIVE ENGAGEMENT

In a group, come up with a way of depicting what a classroom that is based on constructivist principles might look like. You might wish to draw a constructivist classroom or create a poem, a rap, or a metaphor to represent your understanding. Share your depictions with the class. Discuss what some of the pros and cons to teaching in this fashion might be.

How Social Constructivism Has Informed My Philosophy of Education

My philosophy of education is based on these five principles of social constructivism. I believe that every teacher candidate is unique and that they come to their teacher education program with different backgrounds, experience, and knowledge that they have already constructed. Learning something new is a process of building on those past experiences and revising that prior knowledge. The learning process is enhanced through active engagement in experiences that are relevant and meaningful, through collaboration, when there are opportunities to explain ideas to others and listen to others' ideas, and to pause to reflect. These beliefs have shaped the learning activities that have been provided throughout the remainder of this book. As you progress through the chapters of this book and share your thoughts with others, continue to reflect on your initial ideas and beliefs about teaching and learning in social studies and add to or change those beliefs.

Chapter Summary

In this chapter, you were introduced to the notion that understanding learning theory is foundational to coming up with your own teaching philosophy that can be used to guide your social studies program planning. You were introduced to two opposing views on how people learn: transmissionism and constructivism. While transmissionism has dominated much of social studies teaching in the past, moving away from a philosophic starting point that focuses on teaching as transmission to one that focuses on learning as knowledge construction is vital to promoting higher level, engaged learning.

As we saw, the term "constructivism" does not mean the same thing to everyone. Two views on constructivism were also examined: cognitive and social. Social constructivism was identified as the philosophical framework that informs this book. An overview of the key principles of social constructivism identified the importance of acknowledging that each learner constructs his or her own meaning on the basis of the learning experiences provided; central to this knowledge construction is beginning with the learner's prior ideas and then immersing the learner in activities that challenge and clarify those ideas through active engagement, social interaction, and ongoing reflection. For the purposes of this book, constructivism is being defined as a theory of learning that recognizes the important role that learners have in constructing their own knowledge and understanding both individually and socially.

While this chapter has discussed the big picture of theory and its application to teaching and learning in general, we will now begin to narrow down the focus to the application of constructivism in teaching and learning social studies. In the next section of this book, we begin by looking at what social studies is all about and the role played by citizenship education. Be sure to keep the discussion about the principles of social constructivism from this chapter in mind as you continue on with your reading and thinking about the kind of social studies teacher you want to be.

Chapter 3

What Is Social Studies?

In the first two chapters, you were challenged to think about how your underlying beliefs about teaching and learning will influence your goals for your social studies program. Before you can firm up those goals, however, you must also thoughtfully examine what you believe the purpose of social studies to be as a subject area in elementary schools. How you define social studies and envision its purpose in schooling will be affected by your past experiences with it in school. Throughout this chapter's investigation of what social studies is all about, you will be encouraged to reflect on your beliefs about teaching and learning and how they are being challenged and perhaps changed by engaging in the activities provided here.

Defining Social Studies

Let's begin looking at the question of what social studies is by examining a number of different views on and experiences with social studies, including those of children, elementary teachers, and other teacher candidates. Then we'll look at some of the official curricular definitions of social studies from across Canada to determine how these definitions are similar to and different from each other and to see how they fit with the views expressed by the teachers, children, and teacher candidates.

ACTIVE ENGAGEMENT

Interview a child about his or her views on social studies. You may want to ask what she or he thinks social studies is all about, what she or he does in social studies, and what his or her favourite and least favourite parts of social studies are.

Children's Views on Social Studies

Several elementary school children were asked to answer the questions, What is social studies and why do you study it in school? Here are some of their responses:

Stephan, a Grade 4 student, sees social studies as being "about mapping and finding countries and their cities and populations on the map." He says that it is an important subject to study in school because "if you went to that country you would know something about it."

Sandy, in Grade 3, says that social studies is about "pioneers and people from the past—where they lived, what they ate, what they wore and how they made stuff." She adds, "I like making apple dolls and dressing up like pioneers and doing skits." To her, social studies is important because "if you don't learn social studies when you grow up and you have kids you won't be able to help them with their homework."

To Kara in Grade 6, social studies is "where you learn about governments like local and provincial governments, and about elections and how to get elected and voting and about politics. It's important because you should know about them because they are an important part of life and they will affect your grades as you get older."

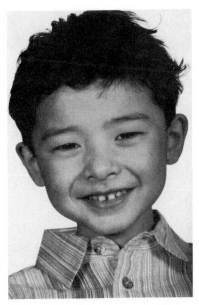

Stephan's favourite part of social studies is geography.

REFLECTION POINT

1. Do you see any similarities in the children's views about what social studies is and why they study it in school? How do the responses of these children compare to the one given by the child you interviewed? What do these responses from children say to you regarding social studies and its purpose as a subject area in elementary schools?

2. How important do you think it is for children to know why they are studying social studies? If you feel that it is important to know why you are learning something, then how might you go about ensuring that your future students could answer the questions, What is social studies and why is it an important subject to study in school?

Teachers' Views on Social Studies

Here are four teachers' responses to the same questions that the children were asked about social studies.

CHAPTER 3 What Is Social Studies? **41**

Ask an elementary teacher what social studies is and why it is an important subject for children to study in school. Compare that teacher's views to the ones expressed by this group of teachers.

Steve, a Grade 5 teacher, says, "Social studies isn't about learning facts and recalling information. It's about understanding why we are the way we are as a country and what our responsibilities are as a citizen. This to me is very important for children to learn especially if they are going to become adults who take their responsibilities as citizens seriously."

A Grade 1 teacher, Lynne, says, "What we are trying to do in social studies is develop good citizens, responsible citizens in society and if we start where it means the most, with your family and how you can be responsible and contribute to your family and go from there, I think it gives the children a better understanding that they are important too, not just their parents, and that they can make decisions and contribute. It's also a very good thinking subject for the child because students are allowed to have different ideas and opinions—there is no right or wrong. None of the other subjects really develop these important thinking skills as well as social studies can so it is very important for children to learn."

Magda feels that the social aspect of social studies is what makes this subject unique.

Magda, a Grade 3 teacher, says, "In the term 'social' itself you get the idea of interaction in society. Children learn through our classrooms how to interact with others and develop positive attitudes toward each other. These social skills are becoming increasingly more important in our multicultural society so our children really need to have positive experiences in social studies."

Frances, who is also a primary teacher, sees social studies as helping "children to understand the social structure of our society, not only so that they will appreciate it but also so that they become active responsible citizens of our society. It's about appreciating the value of interdependence and different social groupings. So what it means to be part of a family, a school, a community and making those connections between what they learn related to their family and how it translates to other relationships."

REFLECTION POINT

Do you see any similarities in the ways the various teachers define and talk about the importance of social studies? How do your thoughts on social studies compare to these teachers' ideas?

Teacher Candidates' Views on Social Studies

Here are some teacher candidates sharing stories about their past experiences in social studies and how those experiences have shaped the way they think about why social studies is included as a subject area in elementary schools.

LOOKING BACK

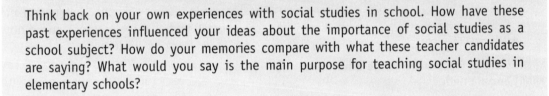

Think back on your own experiences with social studies in school. How have these past experiences influenced your ideas about the importance of social studies as a school subject? How do your memories compare with what these teacher candidates are saying? What would you say is the main purpose for teaching social studies in elementary schools?

Meet Caroline. This is what she recalls about her social studies experiences in school: "As a child in elementary school, I remember learning about people, places, dates, and facts, but giving individual opinions on local issues never had a place in any of my classes. I remember doing research projects on historical figures and countries of the world, but never once did I use any kind of critical thinking or inquiry skills. The educators at my elementary school chose to 'transmit' information to students, resulting in negative attitudes toward social studies and its importance in transforming children into responsible citizens. Sadly, after interviewing my nine-year old cousin, I realized that this trend is still happening. When asked if he liked social studies, my cousin replied, 'not very much because I keep having to remember too many things.' I then asked about what types of things he did in social studies and he responded with, 'notes and tests.' I can remember thinking, 'You're not learning a thing about what social studies really is,' and that's really sad."

Brenda, another student teacher shared this story of her past experience: "My favourite memory of social studies in elementary school was when we studied about China. In this unit our Grade 6 class built a replica of a city in China near the Great Wall of China. For this project we had to build the houses that the Chinese people lived in (and thus had to research their architecture), their crops (and there found out that the rice plantation needed to be built on a slope), and had to build the Wall of China proportionate in size to the other structures. This hands-on activity taught us a lot because we had to find the information out so that we

Robert sees goal setting as his primary responsibility as a teacher.

could apply it to the project and using it this way made us remember it. So social studies, when it is taught right, can be an important subject for learning about our world and how other people live in it. There really isn't any other subject that teaches about that, so it's important."

Here is Suzanne talking about social studies in her past: "For the most part, my own social studies education took the form of transmission. I was fed knowledge about the beliefs and expectations of society while content coverage governed my success. This approach was so boring and uninformative that it is hard for me to recollect what I learned in social studies during elementary school. However, my high school social studies education took a more left-wing approach by teaching us the prescribed content through the process of reflective inquiry. Our development into responsible citizens was accomplished gradually through "hands-on" activities, simulations and other creative assignments. This experience has taught me that how you teach social studies is really important to how important it is seen to be by your students."

FIGURE 3.1 ■ Teacher Candidate Brainstorm Web about Social Studies

Robert had this to say about his experiences with social studies: "For many of us, our social studies consisted of a series of unrelated activities and the memorization of facts and dates. Although some things proved interesting, for the most part I feel my experiences lacked coherence, interest and purpose. I think many teachers lose focus of what they are teaching and why. Instead, they become concerned only with the facts and dates pointed out in textbooks. We teach as we are taught! This is scary because this is not how I want to teach. I realize that elementary teachers are generalists and might take one social studies course before teaching; however, it is still their responsibility to teach the students effectively. In order to become an effective teacher, you need to have a clear understanding of the topics and then create a goal and purpose for teaching these topics."

Shannon, a teacher candidate, was asked to brainstorm what she thought social studies was all about. Figure 3.1 on page 44 presents her response, depicted in a brainstorm web format.

After brainstorming about what social studies entails, the next step is to synthesize all of the ideas about what constitutes social studies into one or two sentences that define what social studies is as a subject area. Synthesis activities such as this are important to refining and bringing clarity to how you think about social studies and to how you represent your understanding of it to others, in particular the children in your future classrooms.

Curricular Definitions of Social Studies

There has always been some level of disagreement amongst educators when it comes to trying to define social studies. As a subject area in Canadian schools, social studies can be traced back to the early 1900s. In its earliest form, social studies was mainly about geography, history, and civics education. The term "social studies" was not commonly found in curriculum documents across most of Canada until the 1930s. One exception now is in Quebec where the term "social sciences" is used in place of social studies and "geography, history and citizenship education" is identified as one of the five core subject areas (Kee, 2002). In other instances, the label "social studies" has been confined to elementary school programs of study. For example, in Ontario, courses in history and geography take the place of social studies at levels beyond Grade 6.

An ongoing tension has always existed between those who envision social studies as teaching the traditional subject disciplines of history and geography and those who see social studies as an interdisciplinary subject that draws from many of the social sciences and focuses on studies of people in society. The role of history as a discipline and its place within social studies has been a particular source of much debate since the inception of social studies as a school subject. Despite these issues, for the most part elementary social studies today is quite similar across the country, although there are some slight differences in how it is defined from province to province.

ACTIVE ENGAGEMENT

As you read about the provincial and territorial views on social studies provided here and visit the weblinks for the various curricular documents, look for similarities and uniqueness in the way that social studies is being defined and the reasons given for including the study of social studies in elementary schools.

In British Columbia, social studies is defined as "a multidisciplinary subject that draws from the social sciences and humanities to study human interaction and natural and social environments." British Columbia is currently in transition between curriculum documents. Teachers can still use the 1998 curriculum; however, optional implementation of the new 2006 curriculum is available, with full implementation slated for 2008. The primary themes that emerge from this new curriculum centre on using social studies to create active, responsible citizens who are able to consider multiple perspectives in their decision-making process. This goal can be achieved by ensuring that students have the ability to acquire knowledge and make connections between current events and the past through the study of issues and cultures.

 Technology Connection On the book's companion website, you will find links to the British Columbia *Social Studies K to 7 2006 Integrated Resource Package* and the 1998 curriculum that is currently being phased out. See if you can identify some of the changes in how social studies is envisioned in the province of B.C. by comparing these two documents.

The province of Alberta is also in the midst of a transition in social studies. The 2005–2006 school year saw the implementation of the new kindergarten to Grade 3 programs of study. The implementation of the new programs of study for Grades 4 through 6 will be staggered between the 2006–2007 and 2009–2010 school years. The Alberta Education document describes social studies as an interdisciplinary study that encourages students to examine issues that occur locally and globally, with the goal of developing identity and citizenship.

46   PART ONE   Why Is It Important to Set Goals for Your Social Studies Program?

NEL

Technology Connection To find out more about how the Alberta social studies curriculum is being defined and what purpose it is believed to serve in schools, visit the book's companion website and follow the links to the province's curriculum documents.

The current Saskatchewan elementary social studies curriculum was implemented in 1995. The Saskatchewan definition of social studies is centred on people and their relationships, as well as on the study of the past as a method of understanding the present to affect the future. Social studies is also seen as a vehicle through which students can acquire the knowledge, skills, and attitudes necessary to become productive citizens within the local and global communities.

 Technology Connection For more information on the Saskatchewan social studies curriculum document for elementary schools (1995), follow the link to the Saskatchewan Learning site provided on the book's companion website.

The Manitoba Department of Education (2003) defines social studies as "the study of people in relation to each other and to the world in which they live" (p. 3). As an interdisciplinary study, social studies in Manitoba examines the past and present with an eye to the future, enabling students to become active democratic citizens who contribute to their local and global communities.

 Technology Connection To view the document *Kindergarten to Grade 8 Social Studies: Manitoba Curriculum Framework of Outcomes* (2003), follow the link to the Manitoba Education site on the book's companion website.

The recently revised social studies curriculum in Ontario is structured differently than its counterparts in western Canada. Students from kindergarten to Grade 6 are taught social studies in which an emphasis is placed on communities. The curriculum states: "Social studies seeks to examine and understand communities, from local to the global, their various heritages, physical systems, and the nature of citizenship within them" (Ontario Ministry of Education, 2004b, p. 2). Students learn about citizenship within the context of a culturally diverse and interdependent world, to develop a sense of identity and an ability to understand multiple perspectives. The Ontario curriculum has also recently emphasized literacy for learning, which is defined as "the ability to use language and images in rich and varied forms to read, listen, speak, view, represent and think critically about ideas" (Ontario Ministry of Education, 2004a, p. 5).

 Technology Connection To have a closer look at the 2004 Ontario curriculum for social studies from Grades 1 to 6 and the Literacy for Learning report, follow the links on the book's companion website.

As noted earlier, social studies is envisioned quite differently in Quebec. Rather than using the term "social studies," reference is made to the social sciences as a subject area. "The social sciences play an essential role in the acquisition of the conceptual tools needed to understand the world we live in, to integrate harmoniously into it and to contribute to its development" (Quebec Education Program, 2001, p. 181). The general objective of the social sciences is "to construct the student's social awareness in order to act as a responsible, informed citizen" (p. 181). The social sciences include the study of history, geography, and citizenship education. The Quebec curriculum document takes an issues focus that examines relationships within and among societies both in the past and present in order to develop students' understanding of diversity.

Technology Connection The Quebec social sciences curriculum document for preschool education and elementary education can be accessed via the link on the book's companion website.

The four Atlantic Provinces are currently in curricular transition. In 1999, the Council of Atlantic Ministers of Education and Training (CAMET) released the *Foundation for Atlantic Provinces Social Studies Curriculum* document. This document served as the basis and vision for the creation of a common social studies curriculum for all of the Atlantic Provinces. The kindergarten to Grade 2 and the Grade 7 curricula have been introduced, with the other ones slotted to be released for the 2006–2007 school year. Until the release of the new curricula, each province will continue to follow its provincially mandated curriculum. The foundation document (Council of Atlantic Ministers of Education and Training, 1999) defines the vision for social studies as the interdisciplinary examination of issues to encourage students to become citizens of Canada and the world who recognize and analyze diverse perspectives.

Technology Connection Links to the following documents are provided on the book's companion website:

- *The Foundation for the Atlantic Canada Social Studies Curriculum*
- *Let's Talk About Social Studies Primary–3,* from the Nova Scotia Ministry of Education
- *You and Your World Curriculum: Kindergarten to Grade 2,* from the New Brunswick Ministry of Education
- *Elementary Program of Studies and Authorized Materials 2005–2006,* from the P.E.I. Ministry of Education
- The Newfoundland and Labrador Ministry of Education social studies curriculum

Of the territorial governments, only the Northwest Territories has its own provincially mandated curriculum. Here, the elementary social studies curriculum focuses on the rights and responsibilities of a citizen of democracy in an ever-changing world and the skills that lead to responsible citizenship.

Technology Connection For an overview of the definition and purposes of social studies in the Northwest Territories, see the document *Social Studies: The Northwest Territories: Our Places, Stories and Traditions* (2006), which is a trial program for Grade 4 Social Studies. (A link is provided on the book's companion website.)

The governments of Nunavut and Yukon have chosen to implement curricula from other regions in their social studies classrooms. The Yukon follows the social studies curriculum of British Columbia, with modifications for local needs made as required. Nunavut has elected to continue to use the curriculum of the Northwest Territories since the creation of the new territory in 1999. However, Nunavut is currently in the process of creating a new curriculum that will contain a focus that is more relevant to the needs of their learners. Specifically, the territory's elders will have a central role in determining the direction of the curriculum; as a result, there will be less focus on student examination of self, and more concentration primarily on understanding family and community. Both Nunavut and the Yukon emphasize that the curricula they borrow are adapted to the needs of their particular learners.

Review the various definitions of social studies that you have read for each province and territory, and then refer back to the views of what social studies is and its purposes as a school subject expressed by the teachers, children, and teacher candidates earlier in this chapter. How do the various ideas expressed in the curriculum documents fit with these individuals' thoughts? Is there anything missing in your personal definition that you would now wish to add? Is there anything that you are concerned about or that you disagree with in the curricular definitions? How might the official definition of social studies that appears in a curriculum document influence how you design your future social studies program?

While the definition of social studies in each of the provinces and territories is unique in some ways, common threads within them do emerge upon closer examination. One such commonality is the envisioning of social studies as an interdisciplinary subject with an emphasis on the historical and geographical. Students are to study the relationships people have within their communities, between communities, with the environment, and with the past to understand the present and affect the future. Another common thread among all the documents is the goal of teaching children to understand the local and global context of their lives and experiences. A third common thread is the perception of social studies as a vehicle to develop students into active citizens who will partake in the democratic process in a meaningful manner.

This latter view—of citizenship education as one of the goals of social studies as a school subject in elementary schools—will be examined further in this last section of Chapter 3 and throughout Chapter 4.

Citizenship Education and Social Studies

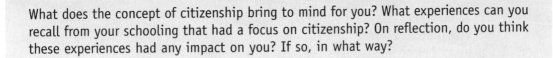

What does the concept of citizenship bring to mind for you? What experiences can you recall from your schooling that had a focus on citizenship? On reflection, do you think these experiences had any impact on you? If so, in what way?

For a long time, the main justification for including social studies as a school subject has been that schools must educate for effective citizenship. It is argued that educating for citizenship is becoming increasingly more important because of mounting political apathy (Osborne, 1997). Youth today are described as knowing less, caring less, voting less, and being less critical of leaders and institutions (Graseck, 2000). This cynicism in the young has been attributed to feelings of alienation from governmental and political matters and a sense of powerlessness to effect change (Sears, 2004). Citizenship in adults has been similarly characterized by passive acceptance of citizenship rights, widespread apathy, a loss of public-spiritedness, disregard for the common good, and little active exercise of citizenship responsibilities (Kymlicka, 1992). As a result, some claim that the rights of the democratic citizenry are falling into disuse (Hughes & Sears, 1996). Even though the teaching of citizenship has long been a goal of schooling, citizenship education has generally failed to take hold in schools. This is of concern because becoming a good citizen does not just happen; it has to be experienced in order to be understood.

REFLECTION POINT

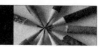

Does the view of youth today described here match with your experience? Why or why not?

ACTIVE ENGAGEMENT

Debate the topic "Youth and voting: What should be the role of social studies?" Support your point of view by using the following articles:

- "Falling Voter Turnout: Is It Linked to Diminished Civics Education?" January 18, 2006. Available at the Canadian Council on Learning website: http://www.ccl-cca.ca/ CCL/Home/index.htm?Language=EN. (Click on Reports & Data and then on Lessons in Learning.)
- "Study: Political Activity among Young Adults," *The Daily*, December 6, 2005. Available at the Statistics Canada website: http://www.statcan.ca/Daily/English/051206/ d051206b.htm.

While educating for citizenship is generally recognized as a school-wide phenomenon, social studies is the school subject that has been agreed upon as the best place to formally carry it out in the curriculum. Unfortunately, citizenship is a vague and contentious concept because everyone has his or her own personal view of what it means to be a "good" citizen. Citizenship is "intensely value laden, embodying a set of ideals that represent what citizens ought to be and how they ought to live" (Osborne, 1997, p. 39). Underlying assumptions about what makes a good citizen as well as about the nature of knowledge and learning influence how social studies is understood and how choices are made about what specific social studies goals best help to develop good citizens. Disagreement about what should be taught in social studies and how it should be taught prevails.

Think of someone you know who is the best example of a "good citizen." List some of their strengths. What do you need to know in order to be a good citizen? How can you become a good citizen?

ACTIVE ENGAGEMENT

Respond to the question, What would you say makes a good citizen? Compile a top-five list of characteristics and then share it with the class. Discuss the similarities and differences among the items generated by classmates as well as the reasons for any differences.

Thinking about What Constitutes a Good Citizen

Nowhere is there an agreed-upon definition of what makes a good citizen. In a discussion paper entitled *Good Schools, Good Citizens* (Caplan, 1998), the Canadian Council of Ministers of Education argued that schools have the important role of communicating proper values to students. The values referred to included "some sense of honesty, truth, civility, social justice and cooperation, and a determination to combat violence, racism, gender inequality, and environmental degradation" (p. i).

In another example, an online poll conducted by the Alberta School Boards Association (ASBA) in 2001 asked members of the public to list characteristics of a good citizen. (See the full report entitled *Shaping Young People into Good Citizens: A Public Consultation* at the ASBA website: http://www.asba.ab.ca. Click on New and Views and then on Research Papers.) The responses included the following characteristics:

1. Respectful and responsible, including respect for selves, for others, for authority and the law, for other cultures, for the environment, for the elderly, for property, and for the community;
2. Hard working, self-reliant and goal directed;
3. Gets along with others;
4. Tolerant of others' beliefs and values; and
5. Patient, kind, humble, compassionate, and optimistic.

In a third example, a publication entitled *A Look at Canada, 2006 Edition*, prepared by Citizenship and Immigration Canada (2006) and intended for people applying for Canadian citizenship, identifies Canadian values as including equality (i.e., respect for everyone's rights and the right to speak out and express ideas that others may not agree with), respect for cultural differences, freedom (of thought, speech, religion, and peaceful assembly), peace, and law and order. New Canadians are encouraged to protect the environment and to contribute in some way to Canada's social and economic well-being.

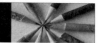
Are there any commonalities in terms of the views of citizenship expressed in these documents? How do the citizenship qualities identified in these sources compare to the characteristics of a good citizen that you came up with earlier? Do you believe that there are commonly agreed-upon values that help to define a good Canadian citizen?

Narrowing the concept of citizenship down to examining what it means to be a good *Canadian* citizen also presents challenges for social studies teachers, as people have differing ways of identifying with and understanding national identity.

ACTIVE ENGAGEMENT

Working with a partner, respond to this challenge: You are being asked to fill a time capsule (to be opened in 100 years) with things that represent what it means to be Canadian. What would you include? Why? What does this exercise tell you about what being Canadian means to you? Does this exercise tell you anything about what you believe children should learn about being Canadian?

 Technology Connection The National Capital Commission provides a resource entitled *The Gathering Place: An Exploration of Canada's Capital* that contains lessons on Canadian citizenship, culture, symbols, and identity. Citizenship and Immigration Canada's *Cultivate Your Commitment to Canada* is a similar resource. Links to these documents are provided on the book's companion website.

Some other websites that have material on Canadian citizenship are as follows:

- Government of Canada: http://www.canada.gc.ca
- Association for Canadian Studies: http://www.acs-aec.ca
- Statistics Canada: http://www.statcan.ca
- Canada's cultural gateway: http://www.culture.ca

Look back at the curriculum documents for social studies described earlier in the chapter and find references to what Canadian citizenship entails. How do these descriptions fit with your list of the characteristics of a good Canadian citizen? How does this activity help you to think about citizenship education as a goal of your future social studies program?

ACTIVE ENGAGEMENT

Schools in Canada have been publicly funded for more than a century. Since elected government officials who are responsible to the public make many of the decisions about curriculum and other aspects of schooling—which can be seen in the current accountability movement, for example—decisions about schooling are often beyond the control of teachers. Discuss the following question: What are the connections among publicly funded schools, social studies, and citizenship education, and how might these connections affect you as a future teacher?

Children's Views on Citizenship and Social Studies

Not only do members of the public, government officials, the official curricula, and you as future teachers have differing views on citizenship, but so do the children whom you will be teaching. Figure 3.2 presents an example of an activity that Ms. Manning, a Grade 6 teacher, carried out at the

FIGURE 3.2 ■ Citizenship and Social Studies Brainstorm Activity

Task Card #1
This is a small group activity for which you will need a piece of chart paper and felts. On your chart paper, record the following two questions, making sure to leave space for the responses under each one:
1. **What is citizenship?**   2. **How is citizenship related to social studies?**

beginning of the school year to find out what ideas her students brought with them about citizenship and its connection to what they do in social studies.

FIGURE 3.2 ■ *(Continued)*

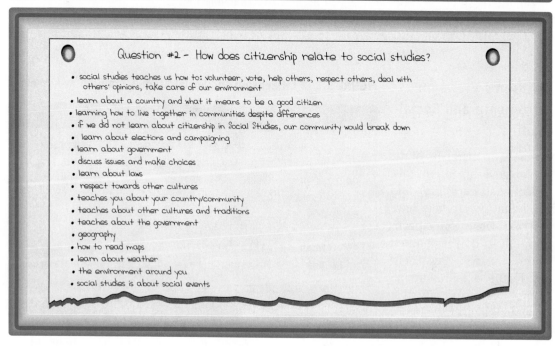

Question #1 – What is citizenship?

being counted equally	working together
belonging to something	human rights
taking part in city events	democracy
being part of our community	citizens take responsibility for their own actions
be respectful	cooperation
not being racist	do not litter
do not vandalize	take care of the environment
to help others	being able to vote
being nice to others	getting along with people
knowing the rules of your community	performing expected duties
to vote in elections	to obey laws
help your elders	justice
citizens keep the community in good order	jobs
being responsible in the community	knowing about your community, country and the world.

Question #2 – How does citizenship relate to social studies?

- social studies teaches us how to: volunteer, vote, help others, respect others, deal with others' opinions, take care of our environment
- learn about a country and what it means to be a good citizen
- learning how to live together in communities despite differences
- if we did not learn about citizenship in Social Studies, our community would break down
- learn about elections and campaigning
- learn about government
- discuss issues and make choices
- learn about laws
- respect towards other cultures
- teaches you about your country/community
- teaches about other cultures and traditions
- teaches about the government
- geography
- how to read maps
- learn about weather
- the environment around you
- social studies is about social events

REFLECTION POINT

Can you categorize the children's responses to the questions in Ms. Manning's activity? What do the children in this class appear to know about citizenship? What do their lists tell you about the children's understanding of social studies and the place and purpose of citizenship education?

After examining the results of this activity, Ms. Manning had this to say about the children's responses: "The children were able to tell me what a good citizen is or does, but they didn't seem to understand the relationship between citizenship and social studies. They were able to repeat the facts—for example, a good citizen does not vandalize, is not racist, etc.—but they didn't really know what it meant and what it had to do with what we learn about in social studies and why we study it as a school subject. They had the head but not the heart."

REFLECTION POINT

What do you think Ms. Manning means when she says her students "had the head but not the heart" of citizenship? Is this an important distinction in your opinion? How might you be able to address this concern in your future social studies program?

As a social studies teacher, deciding what constitutes a good Canadian citizen is only the first challenge of educating children about citizenship. The next concern is how to engage children in citizenship education so that they not only understand what it means to be a good citizen but also are willing to act on that understanding in the way in which they live with others. It is this question of how to educate to encourage citizenship that we will examine more closely in Chapter 4.

 ## ACTIVE ENGAGEMENT

Go back to the survey report *Shaping Young People into Good Citizens* at the ASBA website and find out which schooling experiences the members of the public who responded felt would provide the best educational experiences to develop the characteristics of a good citizen. What do their responses tell you about the public's perception of effective citizenship education? Do you agree or disagree with their ideas? How does this survey help you to think about the way to teach social studies as citizenship education?

Chapter Summary

In this chapter, we got down to the work of beginning to identify goals for your social studies program. The initial step in that goal setting was identified as being able to define what social studies as a school subject is all about. We began by examining the differing personal viewpoints of some teachers, children, and other teacher candidates, as well as your own, on what social studies is and why it is perceived to be an important subject. We then looked at the official definitions of social studies as articulated in curriculum documents from across Canada.

Equally as important as being able to define what we mean by social studies is being able to state the reasons for including it as a subject area in elementary schools. Citizenship education was identified as the one of generally agreed-upon goals of social studies throughout the provincial and territorial curriculum documents. However, defining what constitutes a good Canadian citizen presented the next challenge, as we saw that citizenship is a highly personal concept that means different things to different people. Nonetheless, deciding on what citizenship education encompasses is important to setting goals for your future social studies program.

In Chapter 4, we will continue the exploration of social studies as citizenship education as we examine a number of ways of thinking about teaching for citizenship. Here, we will return to the subject of differing philosophic starting points as we examine views on citizenship education that vary according to what is believed to be important for children to know as citizens and the roles of the children and the teacher in acquiring that knowledge.

Chapter 4

What Does Citizenship Education Have to Do with Elementary Social Studies?

The most widely accepted curricular goal of social studies is citizenship education. However, as you saw in the last chapter, there are many different views of what it means to be a good citizen. Here, you are about to learn that there are even more diverse ideas about what citizenship education as a goal of social studies entails. In this chapter, seven different ways of thinking about citizenship education as a goal of social studies are presented. Each of these orientations represents a different view of what constitutes a good citizen, what that citizen needs to know, and how that important knowledge is best acquired.

ACTIVE ENGAGEMENT

As you read about the seven ways of thinking about citizenship education as a goal of social studies, try summarizing what you are learning about each view. You may want to think about how each view answers the following questions:

1. What is a good citizen?

2. What does the good citizen need to know, and for what use?

3. What is the best way to acquire that important knowledge?

4. What are the teacher's and the students' roles in that learning?

Differing Views of Citizenship as a Goal of Social Studies

Orientation #1: Social Studies as Educating Citizens for Cultural Conservation

The approach of using social studies to educate citizens for cultural conservation has as its primary goal the creation and sharing of a common vision of national identity as one homogeneous people. This view holds that a distinct conception of the ideal society and what it means to be a citizen of that society exists and can be pointed to. Through consensus of authorities, certain knowledge, assumptions, and beliefs are deemed to accurately represent important cultural universals and core values of this ideal society. These are treated as self-evident truths and are thought to remain relatively constant over time. It is believed that all citizens need to be socialized to and internalize this common core of knowledge, as uniformity of knowledge and understanding leads to the maintenance of accepted societal norms and practices. According to this view, the good citizen is passive, law abiding, and loyal to the nation and its institutions, and shares the society's common cultural values (Sears, 1997).

The main goal of social studies as citizenship education for cultural conservation is to pass on the core knowledge, values, and beliefs that hold a society together in order to raise a future generation of citizens who will guarantee the society's survival by developing loyalty and commitment to the nation and ensuring conservation of culture and social unity. To reach this goal, all children of a nation need to be indoctrinated with a common identity and a strong sense of community and loyalty to country. The social studies curriculum ensures adherence to democratic principles by passing on to the next generation the ideas and accomplishments of influential people that have been most influential in shaping a nation.

Citizenship education for cultural conservation is teacher centred and textbook driven. As an authority figure, the teacher's job is to transmit the official curriculum containing a well-defined core body of content to the students. It is assumed that teachers are highly knowledgeable about the official content and beliefs and that they are able to be value neutral and objective. Strategies such as lecturing, note taking, worksheet completion, textbook reading, and structured question-and-answer sessions are employed to pass on the official content. The textbook is also recognized as an authority as it presents the identified core knowledge in an orderly, logical, and usually chronological way.

Students primarily take a passive role in a social studies program that has the goal of cultural conservation. They receive the important knowledge as delineated in the textbook and from the teacher as experts and are to accept that knowledge and internalize it. Recall and retention of the content is frequently checked through testing. It is assumed that indoctrination, memorization, and retention of the core knowledge will lead to application of these ideas to real life, which will in turn ensure conformity to the status quo and the development of citizens who think and behave in socially acceptable ways.

An advocate of this approach, Hilda Neatby, in her book *So Little for the Mind* (1953), condemned the progressive education movement of the 1940s and 1950s and called for a return to the basics in primary education and a focus on a traditional approach to learning and teaching. Another advocate, E. D. Hirsch, in *Cultural Literacy: What Every American Needs to Know* (1987), asserted a common body of information is possessed by the general society and it is the responsibility of the elementary schools particularly to impart this shared information in order that children have "a common base for communication" (p.14).

Critics of this approach to citizenship education argue that this approach perpetuates a constricted and uncritical view of citizenship in which children are taught "*what to think*" (Segall, 1999, p. 366 [italics in original]). Others contend that it presents an overly narrow, elitist, and Eurocentric definition of citizenship. By making the assumption that there is one commonly shared reality, this view excludes the experiences of many groups, such as women, cultural minorities, and the working class. Other critics argue that knowledge alone does not lead to good citizenship (Smits, 1997). Still others assert that the passive knower model of citizenship ignores the importance of political efficacy and ultimately subverts effective citizenship education. By promoting this transmissionist approach, social studies does little to subvert the reproduction of a society in which the larger, more passive working class is dominated by a smaller but well-educated and wealthy elite (Chamberlin, 1992). Lastly, this orientation has been criticized for ignoring the needs and interests of students.

CLASSROOM APPLICATION

Mrs. Zinder's Grade 2 social studies class is learning about Canadian citizenship. Mrs. Zinder begins the lesson with a talk on the symbols that represent Canada. She shows pictures of each symbol—e.g., the Canadian flag, a beaver, a Mountie, a loonie, a maple leaf, etc.—and asks the class to identify them. Next, the children copy from the blackboard a paragraph entitled "The Symbols of Canada." Finally, they are directed to draw a picture of what it means to be a Canadian and to include things that represent Canada. Mrs. Zinder collects the drawings and checks for neatness, effort, and accuracy. She concludes the lesson by restating the important symbols of Canada. Figure 4.1 presents an example of one student's drawing.

What does this drawing tell you about the child's understanding of the concept of Canadian identity?

FIGURE 4.1 ■ Child's Drawing of Things That Represent Canada to Her

What do you think of the cultural conservation orientation to citizenship education? Have you had any experience with this approach? What might social studies taught from this orientation be like for the children in the classroom? How would you respond to the claim that teachers are neutral vessels filled with objective information?

Orientation #2: Social Studies as Educating Citizens to Be Social Scientists

The educating citizens as social scientists orientation is based on the structure-of-the-disciplines movement that was most prominent in the 1960s. The approach is grounded in the assumption that there is a body of knowledge outside of the knower that is important for citizens to know, and it is believed that this knowledge can be found in the various social science disciplines. Adherents of this approach argue that these disciplines have generated the best approaches to thinking about the world as it really is, as well as failsafe techniques for gathering knowledge through discipline-based forms of inquiry. The purpose of this approach is to develop citizens who can apply discipline-based knowledge and methods to solve problems, thereby gaining a better understanding of their world and becoming more effective decision makers.

The goal of using social studies to educate citizens as social scientists is best promoted through the mastery of concepts and processes from the major social science fields of study as students learn to "see the world through the eyes of social scientists" (Vinson, 1998, p. 58) and learn to think and act like historians, archaeologists, geographers, or economists. The official social studies curriculum presents the important discipline-based knowledge in a problematized yet organized and systematized way so that learners can "discover" the solutions to problems from the various social sciences using the inquiry methods of those social sciences. It is assumed that the teacher is knowledgeable about these discipline-based bodies of knowledge and procedures. The teacher's role is to assist students in developing the techniques of a social scientist such as using original sources, including statistical information; observing behaviour; gathering data; and using verification processes to draw upon the "right" sets of concepts, processes, and structures to solve a problem. Students are guided toward the correct interpretation of the information they collect using these techniques. It is believed that mastery of these concepts and methods of scholarly inquiry in the social sciences disciplines assists in building a knowledge base for future learning and will transfer to the process of assuming the duties of a citizen in adult life. This approach holds that a better understanding of how social scientists gather knowledge will enable students to draw on the right set of concepts, structures, and processes when faced with a particular problem in their future.

The teacher is the representative of the disciplined knowledge in the classroom and must model the intellectual skills and dispositions of the discipline for students. A predetermined question from one of the various social sciences is presented, the process to be followed in addressing it is identified, and then students are guided through the process of discovering the essential knowledge and skills using the tools of the discipline. The student's role is to act by taking the information and using it according to the dictates of the teacher to "discover" the pre-determined solution to a selected problem. The student is to accept and incorporate the identified social science model that he or she is being asked to use to complete the research.

One advocate of this view of social studies, Jerome Bruner (1960), asserted that young children could and should learn the structures and processes that scholars used to arrive at new information in their discipline. He stressed the necessity for learning to proceed in an orderly way from the fundamental structure of a subject to the details.

CLASSROOM APPLICATION

Bruner assisted in developing the elementary social studies program *Man: A Course of Study* (1965), which immersed children in anthropological research to compare and contrast the lives of the Netsilik Eskimos from the Pelly Bay region with those of animals, including salmon, herring gulls, and baboons. The goal was to help children to better understand human behaviour and human culture by examining the differences between humans and other animals. The children used anthropological tools such as observations, field notes, primary source data, visual aids, and artifacts to systematically study how the humans and the other animals met their needs.

A criticism that has been aimed at the educating citizens as social scientists orientation is that it assumes that young children are capable of thinking and reasoning in ways similar to experts in the various social science disciplines. Another criticism is that control of *what* and *how* to learn is in the hands of the teacher and the official curriculum, as the children are steered toward pre-selected answers to predetermined questions. It is argued that this presents a very limited view of the learning process and a highly static representation of knowledge, and that the process is neither exploratory nor open ended. A further criticism is that the children's needs and interests are overlooked as teachers pre-select content and processes rather than focusing on what the child already knows and wants to know about these disciplines. Other critics claim that issues of social studies do not fit the logical tidiness and standardized procedures of the methods of inquiry represented in this model. Also, it is pointed out that knowledge is not neutral, objective, and universal, but rather is a dynamic and changing social construction that reflects the experiences, perspectives, and values of the people who construct it, including social scientists. Lastly, there is no evidence to support the assumption that good citizens will emerge from the rigorous and linear study of the knowledge, skills, and methods of the social sciences.

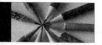
How might thinking like a social scientist be useful or problematic for elementary children? Does this approach to teaching social studies assume that teaching is value free? Would the teaching of selected content and processes from each of the social science disciplines be adequate citizenship education in your opinion?

Orientation #3: Social Studies as Educating Citizens to Be Reflective Inquirers

Social studies from a reflective inquiry orientation is based on the belief that effective citizens are those who participate in social, political, and economic decisions that affect their lives. Democracy necessitates a citizenry capable of identifying societal problems, collecting, evaluating, and analyzing information about those problems, and making choices based on sound reflective thought and inquiry rather than on impulse. Citizenship is envisioned as decision making in a sociopolitical context in which people analyze choices, envision consequences, and make good decisions on issues they view as having an effect on the quality of their lives (Allen, 2000). It is recognized that problems rarely have a single correct solution, but rather that citizens are required to make decisions among several possible solutions. Central to this view of citizenship is the belief that people must interact with ideas in order to make sense of the world for themselves. Knowledge is not seen as something static and "out there" to be discovered but instead as something that is constructed as the individual attempts to make sense of a perplexing situation through reflective inquiry. The search for knowledge is seen as an open-ended, continuous process.

Teachers who hold a reflective inquiry orientation to citizenship education engage their students in real-life decision-making situations. They recognize that understanding social studies and the issues inherent in it is both a socially constructed and a highly reflective process that is different for each student. The process of inquiry is the most important aspect of the learning experience. Teachers adopt a skill-based approach to develop their students' competence in inquiry, communication, critical thinking, reflective thinking, and problem solving and decision making. They solicit issues for study from the students' perceived needs and interests because problems that directly affect students' lives within a specified sociopolitical context hold the greatest importance for those students (Patrick, 2000).

In this approach, students play a more active role in learning about citizenship as they practice the skills needed for their future roles as citizens. They use a generic inquiry process to engage in investigating problems. Students share information, analyze choices, examine consequences, and make informed decisions. The outcome of the investigation is not known ahead of time.

One of the earliest advocates of this orientation, John Dewey (1916), in his book *Democracy and Education*, advocated for "learning by doing" in schools. Dewey believed that schools should reflect the real world of the child and that children should be actively involved in investigating their worlds along with other learners. The progressive education movement, which is based on the principles of student choice and experiential learning, emerged from Dewey's ideas. Other advocates argue that this way of thinking about social studies as citizenship

The teacher acts as a facilitator of the inquiry by ensuring that multiple and suitable resources are available for the students to use in their research and by helping them to build on or rethink their initial ideas as they uncover new information.

education can go a long way to bringing to light the views of marginalized groups that were previously excluded from the curriculum.

One criticism directed toward this orientation comes from those who feel that children are not capable of the level of social and intellectual reasoning that is required to engage in reflective inquiry. Others claim that this orientation does not go far enough, for although nurturing the abilities for meaningful decision making is important, this approach does little to promote students' feelings of efficacy and their ability to bring about change. Students, it is argued, must put democratic principles into immediate practice through direct involvement or they will have no true understanding of citizenship. Still other critics decry the emphasis on process in this orientation, as it does little to help children to build the critical knowledge base necessary for good citizenship. A final criticism is that the issues chosen for investigation can tend to be mindless and of little importance, as teachers are often hesitant to take on problems and issues of a controversial nature and that would involve personal valuing and moral debate.

CLASSROOM APPLICATION

As part of their current events program, children in Mr. Moncrief's Grade 5 social studies class have been talking about a recent story in the news on the depleting fish supply in the oceans. They express a curiosity about what is happening to all

(Continued)

the fish. A decision is made to inquire further into the problem of over-fishing. The question that is decided on to guide their investigation is: Should all countries put restrictions on the amount and type of fishing that is allowed? The teacher refers the children to a poster that outlines a model to help them to work through the stages of inquiry:

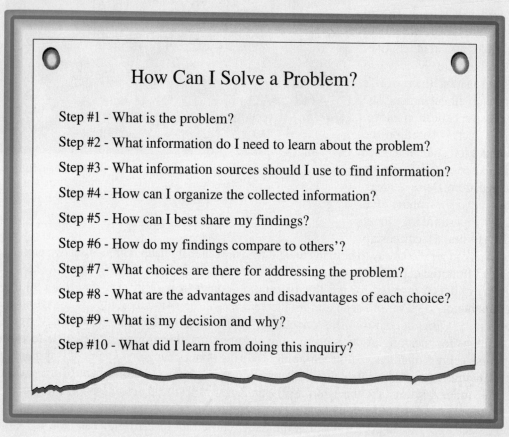

How Can I Solve a Problem?

Step #1 - What is the problem?

Step #2 - What information do I need to learn about the problem?

Step #3 - What information sources should I use to find information?

Step #4 - How can I organize the collected information?

Step #5 - How can I best share my findings?

Step #6 - How do my findings compare to others'?

Step #7 - What choices are there for addressing the problem?

Step #8 - What are the advantages and disadvantages of each choice?

Step #9 - What is my decision and why?

Step #10 - What did I learn from doing this inquiry?

REFLECTION POINT

Think about this method of inquiry as it relates to your prior experiences with social studies. Were you engaged in similar inquiry in elementary school? How effective would social studies taught from this orientation be in your opinion? How important is it to have a citizenry who can inquire into issues and make reasoned decisions?

Orientation #4: Social Studies as Educating Citizens for Cultural Transformation

The educating citizens for cultural transformation approach is based on the belief that effective citizens need to be actively involved in social criticism and willing to stand up and take social action when necessary. The primary goal of this orientation is to create a citizenry that is not simply more active in public affairs but whose involvement is guided by and informed by morally reflective judgment based on critical discourse (Clarke, 1990). This orientation is rooted in a broad concern with issues such as social justice, freedom, equality, human rights, and power. It seeks to encourage understanding, emancipatory learning, and the development of critical consciousness through analysis of repressive social conditions. At the heart of this orientation is a belief that society needs to be transformed, as current social arrangements are unjust and unequal. It is believed that humans are capable of resisting the pressure of the dominant social, political, and economic institutions and of acting upon and changing these institutions. However, while humans have the potential to change their situations, the realization of this potential is dependent upon the awakening of their awareness to their situations in order that they may broaden their choices of action.

Social studies as citizenship education for cultural transformation is aimed at providing opportunities for examination, critique, and revision of past traditions and existing social practices. The teacher's role is to help students to identify issues for examination and to provide an inclusive classroom that is open and safe and where all voices are recognized. Students are taught the importance of perspective consciousness for recognizing, examining, evaluating, and appreciating multiple perspectives on issues. They are encouraged to detect hidden forms of domination and oppression within the school and the society at large. The students' role is to investigate issues from multiple perspectives with an eye for social injustice and then look for ways to put democratic principles into practice. They learn to see themselves as empowered, active agents of change and are encouraged to let their views be heard in the classroom and beyond.

One way this orientation has been enacted in classrooms is through engagement in service learning projects. Service learning comes from the belief that *understanding* democracy comes from *doing* democracy. It can take the form of service as altruistic duty (learning about civic duty, volunteerism, and the value of altruism) or service as social action (including critical reflection about social policies and the acquisition of skills to exert influence in public affairs). Teachers who engage their students in social action aim to help them to develop a strong sense of political efficacy by

Being a good citizen can begin in the classroom by students' taking responsibility for making the classroom an enjoyable and comfortable place for all to learn.

identifying personal values held in relation to issues and then acting on those values. The emotive component of being a citizen comes into play as students learn to make choices and take action that is "informed by passion without being ruled by it" (Grumet, 1996, p. 7). Learning about issues related to how we should live with others in our world, for example, allows students to experience relevant ethical decision making and actions that are embedded in caring for others (Smits, 1997). Investigating issues of inequity and oppression and the social, economic, and political forces that cause oppression can raise consciousness, which in turn becomes the catalyst for activism.

ACTIVE ENGAGEMENT

Jason, a teacher candidate, shared this story about his social studies experience during his student teaching: "While I was doing my practicum, the school was doing a project where the children had to decide on an area in their school's neighbourhood that they wanted to clean up. They didn't just pick an area to clean but they also had to write about why this would be a good area to clean up, who would benefit from it and how it would affect people in the neighbourhood. Most of the children loved the project because not only were they getting to physically do something for their community, but also they were able to use their problem solving skills to do something meaningful. The children also got to experience that their opinions could make a difference." What do you think of this activity? How effective do you think it would be in educating children to be or become cultural transformationists?

The most common criticism of the cultural transformation orientation is that engaging children in action just for the sake of action can do them a disservice (Hughes & Sears, 1996). More importantly, emphasis needs to be placed on making wise choices about what action to take and when to take it, and on enhancing students' sense of political efficacy through trust and support (Glasford, 1992). Another criticism is that while community service is a part of being a good citizen, learning how to be a good neighbour does not necessarily promote an understanding of how to be an effective and politically active citizen (Kymlicka, 1992). Other critics fear that supporting this approach to citizenship education poses a threat to civil peace and stability by encouraging student activism. Still others fear a loss or weakening of the important knowledge base of students, as they argue that too much time is spent on process over content.

Figure 4.2 presents a letter written by a Grade 2 student regarding a problem of concern to her.

FIGURE 4.2 ■ Dear Mr. Mayor Letter from Grade 2 Student

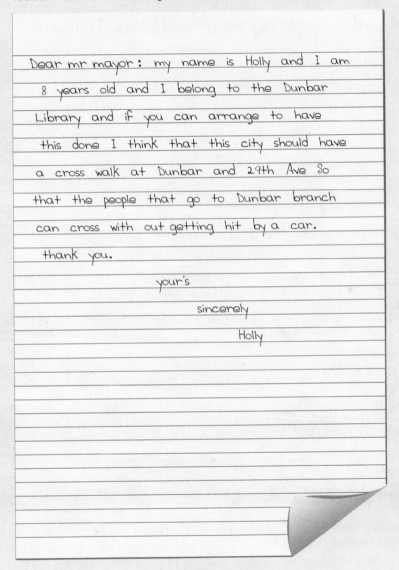

Dear mr mayor: my name is Holly and I am 8 years old and I belong to the Dunbar Library and if you can arrange to have this done I think that this city should have a cross walk at Dunbar and 29th Ave so that the people that go to Dunbar branch can cross with out getting hit by a car.

thank you.

your's

sincerely

Holly

Answer the following questions on your own citizenship practices and beliefs.

How strong is your sense of political efficacy?

1. Did you vote in the last provincial election?	Yes	No
2. Have you talked or written to a mayor or councillor about a broad community issue?	Yes	No
3. Have you ever signed a petition?	Yes	No
4. Have you ever participated in a protest rally?	Yes	No
5. Have you worked for a candidate in an election? (Municipal, provincial, or federal?)	Yes	No
6. Do you believe that if you did try to influence government decisions, you would be able to?	Yes	No
7. Do you believe that if you asked for help with a grievance from a politician, you would get help?	Yes	No
8. How much influence do you think people like you can have over local government?	A lot	Very little
9. Have you participated in any type of political activity other than voting?	Yes	No
10. How responsible do you feel for the quality of governance in our society?	Accept full responsibility	Accept no responsibility

Reflect on your responses. How strong is your sense of political efficacy? Do you think your teachers influenced your beliefs and practices? Could your teachers have had more influence on your views? How? Should they have? What does this activity tell you about your citizenship education? How important is it that citizens have a sense of political efficacy?

68 PART ONE Why Is It Important to Set Goals for Your Social Studies Program?

NEL

Orientation #5: Social Studies as Educating Citizens for Personal Development

The approach of social studies as citizenship education for personal development has at its core the belief that good citizens need to understand how to function in both their personal and social worlds and recognize the importance of cooperation to the survival of democracy. Central to this orientation is a belief that concern for the development of self is foremost in the preparation of citizens. Self-esteem and a strong sense of identity are essential in the lives of good citizens and are necessary foundations for effective and productive social relationships. This orientation also emphasizes the formation of personal standards, values, and beliefs to ensure that citizens develop a strong sense of right and wrong that will guide them in their problem solving, decision making, and actions. The knowledge and skills belonging to the private sphere of family membership and homemaking are believed to be as important to citizenship as the skills of political organization and social action.

Educating citizens for personal development focuses on fostering concern and caring for others. Learning about decent, caring, responsible behaviour in personal and family relationships is considered a way to prepare children for being neighbours, mates, siblings, friends, parents, and pet owners (Noddings, 1992). The creation of caring communities begins in the social studies classroom in the interactions between teachers and students and between students. The children learn how to work effectively as a group and how to develop a positive self-concept and feelings of personal efficacy (Sherman, 2004). The teacher engages the children in exploring social issues that shape the quality of life, such as concern about families, reproduction, housework, health, sexuality, marriage and divorce, the environment, needs of the elderly, and needs of children, as these are seen to be more inclusive of all citizens' experiences (Bernhard-Powers, 1996). The children are encouraged to search for their own meaning within their personal experiences and to understand the significance of these social issues to their own lives.

Citizenship education as personal development can be enacted in social studies through a focus on character education. Character education works on the premise that students need to be indoctrinated with a core set of universal values that are important to developing character—such as truth telling, goodness, sharing, compassion, respect for persons, justice, and diligence—in order to become committed to them. The teacher's role is to teach these values that are believed to develop character through repetition, reinforcement, appeals to the heart, and teacher modelling. The students' role is to adopt the values being taught and apply them to the way they live their lives both in and outside school.

Values education and moral education are two other ways of incorporating the personal development orientation in social studies. A teacher who teaches values education in social studies helps children to develop an ethical framework from which decisions can be made. Values clarification activities are used to help children uncover and clarify the values they hold. A values analysis approach urges students to think about their values and attitudes and assess the adequacy behind their reasoning by presenting opposing arguments and looking for inconsistencies in their attitudes. A moral education approach is based on the premise that students need to explore the moral system of rules that they live by in order to understand the morality of civic life and the balance between rights and responsibilities. The teacher uses moral dilemmas and discussion to assist students in resolving issues of moral conflict so they can judge which values are better than others.

 Technology Connection One strategy for teaching values in social studies is to use children's literature. Some suggestions for books that can help to teach the value of cooperation can be found at the AnswerPoint.org website. Follow the link provided on the book's companion website.

The personal development orientation has tended to generate a great deal of criticism, particularly regarding how decisions are made about what values and character traits are to be taught and how best to teach them. Teaching is never a neutral, value-free endeavour. Teachers bring their own values to the classroom and model those values for their students both overtly and covertly. They need to carefully examine the values they portray in their teaching, especially since students can be strongly influenced by teacher modelling. While current directions in values education favour the character education movement, there is a fine line between inculcating specific character traits and dictating right answers to children without giving them the opportunity to think carefully about the issues and come up with their own answers. Listing values and associating them with behaviours gives the misleading impression that the relationship between values and behaviour is simple and direct; however, the acquisition of these values does not guarantee the resulting behaviour that character educators suggest.

ACTIVE ENGAGEMENT

What experiences have you had with character education programs in the schools that you have visited? Share those experiences with a small group. How effective was this approach in helping children to learn about being a good citizen? Can you find evidence of this orientation in your provincial/territorial curriculum guide?

Orientation #6: Social Studies as Educating Citizens to Respect Diversity

The educating citizens to respect diversity orientation to social studies is based on the premise that good citizens need to appreciate and be accepting of diversity. This orientation moves beyond the idea that the purpose of citizenship education is to establish a national identity of one people to the acceptance of diverse cultural understandings and of a mosaic of different belief systems that resonate for all citizens (Ghosh, 2001). The goal of this approach is to present a truthful and meaningful rendition of human experience.

Social studies with a focus on respect for diversity has as its goal the development of students who recognize and appreciate the interdependence of all people and the importance of cross-cultural communication and relationships to a democracy. It is believed that students are culturally encapsulated: they take their culture, with its values, beliefs, and stereotypes, for granted. They look at culture through lenses and categories that are familiar to them, and assume that all needs and wants are basically the same, which does little to move them beyond their own cultural frames of reference. The teacher's role is to engage children in experiences that help them to become conscious of their culture and be able to step outside of themselves to look critically at the habitual norms, values, and practices that make up that culture in order to see that their way of doing things is not the only or the "right" way, and to understand that others have their own, different ways (Suleiman, 2000). Students also need to develop an understanding of "how cultural, gender, class, religious, ethnic, racial, handicapped and age differences contribute to the unified whole of a democratic nation" (Nakagawa & Pang, 1997, p. 117).

Social studies content and experiences that address respect for diversity can be designed to teach students "about the multiplicity of the heritages that comprise Canada," and help them to appreciate and celebrate Canada's multicultural nature. As Price (1992) argues, "The intent behind multicultural education is to demonstrate that cultural differences are a positive thing, and that they should be recognized and respected" (p. 10). However, critics of this approach contend that limited and superficial exposure to cultures that focuses on celebrations of the food, dress, and music of individual cultures or the "tourist approach" to diversity, perpetuates stereotypes and misrepresents cultural realities (Banks & Banks, 2007). "Simply providing material that exposes students to difference will not sufficiently decrease discriminatory attitudes or increase equal opportunities" (Varma-Joshi, 2004, p. 151). As well, studying groups in isolation from one another teaches children that these cultures are separate from others rather than part of a common whole. What is more important is that students are taught to know, to care, and to act in ways that will develop and foster a just society in which all groups experience democracy and empowerment. Children also need to learn to recognize and be able and willing to combat prejudice and stereotyping both within the classroom and beyond.

LOOKING BACK

Jon, a teacher candidate, had this to say about his experiences learning about Canada's First Nations peoples in school: "I recall that what I learned about Aboriginals was solely from a European perspective, and First Nations peoples were clumped together as if they were all the same. We made teepees and masks, read legends and learned about the importance of the buffalo, but this did little to develop my appreciation of the diversity of Aboriginal cultures. Also, most of what I studied about First Nations peoples was from an historical perspective, reinforcing the notion that they only existed in the past. I think that it is imperative that social studies demonstrates contemporary conditions and contributions of First Nations peoples to Canadian society."

(Continued)

How do your experiences with multicultural education compare to Jon's? What do you think of his last statement about the contemporary study of First Nations issues?

Another way of using social studies to develop citizens who respect diversity is by taking an anti-racist approach. The teacher's goal in this case would be to attempt to eradicate racism by equipping students with the analytical tools to critically examine the origins of racist ideas, to develop awareness of the socially constructed role they play, and to understand the implications of their own race's actions in supporting racism. Anti-racist educators caution that engaging in such studies is not about those who are of white, European descent feeling guilty for the sins of their ancestors but about taking responsibility to ensure that injustices against those who are not white don't occur again. Through an anti-racist approach, the deeper issues of race, prejudice, stereotyping, and discrimination (both past and present), which cause rifts between people, are overtly addressed in the classroom. The teacher provides a range of experiences that help students to understand that ethnic and cultural prejudice and discrimination can take diverse forms. Such experiences can encourage students to begin to see that differing viewpoints about race exist and are part of broader, more complex socioeconomic and political issues. The students' roles are to develop the ability to recognize injustice, to identify causes of it, and to be willing to challenge and change it.

Much of the criticism of the respect for diversity orientation comes from the tension between achieving cohesion as a society on the one hand and enabling people to live lives consistent with their own identity on the other. Some believe that there is a core body of knowledge that every citizen of a nation should learn, while others acknowledge that a society's shared body of knowledge is enhanced through diversity. Others caution against a program that does little more than celebrate diversity and promote an unproblematic national tradition (Werner, 1993). Still others claim that understanding and accepting diversity in terms of national citizenship is too narrow a goal of education for diversity, as we should put more emphasis on how much the citizens of Canada share with citizens throughout the world.

CLASSROOM APPLICATION

At the beginning of the school year, Mrs. Jenkins posts the word WELCOME in different languages in her classroom. She discusses with the children why she has decorated the room in this way and spends part of her first day having them learn how to welcome each other in different languages. (See http://www.freelang.net/expressions for translations of such common expressions.)

ACTIVE ENGAGEMENT

The research in multicultural education claims that not only are students culturally encapsulated but that teachers are as well. What does that mean to you? Discuss your thoughts with a partner. How might you address this concern?

Orientation #7: Social Studies as Educating Global Citizens

The global orientation to citizenship education in social studies is based on the belief that in the twenty-first century, the need is ever increasing for people to be global citizens who understand their place in a world characterized by growing interdependence among nations. The globalization of the world economy, the increasing spread of democratization, the emergence of powerful trading blocks, the heightened movement of people across national boundaries, and the breakdown of time and space barriers afforded by communications technology have all contributed to the need to develop a broad worldview about global issues, global systems, and common elements of human values and cultures (Osborne, 1996). Citizens of the future will increasingly be required to understand and interact with people, cultures, and ideas throughout the world.

The goals of social studies as global citizenship education are to provide students with the knowledge, skills, and attitudes necessary to be effective global citizens who deal thoughtfully with rapid global changes, who recognize the impact of those changes on their own lives, who understand that their actions can attribute to world problems as well as the solutions to those problems, and who participate actively in making this world a more peaceful and just place for all of its citizens. It is believed that children need to learn about the interconnected nature of life on a global scale, and that emphasis should be placed on experiences that tie all humans together in order to better understand and appreciate the delicate relationship between humans and the

Children need to learn about the world and how they are connected to others around the planet as a part of a global community.

natural world. Young learners need not only to understand and celebrate our common humanity and how much citizens in Canada share with citizens throughout the world, but also to develop awareness that their view of the world is not necessarily shared universally.

Teachers who adopt a global perspective toward social studies education provide opportunities for direct experience in which children have opportunities to connect with problems of a global nature and engage in caring and protecting activities that hopefully become habits. By addressing global issues in the classroom, children are assisted in making the connections between their daily reality and what is happening around the world. Teachers recognize that they need to help to evoke in children sensitivities to important global issues and to counter feelings that there is nothing they can do to help to solve large, international-scale problems.

Social studies as global citizenship focuses on the study of global issues such as peace, security, international development, human rights, and environmental problems, and on developing children's problem-solving skills for use in dealing with these global issues. Since there is a strong moral focus to studying global issues, children also need opportunities to examine their attitudes and values about how individuals should be treated and understood and to assess the adequacy of their reasoning. Putting a focus on environmental issues can help children to learn about the character and complexity of the global community and its interconnectedness, as well as to develop an understanding of the human impact on the environment, the need for stewardship regarding the management of resources, and the importance of taking responsibility for protecting and caring for living things that are dependent on humans for survival. A peace education focus on the other hand can develop children's knowledge of possible ways to deal constructively with the issues of violence and conflict (Bickmore, 2004) and can increase their awareness of what a cooperative and caring planet would look like. Activities are designed to help them develop empathy skills, anger management, conflict resolution, peer mediation, and cooperative and social skills.

 Technology Connection Canadians Mark Evans and Cecilia Reynolds (2004) assisted in the development of a teacher's resource handbook entitled *Educating for Global Citizenship in a Changing World* that provides extensive background on citizenship in a global context as well as numerous teaching ideas and weblinks to other global education related sites. To download this handbook for free, follow the link provided on the book's companion website.

Critics of social studies as global citizenship education contend that global issues are too immense and complex for young children, as these issues require much greater economic, political, and social awareness than they are capable of. Others argue that social studies programs that teach peace and conflict resolution do not reduce rates of violence or develop people who are able to resolve conflict, as accomplishing such goals requires much more concentrated and long-term effort. Still other critics of this orientation fear the loss of a shared national identity that could result from a focus on our common global humanity. They claim that this focus could undermine the development of a national consciousness that is dependent upon creating a shared sense of place, heritage, and solidarity with other fellow citizens and that results from the study of cultural beliefs and practices within the nation state. A further concern is that such programs threaten the status quo by encouraging children to see themselves as agents of change.

What do you think of the contention that young children are not aware of or able to deal with today's global issues?

ACTIVE ENGAGEMENT

Debate this assertion: The promotion of a national identity narrowly defined as "national citizenship" contrasts sharply with the economic priorities of the new world order.

CLASSROOM APPLICATION

Libby's Grade 4 social studies class went on a field trip to a museum to see an exhibition entitled "Our Global Village," which focused mostly on developing countries and the problems they are facing. Figure 4.3 presents her reflection on the field trip.

What does Libby appear to have learned from this experience? Do you think this activity helped to develop her understanding of global citizenship?

FIGURE 4.3 ■ Libby's Reflection on Her Museum Visit

> Libby
>
> I like the kind of cothing that they wear, It has paterns that look very nice. I learned that they have no docters so they have a child to child program. I also learned that what happens in this program they have older children checking the heath of younger children. I liked the toys they have and I like how they make toys out of things we throw away.

Throughout this chapter you have been examining alternative orientations toward citizenship education as a goal of social studies. Look back at your own initial thoughts about your goals for your future social studies program. Do your personal professional goals for your social studies teaching match these orientations in any way? Is there anything missing in these orientations that you feel is important to your teaching of social studies? Do you wish to keep your prior goals or would you like to change them? If you have chosen to rethink your goals, why did you do so? If you have decided to retain your initial goals, think about why.

Which of the orientations discussed in this chapter do you feel would best support the constructivist learning principles identified in Chapter 1?

Chapter Summary

This chapter focused on examining differing ways of thinking about social studies and its primary goal of citizenship education. The intent of this chapter was to help you to better understand that there are multiple ways of envisioning the purpose of social studies for citizenship education and to see that the orientation or combination of orientations that you identify most with should closely match your beliefs about teaching and learning. When deciding on their goals for their social studies programs, most teachers use a more eclectic approach that is a blend of several of these orientations, rather than relying on one view of citizenship education.

Deciding on which orientation or combination of orientations regarding the role of social studies in citizenship education best represents your beliefs about the purposes of schooling is an important first step in setting your personal professional goals for your social studies program. Since students learn different roles, norms, values, and expected behaviours through cultural conservation methods than they do through cultural transformation methods, the hidden curriculum varies from one approach to another. Determining which orientation best fits with your belief system will help you to define what you believe is important for your students to learn and help you to think about how you can best shape that learning. Being clear about the beliefs behind these decisions and maintaining a reflective disposition will ensure that you are constantly aware of how your beliefs are shaping what is happening in your classroom. Understanding the premises that inform the orientation(s) you adopt should hopefully move you one step closer to being able to define what your goals for your social studies program might be.

As we have seen in this first part of the book, goal setting is a very important component of the planning process as it helps you to be clear about where you want to end up and what will to be the best route to take to get there. We now move on to the second piece of the planning puzzle: how to select content that will enable you and your students to move towards the goals that have been set for your program.

Part Two

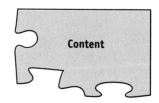

Content

How Do You Select and Organize the Content of Your Social Studies Program?

Part Two of our planning journey turns to the subject of what should be taught in social studies. Here, you will examine a range of differing views on how to select and organize the content for your social studies program. Every social studies teacher must decide what knowledge will best help to achieve both the curricular goals and their personal professional goals. Some things to consider when inquiring into content selection are whose knowledge should be learned, what use knowledge should serve, and what kinds of topics, questions, or issues would be most valuable for preparing future citizens. These questions have different answers for teachers with different goals. The content in Part Two is intended to help you think about how to make content choices that are consistent with your goals.

Chapter 5 begins by considering what is meant by the terms "content" and "content knowledge." Some of the influences on your content choices are then examined, including your provincial or territorial curriculum and the various discipline areas that make up social studies. Chapter 6 investigates other factors that may influence your content choices, including your goals and interests, your students, your teaching context, the available resources, and local, national, and world events. The chapter concludes with a review of a number of approaches to organizing the selected content for instruction.

Chapter 5

What Constitutes Social Studies Content and What Are Some Factors Affecting Your Content Choices?

In order to present a coherent social studies program, after setting goals, you as the teacher will need to decide what your students will be learning about in social studies. As you examined the seven orientations of social studies for citizenship education described in the previous chapter, you may have noticed that each view reflected different answers to the question of what good citizens need to know and for what purpose. The first thing we need to do in unpacking the issue of content selection is to figure out what is meant by the term "content." Then, we need to look more closely at what content should be taught in elementary social studies and who or what might influence the selection of that content. As you read this chapter and engage in the activities provided, continue to think about what you believe students need to know to act intelligently and responsibly both as present and future citizens. You will then be in a better position to answer the question of which content is of most importance for you to address in your social studies program.

Thinking about Social Studies Content

The content of social studies is made up of all of the skills and processes; values, attitudes, and dispositions; and knowledge that you hope to address in your social studies program. All three of these components of social studies content work together to develop the effective citizen who knows, feels, and acts responsibly. The three components need to be weighed equally in your content selection in order to present a balanced social studies program. The first two are usually addressed through the teaching of the content knowledge rather than as separate focus areas.

Skills and Processes

Skills or competencies are defined as the learner's ability to apply knowledge to perform tasks or actions, while processes are the procedures and steps that a learner takes in order to achieve a desired outcome. Skills and processes are acquired through direct experience and practice. Generally, the skills and processes to be taught in social studies fall into the categories of inquiry and research, thinking skills, communication and participation skills, and technological skills.

One of the most critical processes that students can learn in social studies is how to engage in inquiry. To become effective and efficient inquirers, children need to learn a number of skills. The first stage of inquiry involves getting the children interested in and enthused about the focus of the inquiry. In this phase of inquiry, children can be taught about what makes a researchable question and how to plan an inquiry into that question. The next phase of the inquiry involves the development of processing skills, including information gathering, organizing, analyzing, interpreting, and synthesizing, as well as critical thinking skills for evaluating the appropriateness and relevance of the information being accessed. Once data has been collected and analyzed, the next phase of the inquiry involves developing problem-solving and decision-making skills by examining alternative solutions, considering consequences, and learning about making informed decisions based on evidence. A final phase of the inquiry process is the sharing of solutions and decisions. Creative-thinking skills come into play here when original ideas are presented and unique solutions to problems are identified. Students can also develop technological skills and competencies throughout the various stages of inquiry as they use computers to search for information, to synthesize selected information, and to share their findings.

Other important thinking skills taught in social studies are reflection (looking back at changes in one's ideas) and metacognition (thinking about one's own thinking).

Another area that can be easily addressed in social studies is communication skills, such as sharing information with others and being able to express ideas in a way that conveys meaning. Participation skills are also a major part of social studies as children learn to work together and develop group relations and processes that allow them to interact effectively and cooperate with others.

(Chapter 11 presents ideas for teaching to develop all of these skills areas, as well as historical and geographical thinking skills. Teaching technological skills is addressed in Chapters 9 and 12.)

In order to determine the skills and processes to be taught in social studies, you as the teacher need to have a clear understanding of what you feel it is important for an effective citizen to be able to do in his or her world. What do you think are some of the important skills that children should learn in social studies? Compare your list with those identified in your elementary social studies provincial/territorial curriculum document. What do you notice about the number and range of skills identified? Which ones do you feel would be most essential for young children to learn in social studies?

Values, Attitudes, and Dispositions

A second component of social studies content includes attitudes, values, and dispositions. Values are the beliefs that a person holds about what is right and wrong, good and bad, or desirable and undesirable. Attitudes, which are based on values, refer to the biases, inclinations, or tendencies that influence peoples' response to other people and situations. These values and attitudes in turn can influence a person's disposition to act in certain ways (behaviours).

Many of children's attitudes will develop in their interactions with others in the classroom. Of primary importance in social studies is engaging children in learning experiences that develop positive attitudes towards self and others. These attitudes include acceptance, tolerance and respect for others, open-mindedness, a willingness to share with others, a valuing of others' ideas and contributions, cooperation, honesty, industriousness, creativity and intellectual curiosity, care and concern for the environment, and thoughtful use of technology. These attitudes are all deemed to be important to good citizenship.

Social studies programs can also be used to develop children's positive attitudes toward learning and their willingness to take responsibility for their own learning.

LOOKING BACK

What attitudes and values do you recall being most emphasized in your social studies school experiences? How important were cooperation and caring for others, for example? How do you recall learning about attitudes and values? Were they a part of the hidden curriculum or were they overtly taught?

CLASSROOM APPLICATION

Students in Mr. Snow's class are asked to share in groups what being a citizen of Canada means to them. A classroom declaration entitled "Celebrating Being a Citizen of Canada" is then created, on which students' diverse views on citizenship are recorded. A class discussion is held about why people have different ways of experiencing citizenship. What attitudes do you think that the children in Mr. Snow's class would learn by engaging in this social studies activity?

Knowledge

A third component of what makes up social studies is content knowledge. Knowledge is the information that we acquire through our experiences and that we use to organize our world. It is comprised of facts, concepts, and understandings or generalizations.

Facts are specific statements containing discrete pieces of information about people, events, and things, and that apply to particular situations. We construct our factual knowledge from both firsthand sensory experiences in our environment and secondhand sources, such as another person's account of an experience. Facts acquired in the latter manner can contain bias, and children therefore need to learn the skills of detecting bias and sorting out accuracies from inaccuracies. Children also need to learn that facts can change, especially historical ones that are influenced by the unearthing of new evidence. It is important therefore that they learn to always consult more than one source of information in order to check the accuracy of facts.

While children need information upon which to construct their knowledge, memorization of discrete facts without meaning has very little relevance for them and even less staying power. The brain naturally looks for patterns that connect information (Caine & Caine, 2005). Using concepts is one way to organize our experiences into such patterns. Concepts are mental representations that show an association between two or more facts. They denote all objects in a given category or class that share a common set of characteristics. Even though concepts are mental abstractions, they can be labelled and examples can be pointed to.

Vygotsky (1986) reminds us that children come to school with what he referred to as "spontaneous" concepts that are derived from their direct experiences with their world. Changing, refining, and developing new concepts happen as a part of formal schooling. Conceptual understanding is constructed by the learner with the guidance of the teacher, but the formation of accurate concepts is dependent upon a solid background of factual knowledge. Sometimes the understandings that students construct are faulty, and this is where the teacher plays an important role. Since students use their prior understanding and experience to try to fit new experiences with what they already know (the conceptual categories they have already formed), the teacher needs to continuously work at uncovering the flaws in the schemata that the children bring to the learning situation. One particularly powerful tool for getting at these initial ideas of children is the use of concept mapping.

Joseph Novak and colleagues (1984) have been credited with coming up with the concept mapping technique as a way of visually representing knowledge. Concept maps are knowledge representation tools that are valuable for helping students to synthesize their knowledge, clarify their thinking, and look at information in new ways. Using visual representations of their ideas can help children to see the relationships between their previous ideas and the new ones they are constructing. Such tools help to develop important visual literacy tools, for children learn to represent their ideas in varied ways as they develop new knowledge and deeper understanding (Literacy for Learning, 2004). In the example provided in Figure 5.1, you can see evidence of this early Grade 1 student's ideas about what constitutes a family.

FIGURE 5.1 ■ Family Concept Map

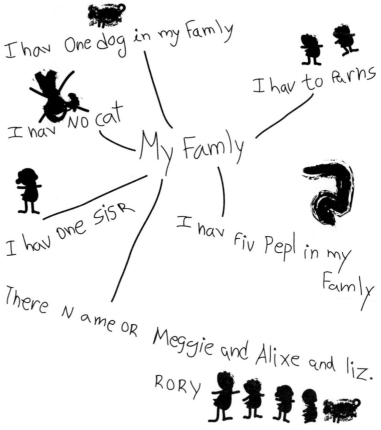

Technology Connection Concept maps come in many forms. Links to websites that provide examples of a variety of concept mapping tools can be found on the book's companion website.

Children need to be able to work with examples of concepts in order to construct understanding of those concepts. The most effective strategies for attaining concepts are to have children figure out for themselves what goes together to form a concept. This strategy not only helps children to learn the concept better but also develops the skill of learning how to learn. Concept formation involves learning the skills of classification, looking for commonalities, discriminating among ideas, seeing relationships and patterns, grouping information, and providing labels for groupings. By exposing children to examples, events, and objects that represent the concept and identifying critical (essential characteristics) and non-critical attributes, the concept can be defined and given a name. In this way, the teacher can assist in students' construction of conceptual understanding.

One approach to teaching concepts is to help children to understand the concept by having them work with examples and non-examples. When teaching the concept of "natural resource," for instance, Ms. Gervais asked her Grade 4 class to write down what they thought the difference was between a natural resource and a human-made one and to give several examples of each type. She then challenged the class to find pictures of a variety of human-made and naturally occurring resources in magazines, newspapers, and online and place them on a T-chart like the one below, which she had posted on the front board.

Resources

NATURAL	HUMAN MADE

The children were encouraged to discuss any pictures that they felt were incorrectly placed on the T-chart and to defend their choices. Once everyone was satisfied with the chart, to help the students come up with a list of the defining attributes of a natural resource, Ms. Gervais asked the class to consider questions such as, What do you see in the pictures under the 'natural' column?, Why do you think they go together?, and What things do all of the pictures in this group have in common? The class then used the common attributes they found to come up with a definition for the concept of natural resource. The children were then asked to look back at their initial ideas about the concept of natural resource to see how their ideas had changed. Ms. Gervais then provided practice with the newly learned concept through a review game using pictures of other examples and non-examples, to check that the children understood the important characteristics of the concept and were able to apply that understanding in new situations.

Miss Bell, a Grade 1 teacher, had this to say about teaching social studies concepts: "The curriculum is too abstract and the terminology is hard to teach. To teach social studies to Grade Ones you have to use terms like "tradition" and "culture," but they are very difficult. You have to be creative and come up with a practical activity that the children can relate to in order for those terms to make sense to them. They have to have concrete examples first before they can make sense of a term like tradition, for example. I think they can only come to understand it over time. They have to hear about it a lot and see examples of it and then eventually it will start to make sense."

Look over the concepts identified in the elementary social studies curriculum for your province or territory. Do you agree with Miss Bell that some of the concepts recommended in the curriculum are very difficult for young children? With a partner, come up with a creative idea for teaching one of the difficult concepts that you have identified. What critical attributes of the concept would you want the children to know? How would you be able to determine if your students understand the concept?

CLASSROOM APPLICATION

To help his Grade 6 students learn about the concept of immigration and to personally engage them and motivate them to want to learn more about the concept, Mr. Thai immersed them in stories told from the perspectives of immigrants. His goal was to develop in the students an understanding of why people immigrate and what it is like to be an immigrant, before trying to unpack the concept. He used two children's books, *Onion Tears* by Diana Kidd and Betty Bao Lord's book *In the Year of the Boar and Jackie Robinson*. He felt that these two selections would teach his students the importance of exploring a variety of differing perspectives on an issue and of taking a participant's view of history to see historical events through the eyes of someone who experienced them.

Ultimately, what we are striving for with regard to the content of social studies is to help children to understand the big ideas that result from connecting concepts so that they can use these ideas to help make sense of their world. The term "generalization" is one label that can be given to these big ideas, rules, or principles that show relationships between two or more concepts. Generalizations can be used to predict cause and effect and to encourage thinking at higher levels.

ACTIVE ENGAGEMENT

Here is an example of how generalizations, concepts, and facts work together:

GENERALIZATION:

All members of a family have certain roles and responsibilities.

CONCEPTS:

Family and responsibility.

FACTS:

a) *My mother works as a doctor.*

b) *I have two sisters.*

c) *My grandmother lives with us.*

d) *I empty the dishwasher every day.*

e) *My oldest sister helps my grandmother cook dinner.*

Can you come up with another example of a big understanding (generalization) that you feel should be part of the content children learn in social studies? Why do you feel this is important? What concepts and facts make up this generalization? How might you guide the children toward an understanding of this generalization?

As with concepts, understandings and generalizations have to be constructed by the learner. Each individual develops his or her own unique understandings based on prior learning and through engagement in new learning experiences, particularly those experiences that engage the senses. Children learn at different rates and in different ways, and they construct their own individual meaning. Sometimes this meaning might seem to be illogical to you as the teacher, but it makes sense to the child. As the teacher, your role is to provide access to a variety of different activities that encourage children to explore, refine, and sometimes completely rethink their concepts and understandings. Ultimately, the goal is for students to be able to articulate and support these understandings, to be able to apply their new knowledge in different learning situations, and to be able to use it to help make sense of their worlds.

The Influence of the Official Curriculum on Content Selection

A major problem for social studies teachers when it comes to selecting content is that a massive amount of content is available to be chosen, but the school year affords only time enough for a very tiny portion of that mass to be studied (see Figure 5.2). Most of the existing knowledge about history will not be learned simply because there have been too many events over too many years in too many different continents to allow for a comprehensive approach to the subject. Similarly, most present-day issues and problems cannot be addressed because there are too many local, global, social, and environmental problems. Nor can all the skills and attitudes that go into the making of a good citizen be covered, as there is just too much content to try to teach it all. Furthermore, we must also accept that not everything is worth teaching.

FIGURE 5.2 ■ Knowledge Representation

☐ Knowledge we have time to teach in school
 All the knowledge there is that won't be taught

ACTIVE ENGAGEMENT

In small groups, brainstorm a list of what the citizen of tomorrow might need to know and be able to do and feel? Indicate why you think these things would be important. How does this important content connect back to your goals for your social studies program? How much of this important knowledge do you see reflected in your provincial/territorial curriculum guide?

Since there is far too much content to find time to teach in a social studies program, you will have to choose what to include and what to exclude when selecting the content of your program. It is important to keep in mind this advice from Grant Wiggins (1989): "Students cannot possibly learn everything of value by the time they leave school, but we can instill in them the desire to keep questioning throughout their lives" (p. 44).

Your provincial or territorial curriculum guide for social studies outlines what is considered important for children to learn at each grade level. However, teachers often express concern about the breadth of the curriculum and the large amount of content to be covered in a year. Their concerns are justified, as the experts have found that marginal coverage of a lot of content allows very little room for in-depth investigation in any one area, and it is this deeper learning that the latest brain research shows to be the longest lasting (Levine, 2002). Experts have also found that content that is too abstract and difficult can lead to frustration for young learners and discourage them from wanting to learn (Jensen, 1998). This is one reason why you as a social studies teacher will need to be selective in what you decide to emphasize in your program planning. You will need to ask your students what they think would be most important and interesting for them to learn, and you will need to decide what is attainable to help them feel successful as learners.

REFLECTION POINT

According to Ben-Peretz, "a curriculum offers a series of "potentials," not a straitjacket that dictates what a curriculum "means" (in Thornton, 2004, p. 11). Thornton adds that, "Curriculum is not merely a product developed by distal 'experts' as a script for teachers, but a classroom enactment, properly differing from one classroom to the next. The same curriculum can be arranged and taught in countless ways. . . . Prior to and during its classroom enactment, teachers have great leeway to interpret a prescribed curriculum" (p. 11).

What do the statements from Ben-Peretz and Thornton tell you about the place of the curriculum in your planning of your social studies program? Is there ever disparity between what is written in the official curriculum and what is actually taught in schools, and, if yes, what can you do about it?

Constructivist theorists would argue that all teachers interpret curricula in their own way as they construct an understanding of what content to teach. The purpose of a curriculum document, then, should be to act as a guideline or a map for your social studies program.

Curriculum documents provide you with the all-important big picture of what is recommended for each school year. Usually included in these documents are an overview of the rationale for studying social studies from the position of the provincial ministry of education, a statement about how social studies is being defined, a synthesis of beliefs about teaching and learning that shape the document, and the overall goals of social studies as a school subject. While these curricular goals are important stepping stones in the planning process, they are usually broad statements that need to be broken down into more specific terms in order to guide the planning process. Curriculum documents provide general objectives, learning outcomes, or learner expectations that describe what students should come out of their social studies experiences knowing, being able to do, and feeling or valuing as a result of their learning experiences. Outcomes are achieved objectives. They range from general outcomes to more specific ones that identify the specific content to be addressed at each grade level. The content is then refined further, and specific content is identified in terms of knowledge or understandings, skills or processes, and attitudes, values, or dispositions to be addressed at each grade level.

Figure 5.3 (p. 92) provides an overview of the content for Grade 1 from each of the provincial and territorial curriculum guides for social studies. In terms of knowledge outcomes, the common focus for the primary grades is on concepts such as the family, the school, and the community; cooperation, needs, and wants; roles and responsibilities; and interaction and interdependence.

At the upper-elementary level, the focus shifts beyond the child's immediate surroundings to communities in Canada and the world, with an emphasis on Canada's past exploration and settlement, Canadian geography, and Canadians interactions with others in the world. Concepts included are governance; identity; culture; heritage; worldview; and time, continuity, and change. Figure 5.4 (pp. 94–101)provides an abbreviated overview of the content for Grade 2 to 6 social studies across the country.

The Place of the Social Sciences in Social Studies Content

As you probably noticed in your perusal of the provincial and territorial curriculum documents, social studies draws its content from a number of the social sciences disciplines, as depicted in Figure 5.5 (p. 102). Each of these disciplines has its own integral structure and underlying concepts, as discussed in the following sections.

History

Of all of the social sciences from which social studies draws its content, the most influential is history. History involves studying past human behaviour and events to develop an understanding of how the past is related to and influences the present and the future. Some of the concepts from history that are included in the content of social studies are time, chronology, change, and continuity; cause and effect; and power and governance. Also included in social studies content are skills such as historical thinking, or how we understand the past and are able to use the documents and records of the past to construct historical knowledge. Another important skill is the development of historical empathy, which involves being able to view and attempt to understand history from the perspectives of those who experienced it.

FIGURE 5.3 ■ Canada-wide Comparison of Content for Elementary Social Studies: Grade 1

BRITISH COLUMBIA AND YUKON	ALBERTA	SASKATCHEWAN	MANITOBA	ONTARIO	QUEBEC	ATLANTIC PROVINCES	NORTHWEST TERRITORIES AND NUNAVUT
Identity, Society, and Culture • Changes in their lives • Similarities and differences among families • Social structures • Ways people work together in groups • Symbols of Canada **Governance** • Roles, responsibilities, and rights at home and at school • Purpose of classroom and school rules **Economy and Technology** • Basic human needs and how they are met • Types of work in the community • Purpose of money • Ways technology makes lives easier	**Citizenship: Belonging and Connecting** **1.1 My World: Home, School, Community** **1.2 Moving Forward with the Past: My Family, My History, and My Community** • Introduction to active and responsible citizenship • Introduction to the concept of community • Examines how communities change over time • Examines children's own identity in relation to others • Historical thinking is employed	**Identity** • Self • Groups—families, classroom • Similarities, differences • Cooperation **Heritage** • Family traditions, rites, rituals, and celebrations • Families of the past • Multicultural heritage **Interdependence** • Family meeting needs and wants • Agriculture • Responsibilities, roles • Conservation **Decision Making** • Changes in the family • Making decisions at home and school • Family, school rules • Decisions for change • Conflict resolution	**Connecting and Belonging** **Cluster 1: I Belong** • Examine relationships with others through groups in the community • Discover family and community expressions of culture and identity • Explore how traditions, celebrations, and personal stories connect them to the past **Cluster 2: My Environment** • Explore their environment using maps and globes • Discover aspects of their community, including natural environment, landmarks, and important places	**Heritage and Citizenship: Relationships, Rules, and Responsibilities** • Identify relationships, rules, and responsibilities in the home, school, and communities • Examine how and why relationships, rules, and responsibilities may change over time and in different places **Canada and World Connections: The Local Community** • Investigate physical features and community facilities • Investigate how people live and interact within their community	**Cycle One (Grades 1 and 2)** Competency: To construct his/her representation of space, time, and society • Refer to aspects of everyday life here and elsewhere, from the past and the present • To orient himself/herself in space and time • To recognize some characteristics of the social organization of a group • To explore places here and elsewhere, from the past and the present	**Interactions Unit One: Groups** • Understand the importance of interactions between people • Understanding the similarity and diversity of social and cultural groups, including Aboriginal peoples • Understand that people within groups have rights and responsibilities **Unit Two: Environment** • Recognize that environments have natural and constructed features • Describe how people depend upon and interact with different natural environments • Practice responsible behaviour in caring for the environment	**People around Us** **Theme A: Home and Family** • Family • Respect • Tradition • Sharing • Responsibility • Relatives **Theme B: Home and School** • School • Rules • Authority • Education • Differences **Theme C: Home and Community** • Change • Community • Neighbourhood • Cooperation

Human and Physical Environment
- Characteristics of environments
- Characteristics of local human-built environments
- How the environment affects daily life
- Ways to care for their environment
- Recognizing maps of Canada

- Explore national aspects of official languages and anthem
- Distinguish between needs and wants
- Explore how media influences choices

Cluster 3: Connecting with Others
- Explore responsibilities and rights as members of communities
- Consider diverse and similar ways people live, meet needs, express themselves, and influence each other
- Explore the purpose of rules, as well as solutions to conflict

- Recognize the role that community plays in meeting human needs

Unit Three: Place/Time
- Understand that signs, symbols, direction, and scale are used to represent landmarks and locations
- Understand that the way people live in their community evolves over time
- Understand that Aboriginal peoples' relationship with place has changed over time
- Explain how interactions between communities have changed over time

Unit Four: Needs and Wants
- Identify the difference between needs and wants
- Understand the factors that influence how needs and wants are met
- Understand how communities depend on each other for the exchange of goods and services

- To compare places and social phenomena here and elsewhere, from the past and the present

CANADIAN SOCIAL STUDIES TOPICS

GRADE	BRITISH COLUMBIA AND YUKON	ALBERTA	SASKATCHEWAN	MANITOBA	ONTARIO	QUEBEC	ATLANTIC PROVINCES	NORTHWEST TERRITORIES AND NUNAVUT
K	• concepts of change, groups places and families • roles and responsibilities in school, purpose of classroom and school rules • human needs and technologies in daily life • characteristics of local natural and human-built environments; caring for their environment	Being Together • K.1 I Am Unique • K.2 I Belong		Being Together • Cluster 1: Me • Cluster 2: The People around Me • Cluster 3: The World around Me			Connections • Unit One: Social Connections • Unit Two: Roots • Unit Three: Place	

	Communities in Canada	Local Communities	Communities in Canada	Heritage and Citizenship: Traditions and Celebrations Canada and World Connections: Features of Communities around the World	Cycle One (Grades 1 and 2) Competency: To construct his/her representation of space, time, and society	Change	Our Community
• contributing to community, personal identity, language and cultural characteristics of Canada • group decision making • jobs in school, money, affects of technology on individuals and schools • bodies of water and landforms, how the environment affects human activities	• 2.1 Canada's Dynamic Communities • 2.2 A Community in the Past	• Identity • Heritage • Interdependence • Decision Making	• Cluster 1: Our Local Community • Cluster 2: Communities in Canada • Cluster 3: The Canadian Community		• Refer to aspects of everyday life here and elsewhere, from the past and the present • To orient himself/herself in space and time	• Unit One: People • Unit Two: Technology • Unit Three: Economics • Unit Four: Environment	• Theme A: Living in Our Community • Theme B: Working in Our Community • Theme C: Transportation and Communication in Our Community

(Continued)

FIGURE 5.4 ■ *(Continued)*

GRADE	BRITISH COLUMBIA AND YUKON	ALBERTA	SASKATCHEWAN	MANITOBA	ONTARIO	QUEBEC	ATLANTIC PROVINCES	NORTHWEST TERRITORIES AND NUNAVUT
2 (cont'd)						• To recognize some characteristics of the social organization of a group • To explore places here and elsewhere, from the past and the present • To compare places and social phenomena here and elsewhere, from the past and the present		
3	• communities and change • characteristics of Canadian society, cultural similarities and differences	Connecting with the World • 3.1 Communities in the World • 3.2 Global Citizenship	Community Comparisons • Identity • Heritage • Interdependence • Decision Making	Communities of the World • Cluster 1: Connecting with Canadians • Cluster 2: Exploring the World	Heritage and Citizenship: Early Settlements in Upper Canada Canada and World Connections: Urban and Rural Communities	Cycle Two: (Grades 3 and 4) • Iroquoian Society around 1500 • French Society in New France around 1645	Change • Unit One: People • Unit Two: Technology • Unit Three: Economics • Unit Four: Environment	Other Communities • Theme A: Communities in Our Region • Theme B: Communities in the NWT

(Continued)

4

	Alberta: The Land, Histories, and Stories	Saskatchewan	Manitoba, Canada, and the North: Places and Stories	Heritage and Citizenship: Medieval Times				Our Northern Land and Its People
• roles and responsibilities of local governments	• traditional Aboriginal cultures	• Identity • Heritage • Interdependence • Decision Making			• Cluster 3: Communities of the World • Cluster 4: Exploring an Ancient Society	• Canadian Society in New France around 1745 • Iroquoian Society and Algonquian Society around 1500 • Canadian Society in New France and Societies in the Thirteen Colonies around 1745	Explorations • Unit One: Explorations	• Theme A: How Our People Lived Long Ago
• needs and wants, affect of technology on individuals and communities past and present								• Theme C: Working in NWT Communities
• landforms and water bodies and provinces and territories in Canada								
• effect of the physical environment and natural resources on early settlement								

FIGURE 5.4 ■ *(Continued)*

GRADE	BRITISH COLUMBIA AND YUKON	ALBERTA	SASKATCHEWAN	MANITOBA	ONTARIO	QUEBEC	ATLANTIC PROVINCES	NORTHWEST TERRITORIES AND NUNAVUT
4 (cont'd)	• effects of early contact between Aboriginal societies and European explorers and settlers • traditional Aboriginal governance structures • governance structures in early European settlements in Canada, impact on Aboriginal peoples • bartering; traditional technologies used by Aboriginal cultures; technological exchange with European explorers/settlers	• 4.1 Alberta: A Sense of the Land • 4.2 The Stories, Histories, and People of Alberta • 4.3 Alberta: Celebrations and Challenges		• Cluster 1: Geography of Canada • Cluster 2: Living in Canada • Cluster 3: Living in Manitoba • Cluster 4: History of Manitoba • Cluster 5: Canada's North	Canada and World Connections: Canada's Provinces, Territories, and Regions		• Unit Two: Explorers: Past and Present • Unit Three: Exploring the World Today • Unit Four: Exploring Canada Today	• Theme B: The North's Resources • Theme C: The Faces of the NWT

5

- hemispheres, continents and oceans
- location of Aboriginal groups in Canada and their relationship with the land
- key events and factors in the development of Canada; immigration, citizenship and rights
- levels of government, First Nations governance, Confederation
- resources and economic development of communities, transportation systems in Canada

Canada
- Identity
- Heritage
- Interdependence
- Decision Making

Canada: The Land, Histories, and Stories
- 5.1 Physical Geography of Canada
- 5.2 Histories and Stories of Ways of Life in Canada
- 5.3 Canada: Shaping an Identity

Peoples and Stories of Canada to 1867
- Cluster 1: First Peoples
- Cluster 2: Early European Colonization (1600 to 1763)
- Cluster 3: Fur Trade
- Cluster 4: The British Colony to Confederation

Heritage and Citizenship: Early Civilizations

Canada and World Connections: Aspects of Citizenship and Government in Canada

Cycle Three (Grades 5 and 6)
- Canadian Society around 1820
- Quebec Society around 1905
- Quebec Society around 1980
- Canadian Society in the Prairies and on the West Coast around 1900
- Quebec Society and Canadian Society on the Prairies around 1900

Societies
- Unit One: Introduction: Societies over Time
- Unit Two: Place: Ancient Societies
- Unit Three: Social Structure: Medieval Societies
- Unit Four: Tradition: Early Aboriginal Peoples—North America

Our Northern Land and Its People
- Theme A: How Our Northern Territory Came to Be
- Theme B: The North's Resources
- Theme C: Regional Councils and Aboriginal Self-Government Democracy

FIGURE 5.4 ■ *(Continued)*

GRADE	BRITISH COLUMBIA AND YUKON	ALBERTA	SASKATCHEWAN	MANITOBA	ONTARIO	QUEBEC	ATLANTIC PROVINCES	NORTHWEST TERRITORIES AND NUNAVUT
5 (cont'd)	• physical regions of Canada, natural resources, sustainability, environmental affects of settlement in early Canada					• Quebec Society and an Undemocratic Society around 1980 • Micmac Society and Inuit Society around 1980	• Unit Five: Settlement and Immigration: Colonial French Societies • Unit Six: Summative: The World in 1800	Our Place in the Nation • Theme A: Territorial and Provincial Governments • Theme B: The Regions of Canada
6	• Canadian identity, artistic expression and culture	Democracy: Action and Participation • 6.1 Citizens Participating in Decision Making	Canada's Relationship with Its Atlantic Neighbours • Location (Physical Geography)	Canada: A Country of Change (1867 to the Present)	Heritage and Citizenship: First Nation Peoples and European Explorers Canada and World Connections: Canada's Links to the World		World Cultures • Unit One: Introduction: World Cultures • Unit Two: Environment	

- federal government, justice system, the Charter rights and responsibilities
- role of Canada in the world
- Canada's changing economic relationships, communications technologies in effects on lifestyle and environment
- relationship between cultures and their environments; settlement patterns and population distribution

- 6.2 Historical Models of Democracy: Ancient Athens and the Iroquois Confederacy

- Interaction (Historical Geography)
- Identity (Cultural Geography)
- Interdependence (Political/Economic Geography)

- Cluster 1: Building a Nation (1867–1914)
- Cluster 2: An Emerging Nation (1914–1945)
- Cluster 3: Shaping Contemporary Canada (1945 to the Present)
- Cluster 4: Canada Today: Democracy, Diversity, and the Influence of the Past

- Unit Three: Cultural Influences
- Unit Four: Expressions of Culture
- Unit Five: Global Issues
- Unit Six: Summative: Canada—A Multicultural and Multiracial Mosaic

- Theme C: The Faces of Canada Settlement

FIGURE 5.5 ■ The Social Sciences That Make Up Social Studies

Because of their level of abstractness, many of the concepts of history are particularly difficult for children to comprehend. One example is the concept of historical time. Understanding chronology is particularly difficult for young children. At the Grade 1 level, children's understanding of time is mostly comprised of "long ago" and "now." It often takes until Grade 5 for children to be able to use dates in a historical sense (Alter, Monson, Larson, & Morgan, 2000). Experiencing history as long ago through imaginative stories of conflicts between opposites (i.e., good versus bad, love versus hate) can be particularly engaging for young children. Older children are equally as engaged by history as story but are also able to connect empathetically with stories of real peoples' struggles (Egan, 1997).

Another way to begin to develop young children's understanding of the concept of historical time is by having them map out their own lives in terms of the important things that have happened to them since birth. Young children can also be engaged in history through the creation and sharing of personal histories in activities such as making family scrapbooks, interviewing family members, and identifying objects of importance to one's personal history (Levstik & Barton, 2001).

CLASSROOM APPLICATION

The children in Miss Wieronski's class were asked to bring an object from home that represented their past for them. Caroline shared this story about her object with her class: "My special object is a sugar bowl. The sugar bowl is white and has coloured flowers all over it. This sugar bowl belonged to my grandmother. She brought it to Canada in 1910. Her and my grandfather came to Canada from the U.S.A. in a covered wagon. My grandmother had a very small baby at the time. She was 20 years old."

Children know more about some historical topics than others, and they need opportunities to make their previous historical knowledge explicit in order for teachers to identify misconceptions and help them to refine their knowledge (Seixas, 1993). Research on elementary children's historical knowledge indicates that they know the least about political and diplomatic history (i.e., elections, political leaders, and wars, etc.) and find these topics confusing; but their knowledge of social history, including changes over time in the everyday life of people

Children's historical sense is culturally embedded and comes from the sharing of family stories and traditions.

and the way people treated each other, is better developed (Barton, 1997b; Barton & Levstik, 1996; Downey, 1994). For this reason, elementary social studies is most effective when it is taught with an emphasis on social history, which provides a basis for developing understandings of societal institutions and their role in history. This approach involves not only examining famous people and events but also learning about the social relations that made those events and people meaningful (Barton, 1997b).

Children learn a great deal of what they know about history outside of the classroom from television, films, the media, visits to historic sites, and stories told by relatives (Barton, 1997a). Although they may not know the word "history" or connect what they know with school history, their encounters with history outside of school are often positive and interesting and have an impact on promoting interest in and enthusiasm toward history (Barton & Levstik, 1996). Sometimes the history that children possess is in bits and pieces and at other times it includes misconceptions (McKeown & Beck, 1990). It is important that, as a teacher, you recognize, respect, refine, and build on these historical understandings.

REFLECTION POINT

Figure 5.6 presents an example of a piece of writing from a Grade 5 student about her understandings of the fur trade and the relationship between the traders and the Natives.

(Continued)

The fur trade

When Europeans came to Canada they first wanted to trade there metal tools and other goods for fresh food But then they found out that the natives also had furs. So they Built trading posts and they fought for the furs of the natives. The fur trade changed the lives of the Europeans and the natives, It changed the Natives lives Because they hunted more, and the wives were kept Busy By always cooking the meat and skining the animals. The Europeans were Busy trading furs for Guns and food and clothing.

The Natives Hunted more to trade the European than to Eat.

What does this piece of writing tell you about this child's knowledge of this historical event? Is there evidence of misconceptions or missing information? If yes, how could you use that information as the child's teacher?

You will also need to be aware of the kinds of messages children are getting about history from the activities you are involving them in. Exercises that expect them to memorize static facts such as dates, names, causes of events, and other information in order to be successful can give children "a misleading impression of history as inert, disconnected facts" and leave them thinking that "there is a single story about what happened, that teachers and textbooks are neutral sources of information, and that their own judgments about the past are irrelevant" (Hartzler-Miller 2001, pp. 673/675). Developing historical thinking and understanding involves learning to view history as something that is both evolving and biased, as it has been constructed from an individual historian's perspective. Children need to experience history from the perspectives of all who were a part of it, including women, the working class, and ethnic groups so that the history they experience more accurately represents our multi-dimensional, diverse society (Crocco, 1997; Strong-Boag, 1998).

History teaching also needs to place increased emphasis on historical inquiry and the use of primary sources so that children learn that "History is something one does: a process of reasoning using contextual information, texts, empathy and imagination" (Hartzler-Miller, 2001, p. 672). The focus should be on helping students to develop a genuine understanding of historical events, not just on the acquisition and memorization of facts. Students need be taught methods to assess conflicting accounts of the past and actively assess the claims made in those accounts rather than accepting them uncritically (Seixas & Peck, 2004). It is not enough to learn about the past; students must also be able to question all accounts of history they encounter, develop an understanding of why accounts might be different, and recognize them as interpretations in time (Lee, 1998). This requires a radical shift in classroom practice as students are involved in the "doing" of history, including posing questions, collecting and analyzing sources, struggling with issues of significance, being challenged to rethink assumptions about the past, and building historical interpretations (Levstik & Barton, 2001). Involving children through music, drama, dance, games, and simulations that help to stimulate their historical imaginations and develop their awareness of historical interpretation and alternative perspectives can connect children to the history they are learning (Groth & Albert, 1997; Hoostein, 1995).

 **Technology Connection** The following websites provide ideas and lesson plans for approaching the study of Canadian history. (Use the links to specific pages found on the book's companion website.)

- See CanTeach.ca for lesson plans on making personal timelines, interviewing a historical figure, creating war propaganda, and making a graphic organizer to compare different perspectives.
- See the Saskatchewan Department of Learning website, http://www.sasked.gov.sk.ca, for a lesson plan on simulating the lives of Canada's First Peoples.
- See the Histor!ca Foundation of Canada website, http://www.histori.ca, for ideas on how students can plan and carry out a historical fair.

- See the Great Unsolved Mysteries in Canadian History website, http://www. canadianmysteries.ca, for famous mysteries students can learn about and help to solve.
- See the Kids' Stop page at the Indian and Northern Affairs Canada website, http:// www.ainc-inac.gc.ca, for a multitude of learning resources, activities, and games on the subject of Native life in Canada.

Geography

Another discipline that has had a major role in contributing content to social studies is geography. Geography is the study of the earth and the relationship between humans and their physical surroundings. The discipline of geography is divided into the physical aspect, which addresses the natural features of the earth, including climate, vegetation, landforms, and bodies of water, and the cultural aspect, which is concerned with where people live and why. Geographical concepts that are addressed in social studies include natural resources, ecosystems, climate, location, topography, ecology, spatial organization, the environment, the earth, conservation, globalism, and regions. An example of a generalization in social studies that comes from geography is that humans modify and adapt to natural settings in ways that affect their lifestyle and the environment.

CLASSROOM APPLICATION

Here is a sample social studies activity planned by a Grade 5 teacher on the regions of Canada. Can you identify the generalizations and concepts from geography that have contributed to the content knowledge covered in this project?

Canada's Regions Trade Fair Project

Your group is on a sales mission. You want to attract workers to your region. You will need to design a display and prepare an oral presentation about your region of Canada to use at our Regional Trade Fair to try to attract your classmates to your region. Before you begin your research, decide on what needs to be done, a timeline for completing each piece, and job descriptions for each group member. You only have two weeks until the fair, so work hard!

The knowledge outcomes of this project include (a) understanding that Canada is divided into different regions and that the boundaries of these regions are different from the political boundaries of the provinces and territories, and (b) understanding that in each region the geography of the land affects how citizens meet their various needs.

The skills you will be developing include identifying sources of information; gathering information by reading, skimming, listening, and viewing; interpreting relationships and drawing inferences from graphs, tables, charts, pictures, and maps; visually and orally representing ideas; and creative thinking.

The main research question is: How does the geography of the land affect how citizens meet their needs?

Sub-questions to guide your inquiry are: What are the physical features of your region? What natural resources are in your region? What occupations are there and how are they dependent on natural resources? Where are the largest and smallest populations? How are population distribution and transportation related? How do physical features affect occupations, transportation, and population density?

One of the main aspects of geographic learning is the development of mapping skills. Curriculum guides list mapping skills such as legend, latitude, longitude, and scale, as well as the concepts of location (hemisphere, continent, oceans), landform, physical region, political region (continents, countries, provinces, territories), vegetation, and climate, among others. When designing teaching activities, care needs to be taken to address the development of students' mapping skills, as colouring maps or memorizing disconnected information that has minimal relevance to children's lives without knowing the underlying reasoning associated with such information does little to promote students' geographic understanding. As Atler et al. (2000) point out, "Developing in-depth learning on one or two major concepts has a much higher return overall than memorization of names, products and other geographical facts" (p. 36).

When teaching mapping skills, teachers also need to recognize that such skills are developmental—i.e., they build on prior learning. Younger children, for example, have difficulty when it comes to understanding that a globe represents the earth, and even more trouble seeing that a flat map represents a place on the earth (Wiegand & Stiell, 1996). The main reason that mapping is difficult for young children is the fact that maps take a bird's-eye view, looking down onto a surface from above. Hurren (2004) calls for a more embodied way of thinking about location

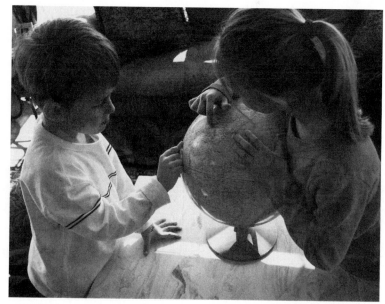

Helping children to understand that the globe is a representation of the earth is an important beginning point for teaching geographical understanding

that acknowledges the child's personal and lived experiences, associated with specific places, through the engagement of the senses, descriptive writing, poetry, stories, and conversation. Younger children can also learn geographic concepts and build geographic skills by using an interdisciplinary approach (Palmer, Smith, & Grace, 1993) and active learning methods, such as setting problems using geographic concepts within a story format (Sowden, et al. 1996), incorporating children's literature (Deir, 1996), participating in field trips and field work (Wright, 1997), creating models, drawing maps from memory (Lenhoff & Huber, 2000), and engaging in simulations, scavenger hunts, and cooperative learning (Whiteside, 2000).

CLASSROOM APPLICATION

Figure 5.7 presents a Grade 2 student's drawing of her favourite route to school.

What mapping concepts are addressed in this exercise? What do you notice about the child's understanding of those concepts?

FIGURE 5.7 ■ Child's Drawing of Her Route to School

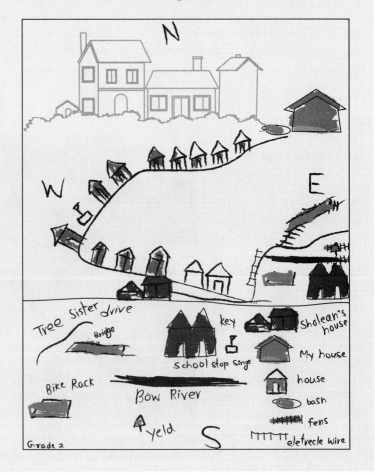

CLASSROOM APPLICATION

Mrs. Wong, a Grade 1 teacher, uses the children's book *Rosie's Walk* by Pat Hutchins, which is about a hen named Rosie strutting around her barnyard, to teach the spatial concepts of over, under, across, past, through, and around. After orally sharing the book, she has the children role play the story by turning her room into Rosie's barnyard and directing the children to follow the path that Rosie takes on her walk while naming the directional term.

Older children develop geographical understanding best through the study of problems and issues with significant geographic dimensions at both the regional and global levels, such as undertaking a local environmental project or studying the issue of global warming collaboratively with a class somewhere else in the world. (See examples of telecollaborative projects in Chapter 11). The ultimate goals are to guide children to grasp the significance of location, to understand the inevitability of change, and to understand the important role that geography plays in their lives.

 Technology Connection Visit the following geography-oriented websites and decide how you might use such sites to engage your students in geographic thinking activities.

- Canadian Geography Network and the Arc Explorer Web: http://www.geographynetwork.ca
- The National Atlas of Canada: http://www.atlas.gc.ca
- Canadian Geographic: http://www.canadiangeographic.com
- Canadian Council for Geographic Education: http://www.ccge.org
- GeoWorld: http://www.geoworld.ca
- CanTeach: www.canteach.ca (For links to specific pages on geography lessons, making papier mâché globes, and creating an edible map, a playground map, and a school map, visit the book's companion website.)
- Environmental Systems Research Institute (ESRI) Canada Schools and Libraries Program (http://k12.esricanada.com), and the GeoCommunity (http://www.geocomm.com): Both of these sites provide students access to Geographic Information Systems (GIS), which allow layers of geographical formations such as countries, bodies of water, and political divisions to be superimposed so that users can manipulate information and do comparing and contrasting exercises.

Economics

Another discipline from which social studies draws content is economics. Broadly speaking, economics is the study of production, distribution, and consumption of commodities. From economics come the concepts of goods and services, division of labour, producers and consumers, supply and demand, needs and wants, scarcity and inflation, interdependence, resources, money, loans, interest, business ownership, and natural and human capital. An example of a generalization in social studies that comes from economics is that supply and demand affect not only our choices as consumers but also the stability of our economy.

For young children, examining the concepts of need and wants can be particularly challenging. Jere Brophy and Janet Alleman (2002) looked at K–3 children's prior knowledge and thinking about the economics of a family meeting its need for shelter. They interviewed children about their views on different types of shelter (i.e., houses, apartments, hotels) and on the differences between owning and renting and reasons for doing each. The study found that the children had little knowledge about renting or buying, and many had misconceptions about the different types of shelters that exist and about differences between rural life and life in the big city (the effects of crime, pollution, etc.). The children were mostly from the suburbs of a small city and they knew little about lifestyles and types of shelter that were different from their own. Brophy and Alleman recommended that exposure to these differences and to the economics of paying for shelter were important to the development of young children's economic knowledge as well as their understanding of citizenship. For older children, learning about consumer skills such as different types and values of money, banking, investing, buying and selling, and learning about how an economy works, both in Canada and around the globe, helps them to understand how the economy affects people's lives and to see that every society faces a struggle between unlimited wants and limited resources.

 Technology Connection Visit the book's companion website for a link to a lesson plan on the economic concept of supply and demand. For more teaching ideas about economic concepts in elementary schools, see http://ecedweb.unomaha.edu/K-12/K-5concepts.cfm. Although this is a U.S. site, it lists a wide range of economic concepts from social studies curriculum documents and provides numerous lessons that could be adapted for use in Canadian programs.

Other Social Sciences

From anthropology, social studies draws its emphasis on the study of the origins of people and their social relationships. Concepts such as culture, customs, beliefs, ethics, artifacts, tools, ways of life, and traditions come from anthropology. The main focus that comes to social studies from anthropology is on understanding different cultures and human behaviours. A generalization that comes from anthropology is that culture is shaped by the contributions of groups that make up that culture; another is that cultures change over time.

From sociology, the study of human behaviour and social relations, social studies derives the concepts of social roles, socialization, belonging, class, groups, norms, interactions and interdependence, cooperation, and social institutions. Understandings about various group structures, such as family, school, community, clubs, etc. and how people act within these groups, as well as how those groups differ in other societies, are typically found in the elementary curriculum.

Political science, the study of government and political institutions, provides social studies with concepts such as law making, power, justice, authority, nation, state, citizenship, electoral process, and democracy. At the elementary level, content drawn from political science is usually focused on learning about concepts such as government, including the various types and functions; how rules are made, interpreted, and enforced in society; the difference between rights and responsibilities; and how people organize themselves to make decisions. A generalization drawn from political science is that all societies establish ways of governing themselves through which decisions are made that apply to all members of that society.

Religious studies provide the moral dimension to examining social issues within social studies. Other concepts are drawn from archaeology, the study of ancient societies; from philosophy, the study of belief systems; from psychology, the study of the human behaviour, the mind, and emotions; and, from law, the study of the function and workings of the legal system and government regulations, and crime and punishment.

While each of the social sciences contributes in varying degrees to the content of social studies, the content of these disciplines is far too extensive for it all to be included in the curriculum, and much of that content is beyond the grasp of elementary children. Since social studies is envisioned as being interdisciplinary, it should represent a blend of content from the social sciences with no single discipline having exclusive domain. Ultimately, learning social studies content helps children to understand the big ideas about humans and their relationships with each other and with the environment.

ACTIVE ENGAGEMENT

Look back at your provincial or territorial curriculum document and list the various social sciences that you see represented in the content to be taught. What are some of the concepts and generalizations that are addressed for each of the social science disciplines? Of all of the concepts listed in this curriculum, which ones do you feel would be most important for your students to learn about in social studies? Why? Are there important concepts that are not listed?

Chapter Summary

As you saw in Chapter 4, citizenship education is recognized as the primary goal of social studies in schools. Deciding on what social studies content would best guide your students to an understanding of what citizenship entails is an important planning task. In this chapter, the meaning of the term "content" was unpacked by first examining what is meant by knowledge, skills, and attitudes and how these three areas contribute to the content of social studies. Content knowledge was explored further by considering facts, concepts, and generalizations.

In the second half of this chapter, the official social studies curriculum was examined as an important influence on teachers' thinking about content selection. An overview of the purpose and types of information provided in provincial and territorial curriculum documents was given. Next, the contributions of the various social sciences to the official curriculum content were examined. While these curriculum documents are available to assist in the content selection process, this chapter emphasized that you as the teacher will ultimately need to decide what content best addresses the needs and abilities of your students and your goals. The most important thing when choosing content is that it is meaningful and relevant to the children who are engaging in social studies learning.

In Chapter 6, we continue our look at the possible influences on your decision making about content, including the interests and developmental learning needs of your students, your goals as the teacher, the context in which you teach and the available resources, and current events.

Chapter 6

What Other Factors Affect Your Social Studies Content Choices?

In the previous chapter, we looked at content selection as the important second step in planning your social studies program, after goal setting. We began by examining the meaning of the term "content" within social studies, as well as the skills and processes; values, attitudes, and dispositions; and knowledge that make up that content.

Next, we examined the role of the official provincial or territorial social studies curriculum in determining your content focus. A number of other factors can also help to shape your thinking about what is important for children to learn in social studies. These include your professional goals as the teacher, as well as your interests, past experiences, and content knowledge; the children's developmental needs, including what we know about these from brain research and multiple intelligences theory, as well as their interests and diverse experiences; and the sociocultural context of the school community in which you are teaching. Each of these factors will be examined in more detail in the following sections. As you read about them and engage in the activities provided, think about their potential influence on your choices of what to teach. Following the discussion of important considerations in the selection of social studies content, some ways to organize this content will be explored.

Your Goals, Interests, and Background as Influences on Content Selection

In Chapter 1, you read about several studies of children's attitudes toward social studies in which it was discovered that they were generally bored by and uninterested in the content of social studies, mainly because of its perceived irrelevance to their lives, both present and future. One of the suggestions coming out of those studies was that teachers should communicate the value of social studies to their students. Beginning your social studies program by providing students with the big picture of what they are going to have the opportunity to explore over the upcoming year and explaining why those things are important can help them to more clearly see a purpose for studying social studies. Giving students the opportunity to provide feedback on the proposed plan is another way to promote their interest in and personal connection with social studies.

ACTIVE ENGAGEMENT

Turn to a partner and discuss whether you feel it is important for children to know why they are learning about citizenship and what it entails. How might you go about explaining the role of citizenship as this is taught in social studies to your students?

CLASSROOM APPLICATION

Mr. Boyle believes that his students need to have input into what they learn in order for it to be meaningful to them. He begins a unit on the study of China by showing the official curriculum goals to his class and by reviewing what the document suggests that his students should know, do,

Meet Mr. Boyle, a Grade 6 teacher.

and feel after completing the unit. He asks the students to vote on what in the curriculum they would be most interested in focusing on and encourages them to add anything else of interest that they might like to explore. He then uses the students' input to design the unit. Do you recall ever being asked for this type of input into what you were learning as a child in school? What do you think your reaction would have been as a student in Mr. Boyle's class? What do you think his students are learning about their roles and responsibilities as learners? What hidden curriculum is at work here?

Part of your being able to communicate the value of social studies to children is understanding and believing in its value yourself, as the teacher. During our investigation in previous chapters of why we teach social studies, we looked at different views on citizenship education as a curricular goal of the discipline. You were challenged to think about differing views of citizenship education and which one(s) best fit with your ideas about social studies and its purpose as a subject in elementary schools. Once you clarified this picture of the purpose of social studies, you were then encouraged to think about your own professional goals for your social studies program using these orientations as a guide. Remember that these goals are influenced by what you believe to be important for children to know, what you believe about how they learn that important knowledge, and what you believe about your role as teacher and the children's roles in that learning.

Each of the orientations to social studies described in Chapter 4 argues for a different approach to selecting content. Content choices are based on how those who view social studies from these orientations would respond to questions such as (a) "What is knowledge?"; (b) "Where and how do we get knowledge?," and, (c) "What knowledge is significant and why?" Figure 6.1 (p. 116) presents some examples of the possible responses to these content questions, based on four of the different orientations discussed in Chapter 4.

In order to encourage your students to value social studies, you will need to help them to understand the importance of being a good citizen and the relevance of social studies to their lives.

FIGURE 6.1 ■ **Content Knowledge and the Orientations of Citizenship Education**

ORIENTATION	WHAT IS KNOWLEDGE?	WHERE AND HOW DO WE GET KNOWLEDGE?	WHAT KNOWLEDGE IS SIGNIFICANT? WHY?
• Citizens as Cultural Conservationists	• What authorities say it is—i.e. teacher, textbook	• Listening to the teacher, reading the textbook	• What teachers say, and what authors put in the text, the curriculum, etc. • Authorities know the culture.
• Citizens as Social Scientists	• Concepts selected by social scientists and scholars	• Concepts from geography, history, sociology, economics, etc. • From directed investigation using primary source materials and various processes of social sciences	• Explanations for why the world works as it does • These explanations have been proven to be foundational by social scientists.
• Citizens as Reflective Inquirers	• Personally constructed meaning built from varied knowledge claims and points-of-view	• From primary sources • Research of interest to the learner	• Steps in problem solving and decision making, knowledge of likely consequences of choices, both positive and negative • Need to be able to use knowledge to predict consequences and make appropriate decisions.
• Citizens as Cultural Transformationists	• As in Reflective Inquiry	• From primary sources, multiple perspectives • Look for bias, value positions	• As in Reflective Inquiry, plus knowledge of how to make decisions then act on them, knowledge of how to plan effective action and how to persuade • Must know how to go about exerting influence and making change.
• Personally Developed Citizens • Citizens who Respect Diversity • Global Citizens			

How would you fill in the remaining three orientations to citizenship education in Figure 6.1? At what points do your current views of social studies teaching and learning fit best with the information on this chart?

When you are clearer about what kind of "good citizen" qualities you seek to promote, you should be better able to make decisions about what content is consistent with that goal. You will also want to strive to select content in a way that fosters the kind of growth in your students to which you give highest priority. Throughout the content selection process, and the entire planning process, it is important that you continually revisit your evolving professional goals and reflect on how they are influencing your decision making.

Introducing Pedagogical Content Knowledge

Your personal interests and past experiences will also influence your selection of content. If you have a particular interest in a topic or feel more confident about your knowledge of that topic—based on either prior travel or educational experiences, for example—you may wish to address it rather than something that you have no interest in, have no past experience with, or lack a feeling of confidence about. At times, you will still need to teach content that doesn't particularly motivate you, so be sure to keep in mind the studies of children's attitudes toward social studies reviewed in Chapter 3, which identified the teacher's enthusiasm for the subject as one of the factors that influenced students' feelings about social studies. Furthermore, because the fact that you may have taken university-level courses in a specific area of a discipline—say, pre-Confederation Canadian history—and you feel that you know everything there is to know about that subject, does not necessarily mean that you know how to translate that material so that young learners will understand it. This is the difference that Lee Shulman (1987) cited between content knowledge and pedagogical content knowledge.

Shulman argued that teachers not only need to know a lot about the content of the subject area(s) they teach but also need to understand the content well enough to be able to create experiences that make the subject interesting and learnable for children. Pedagogical content knowledge is about being able to transform the content to be taught into something students will understand through the use of strategies such as metaphors, analogies, stories, explanations, discussions, and real world examples.

A teacher also needs to have a "feel" for the subject and to be able to convey that feeling to students. A social studies teacher who has a feel for the subject both understands the substantive or structural aspects of the subject, such as "the variety of ways in which the basic concepts and principles are organized to incorporate [the subject's] facts," and knows why certain topics are central while others are less important (Shulman, 1986, p. 9). In addition, such a teacher understands the syntactic aspects of the subject, or the rules of evidence and proof that guide inquiry in the subject. For example, this teacher recognizes the importance of encouraging students to see beyond the generally accepted facts of history to the role that interpretation plays in history, and is able to help students see the relevance of what they are learning to their lives. This teacher not only knows the rationale of social studies and the content to be taught but also continues to reflect on and ask questions about social studies content and models this curiosity for students.

REFLECTION POINT

Look back at your provincial or territorial social studies curriculum document and review the content that has been designated for each of the elementary grade levels. What social studies content do you feel (a) most interested in and (b) most confident about teaching right now? Why is that? What content do you feel least prepared to teach? How can you begin to prepare yourself to teach it?

 Technology Connection Look through your provincial or territorial curriculum document and find a topic with which you are not very familiar. Do an Internet search to locate information about this topic that you could use in the teaching of it. The book's companion website provides a list of links to educational and discipline-specific sites that will be useful to you in this searching activity.

The Influence of Children's Developmental Needs, Interests, and Past Experiences on Content Selection

Other important considerations when deciding on what content to select are the developmental needs, interests, backgrounds, and prior experiences of the children in your classroom. One of the most important things you can do as a teacher is familiarize yourself with your students in terms of what interests and excites them. Learners bring different cultural and religious backgrounds, socioeconomic statuses, genders, sexual orientations, and native languages to the classroom. It is important to familiarize yourself with the makeup of your class to be able to build learning experiences that are meaningful for all of your students. Each learner is also unique in his or her cognitive and social development and preferred learning style. In the inclusive classroom, students can have a range of abilities and disabilities. For example, according to the Government of Canada's report *Disability in Canada: A 2001 Profile* from the Office for Disability Issues, in 2001, 4 percent of Canadian children under the age of 15 had physical and intellectual disabilities, and 72 percent of those children had more than one type of disability. All of these factors need to be taken into consideration when deciding on social studies content that will be most effective for the children you are teaching.

At the beginning of the school year, Mrs. Pringle interviews each of the children in her class to help her to get to know them a bit better. Some of the questions she asks are, If you had to describe yourself and your likes and interests to someone else, what would you say?; Do you speak any other languages?; Who are the people in your family? Describe each of them for me.; Do you have any special traditions in your family?; Have you any ideas about what you would like to do when you grow up?; How do you spend your time after school?; Who are your friends?; What do you like best about school?; What are you really good at?; What do you feel that you need help with?; If you could change some part of your school life, what would it be?

ACTIVE ENGAGEMENT

Constructivists assert that you should start the formal learning process at the point where your students are in terms of how they see the world (Brooks & Brooks, 1999). How might you find out what excites your students and what questions they have about their worlds? Based on your practicum experience and knowledge of children, what questions and content do you think would be of interest to a 6 year old compared to a 12 year old? If you have easy access to children, talk to them about what they are interested in, what they know about the world, and what they would like to find out about in social studies. Compile a class list of these curiosities and keep them in mind as you read this chapter.

Brain Research as an Influence on Content Choice

We know much about children's learning that should be considered when selecting social studies content. Current research on how the brain functions, based on work in neuroscience using tools such as magnetic resonance imaging (MRI), electroencephalogram (EEG), and positron emission tomography (PET) has informed our knowledge about learning. From brain research, we have confirmation that the best learning happens in the early school years. During those years and beyond, teachers "need to teach content within a context that is meaningful for students and that connects to their beliefs and experiences" (Wolfe, 2001, p. 48). Learning that is embedded in the experiences of students and that is hands-on, experiential, and interconnected is the most effective.

We also know that meaning making occurs when the content is relevant to the learner. Relevance can be created by linking with prior learning and experiences, and by helping children to see that their ideas, interests, and curiosities are being acknowledged (Caine, Caine, McClintic, & Klimek, 2004). Since relevance directly influences meaning making, the effectiveness of the learning process is enhanced when it has application to real, practical situations rather than taking place in isolation from the child's life experience outside school. Further, since making meaning requires connecting prior ideas to new knowledge through patterning, the content selected should connect to and build on children's prior learning. Engaging the senses as a part of learning experiences can have positive effects on children's understanding (Jensen, 2000).

CLASSROOM APPLICATION

Mrs. Crow was teaching a lesson on the concepts of rural and urban. She had her class complete the following "engaging the senses" activity. "Close your eyes and imagine that you are standing in a field out in the country, then complete these statements: I see . . ., I hear . . ., I smell . . ., I feel . . ., I touch. . . . Now pretend you are standing in the city on a busy street corner and do the exercise again. Compare and contrast the sensations you experience."

Brain research has also identified the fact that every brain is unique and develops at its own stage of readiness, and that there are differences in the brains of males and females. Learning structurally changes the brain; therefore, the more we learn, the more unique our brains become. Neural pathways that help us to excel at thinking are very specific, and while a student may succeed at one type of thinking, she or he may have difficulty with another. Therefore, student choice, in terms of the complexity, format, and type of activity, as well as whom to work with, at what pace to complete the work, and how the outcomes of the work are to be represented, is crucial to the learning process (Sylwester, 2003).

ACTIVE ENGAGEMENT

Reflect on your own beliefs about how people learn. How do the views of learning drawn from brain research fit with what you believe? How might this research influence your future teaching of social studies?

 **Technology Connection** Visit the following weblinks for further information about brain research:

- New Horizons for Learning: http://www.newhorizons.org
- Brain.org (Educators' website about practical applications for brain research): http://www.brains.org
- "Learning Windows and the Child's Brain," article on SuperKids Educational Software Review website: http://www.superkids.com (Click on "feature articles.")

- "Brain-Based Teaching," article on the Ontario College of Teachers website: http://www.oct.ca
- Caine Learning Institute: http://www.cainelearning.com

The Influence of Multiple Intelligence Theory on Content Selection

There are numerous theories about how children learn. The work of one theorist, Howard Gardner, in the area of multiple intelligences can be particularly useful for informing your views on children's needs and interests when selecting content. Gardner (1983) challenged the standard view that human beings are born with a single fixed intelligence, identifying instead a number of intelligences that he saw as the tools a person uses to represent and ultimately understand the world. To Gardner (2000), intelligence is the human ability to solve problems or to make something that is valued. Gardner's categories of intelligence have continued to evolve over time, and he now distinguishes between nine intelligences, including linguistic, logical-mathematical, spatial, bodily kinesthetic, musical, interpersonal, intrapersonal, naturalist, and existential (see Figure 6.2). Gardner contends that most schooling focuses on students' linguistic and logical-mathematical, and perhaps spatial, abilities, but that it neglects the others.

ACTIVE ENGAGEMENT

Do you agree with Gardner that schooling is mostly focused on linguistic and logical-mathematical abilities? Was this typical of your educational experience? How might you use the information in Figure 6.2 on Gardner's multiple intelligences theory to assist you in selecting social studies content?

 Technology Connection Visit the book's companion website for links to the web pages cited below.

1. Go to these sites' pages on multiple intelligences to find out more on each type of intelligence and to find out how Howard Gardner came up with his theory.
   - Thirteen educational website (http://www.thirteen.org/edonline/concept2class): "Concept to Classroom" Workshop: Tapping into Multiple Intelligences
   - Funderstanding: http://www.funderstanding.com
   - New Horizons for Learning: http://www.newhorizons.org
2. Take an online test to determine what intelligence(s) you have strength in at the Birmingham Grid for Learning website: http://www.bgfl.org
3. Have the children in your classroom take a test to help them determine their own intelligence(s) at the Teaching to the Seven Multiple Intelligences website: http://www.mitest.com.

FIGURE 6.2 Gardner's Multiple Intelligences as Influences on Content Selection

TYPE OF INTELLIGENCE	DESCRIPTION OF INTELLIGENCE	INTERESTS/NEEDS OF CHILD DISPLAYING THE INTELLIGENCE
Verbal-Linguistic	The ability to use words and language to express ideas and to remember information	Likes storytelling, explaining, writing, listening
Logical-Mathematical	The ability to think in numbers, to analyze problems logically, to detect patterns, and to reason deductively	Asks a lot of questions, likes to do experiments, likes problem solving
Musical	The ability to understand and create music and to recognize musical pitches, tones, and rhythms	Likes singing, playing instruments, composing music; taps out rhythms, sensitive to noises
Visual-Spatial	The ability to visualize objects and think in pictures	Likes puzzles, sketching, painting, constructing, manipulating objects, interpreting maps, charts, pictures, movies
Bodily Kinesthetic	The ability to use one's body skillfully and to control physical motion	Likes making models, hands-on experimentation, crafts, acting, miming, expressing emotions through the body, using hands to create, build, or problem solve
Interpersonal Intelligence	The ability to understand and communicate with other individuals	Likes social experience, small group work, seeing things from others' viewpoints, conflict resolution
Intrapersonal	The ability for self-reflection and understanding and appreciation of one's emotions, feelings, fears, and motivations	Likes reflecting and analyzing him/herself and evaluating his/her thinking
Naturalist	The ability to recognize and categorize plants, animals, and other objects as they naturally occur	Likes experience in the natural world, field trips, outdoor experiments and activities
Existential	The ability to ponder deeper questions about life and human existence	Likes to ask and explore "I wonder" questions about life, death and the existence of other worlds

The Diversity of Your Students as an Influence on Content Selection

Children differ not only in the ways they prefer to learn, as Gardner suggests, but also in the background experience that they bring to the learning. The Statistics Canada Ethnic Diversity Survey (2003) examined the ethnocultural backgrounds of Canada's non-Aboriginal population aged 15 and over (see the link to this survey at the book's companion website). The results showed that in 2002, almost one-quarter of Canada's population, or 5.3 million people, were born outside

Canada; of these, 21 percent were of British ancestry, the same percentage were of other European ancestry, and 13 percent were non-Europeans, with the most frequent origins being Chinese and South Asian. The remaining population in 2002 included all Canadians of second generation and beyond, and Aboriginal Canadians. Additionally, the three Aboriginal groups—North American Indian, Métis, and Inuit—represented 3.4 percent of Canada's total population. This figure is predicted to grow to 4.1 percent by 2017. Another finding of the survey was that approximately a quarter of a million newcomers arrive in Canada every year, and by the year 2017, roughly one out of every five people in Canada will not have been born in Canada.

All people have their own unique cultural practices. As well, there may be as many differences among people within a particular cultural group as there are differences between cultural groups. Sociologist Timothy Blair (2003) defines culture as "all of the shared products of human society. . . . Material culture consists of all the artifacts, or physical objects, human beings create and give meaning to—wheels, clothing, schools, factories, cities, books, spacecraft, and totem poles. Nonmaterial culture consists of abstract human creations—language, ideas, beliefs, rules, customs, myths, skills, family patterns, and political systems" (p. 55). The challenge for the social studies teacher where content selection is concerned is

The children in your classrooms will be diverse in many ways, including their socioeconomic and ethnocultural backgrounds, sexual orientations, and lifestyle experiences (i.e., rural/urban location and family structures—adopted, single parent, same-sex parents, foster care, etc.).

to understand that each individual in the classroom has a unique way of seeing the world. You will want to try to draw on students' differing backgrounds, experiences, and cultural practices to enhance each individual's learning but also to benefit all learners in the classroom. Through content selection, students can be helped to recognize that Canada is a multicultural country made up of people with a range of languages, customs, religions, and beliefs. To promote positive attitudes and acceptance of diversity as well as development of positive self-identity, children need to come to an understanding that everyone can make valuable contributions to our country.

REFLECTION POINT

Most of us are unaware of the role that our cultural experiences have played in shaping who we are. And yet, as Pai (1990) notes, "Our goals, how we teach, what we teach, how we relate to children and each other are rooted in the norms of our culture" (p. 229). A critical place to start when selecting content for your social studies program

(Continued)

is with your own cultural perspectives in order to better understand that your way of seeing and doing things might vary from those of some of your students. You can begin to clarify your own cultural roots by thinking about how you would describe each of the material and nonmaterial elements of your way of life, as identified by Blair (2003) on page 123.

The social studies content that you choose for your program needs to address diversity by representing multiple viewpoints, and should help students both to be open-minded and to recognize and counter bias, assumptions, and stereotypes. As well, it should promote understanding and appreciation, and as caring and concern, for others.

CLASSROOM APPLICATION

The children in Miss Birrell's Grade 3 classroom were asked to bring a mystery bag that contained things that were special to them, that represented something about an activity they enjoyed, that told something about their family, and that show something special that they do as a family. These mystery bags were then shared with the class so that everyone had a chance to get to know each other better. How else can teachers draw on children's cultural identities?

w w w **Technology Connection** The book's companion website provides links to the following resources for teaching about cultural diversity.

- Celebrating Diversity activity resource, available on the Classroom Connections website: http://www.classroomconnections.ca; "Helping Children Respect and Appreciate Diversity," article on the Child and Family Canada website: http://www.cfc-efc.ca

- Cultures Canada: http://www.culturescanada.ca/

- Diversity and Multiculturalism page on the Government of Canada's Canadian Heritage website: http://www.pch.gc.ca

- Multicultural Pavilion: http://www.edchange.org/multicultural

- Linguistic Diversity activity on Statistics Canada's Census 2001 website: http://www12.statcan.ca/english/census01; Family Studies Kit and South Asians in Canada: Unit through Diversity lesson plan on the Statistics Canada website: http://www.statcan.ca

- Celebrating Aboriginal Peoples page, on the Indian and Northern Affairs Canada website: http://www.ainc-inac.gc.ca

The School Community and Beyond

The sociocultural context in which you are teaching is another factor that you will need to consider when selecting content for your social studies program. The makeup of the classroom culture, including the backgrounds and experiences that the children bring to the learning, needs to guide your content selection in order for you to design a program that is relevant and meaningful to the children's lives, but the issues and problems unique to the communities from which the school draws its student body should also play a guiding role. Further, teachers need to make and build upon connections with the local community to support students' learning by bringing in guest speakers, including family members, and by taking students on field trips to local community sites. Talking to parents, school staff, and community members, as well as reading local community-based newspapers can help to make you more aware of what is going on in the community and what might be some of the local issues of interest to the students.

CLASSROOM APPLICATION

Mr. Hansen took his Grade 2 class to the local community museum as a part a study of the changes in the community over time, and then had his class complete the reflection "In Canmore's past, you could see . . . ," based on what they observed in the pictures and artifacts available at the museum. Figure 6.3 presents one child's response.

FIGURE 6.3 ■ Child's Field Trip Reflection

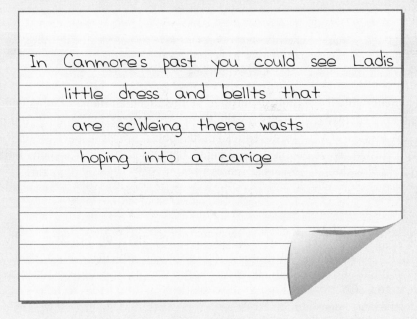

> In Canmore's past you could see Ladis
> little dress and bellts that
> are scWeing there wasts
> hoping into a carige

Addressing Controversial Issues

Sometimes the events that are occurring in the community you are teaching in can be considered controversial. Therefore, you will need to be sensitive to the level of controversy in the content that you choose to focus on and be careful to consider what would work best in your particular setting. Teaching contentious issues can be challenging, but controversy and conflict are everywhere and children are exposed to them whether we as teachers address them or not. These issues can be very confusing for children, which makes it even more imperative that we help them to understand such issues rather than ignoring them. Downplaying or ignoring controversial topics in the curriculum is unwise and contrary to the purpose of social studies (McBee, 1995).

Addressing controversial issues in children's early years is particularly important because young children's self-concepts are being formed at this point and they are more open to diversity and have more tolerance of unfamiliar ideas (Skeel, 1996). All children need opportunities to practise addressing taboo topics and unsettling views (Bickmore, 1999). Children also need to explore issues that may have an emotional impact on them and have the opportunity to express how they are feeling and to hear that others may be feeling the same things regarding these issues.

CLASSROOM APPLICATION

While studying the concept of families, one child in your Grade 1 class states that she has two mommies and no daddy. Another student says, "You can't have two mommies." What would be the best way of dealing with this situation, in your opinion?

ACTIVE ENGAGEMENT

Look at human rights legislation as outlined by the Canadian Human Rights Commission (see the book's companion website for the link to this legislation) and by your province or territory, as well as your local school boards' policies with respect to equity, diversity, and inclusion. What do these documents tell you about your responsibility when it comes to addressing controversial issues in your social studies program?

It is important to remember that there will be diverse views on any issue in the community in which you are teaching. It is critical that you establish and maintain a good rapport with parents and communicate with them about any issues you wish to address that you feel may be of a sensitive nature. Controversial issues must be dealt with in order to help students to learn respect, understanding, open-mindedness, and appreciation of others, as well as a willingness to seek out and develop tolerance for multiple perspectives on an issue. Exploring such issues also helps to develop children's critical and constructive thinking skills and their understanding of how to reach sound, informed, and reasoned judgments based on evidence. When addressing a potentially controversial issue, it is most important to present differing views and ensure that children have ample background information upon which to base decisions.

CLASSROOM APPLICATION

You are a Grade 5 teacher in a small logging community. Your class is studying the forestry industry as a part of a social studies unit on renewable resources. Many of the families of the children in your classroom make their living in the industry or directly from the people who work in the industry. A dispute has recently broken out about logging, and a number of environmental activists are demanding a cutback in logging activities in your area. This would directly affect the income of your students' families. How might you deal with this controversial issue in your social studies program?

Responsible citizens need to be informed about contemporary, controversial issues. Not only can the study of a wide variety of controversial issues be a very effective way of both increasing the relevance of the learning and helping young citizens to better understand and empathize with others; it can also provide opportunities to understand factors that influence how people's views are developed and to encourage students to think about their own views and how they are different from others' (Soley, 1995). By actively involving students in examining controversial issues, static—and, in some cases, unsupported—ideas can be challenged. Exploring issues that are controversial is also a good way for children to learn about values such as peace, justice, and the dignity of the individual and to study value conflicts and peaceful resolution. Addressing controversial issues can also increase students' positive feelings toward social studies and improve their attitudes toward the rights of all people to express their ideas.

CLASSROOM APPLICATION

Your class is studying about a community in a foreign country where women have few if any rights and are subject to abuse. How will you teach about this community, working toward a learning outcome that calls for the development of an appreciation for, understanding of, and respect for people in other parts of the world?

There is no such thing as bias-free teaching. As a teacher candidate, you need to acknowledge that you have views and biases and you need to be comfortable with them and be prepared to grow in your understanding of yourself and others personally and professionally. Who you are as a teacher and your comfort level with your biases will have a major impact on your approach to teaching—and in particular on your willingness to take on controversial issues, the actual questions you select, the length of time you spend on these issues, and the possible action you may want your class to take in response to an issue.

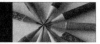

REFLECTION POINT

Visit the book's companion website and follow the link to the article "Teaching Elementary Children about Controversial Issues" on the Educators for Social Responsibility website: http://www.esrnational.org.

What tips does author William Kreidler provide for dealing with controversial issues? Do you agree with the advice given in this article? Do you feel that you should reveal your views on particular issues to the children you teach or that you should withhold them?

Technology Connection Visit the book's companion website for links to the web pages below. How might you use these resources to guide your content selection for your social studies program? What issues identified in these web resources might you have your students investigate?

- Global Issues: http://www.globalissues.org
- Controversial Issues page on the Palo Alto College website: http://www.accd.edu/pac.htm
- Library Media Center list of issues on the Twin Lakes School Corporation website: http://www.twinlakes.k12.in.us
- Hot Paper Topics page on the St. Ambrose University library website: http://library.sau.edu

So far in this chapter, we have been examining a number of factors that will influence the content you decide to focus on in your social studies program. Once you have determined what content will be important for your students to learn, you will need to think about how you are going to organize that content for teaching in a way that will maximize students' learning. We address this topic in the final section of the chapter.

Organizing the Selected Content

Considering Scope and Sequence

Two important considerations when organizing content are scope and sequence. Scope deals with how much content should be covered and is partially determined by what you believe your students need to know to act intelligently and responsibly, as both present and future citizens. You may believe, for example, that a deeper treatment of a few topics is more important than a broader coverage of a larger number of topics, or just the opposite. When making decisions about the scope of what you teach, it is important to keep in mind what we know about the role of the brain in learning. Brain research reminds us that the most effective type of learning focuses on a few ideas in depth and makes connections among these ideas and to the child's life experiences.

Sequence deals with the order in which the selected content is taught. In order to maximize the results of the teaching/learning experience, you will need to make decisions about what aspects of the selected content are necessary beginning points from which to build subsequent learning. It is important to begin by examining how the selected content ties into previous learning and what is to follow. Here is where collaboration with other teachers can ensure that flow and continuity rather than redundancy characterizes what is learned from year to year in social studies. Learning theory reminds us that content should be structured around important ideas and taught with an emphasis on the connections among those ideas. In other words, we build on children's prior learning experiences so that they can assimilate new material into what they already know and believe and/or shift their thinking to bring about conceptual change. The brain has a natural inclination to make connections, so learning should cause students to create connections and allow them to apply what they are learning in different contexts. Content should be relevant to the students and fit with their real-life experiences and should be geared toward a wide range of interest and abilities.

Approaches to Organizing Content

There are a number of possibilities for addressing scope and sequence questions when organizing the content for teaching. Alternative ways of thinking about that organization are presented here, including the textbook as organizer approach, the expanding horizons approach, the disciplines-based approach, the concerns-based approach, and the cross-curricular/thematic approach. Each approach is based on different goals and citizenship education orientation(s) that determine what content is deemed to be most important and how it is best organized.

Textbook as Organizer Approach

One way of organizing the content to be taught in social studies is by using the textbook as the organizing structure. While this is a common approach to organizing content, you need to be cautious when considering it. Textbooks are often written with a very broad scope in order to cover a maximum number of concepts. They have been criticized for causing information overload, for offering sketchy coverage, and for suffering from lack of connection among ideas. Also, textbooks can easily become outdated. Further, taking such an approach to organizing content removes the decision about what content is most important from you as the teacher by giving it to the textbook author. Remember, too, that the author has a certain bias regarding what content is included and whose views are represented.

Expanding Horizons (or Environments) Approach

The organizational approach known as expanding horizons or environments is based on a belief that younger children need to and are capable of learning only about the here and now. This approach involves teaching the content in a developmental sequence that begins with examples

FIGURE 6.4 ■ Spiral Approach to Sequencing Content

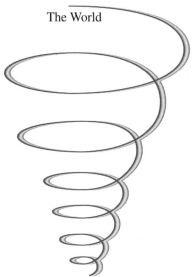

The World

The child's immediate surroundings

from the child's local environment and then expands outward. It proceeds from simple to complex, from familiar to unfamiliar, and from known to unknown. The premise of the approach is that when learning social studies, primary children should begin with what is familiar—namely the home and the school. The horizons of the content then gradually widen to neighbourhoods, cities, regions, nations, and the world as the child's capacity for self-awareness increases.

Hand in hand with the expanding horizons approach to thinking about the scope of the social studies curriculum has traditionally been the spiral approach to sequencing content (see Figure 6.4). This approach was designed to enhance the key objectives of reinforcement, concept and skill development, and transfer of learning from one grade to the next. It requires the introduction of concepts and skills at simple levels in the lower grades and then numerous revisits to that same content at deeper levels of sophistication over the total span of a child's schooling.

One concern that critics have raised about this approach is that its rigid and lockstep implementation does not acknowledge the complexity of the learning process. Another concern is that topics that were once thought to be beyond young children, such as global issues, war, terrorism, and pollution, are now recognized as being part of the young child's world because of exposure through electronic media and more frequent travel. Social studies that limits the scope of the content to be studied to the child's immediate surroundings is no longer considered to be sophisticated enough for future generations of children. A third concern is that the child development principles upon which this approach is based are unfounded. Egan (1986) claims, for example, that beginning with the familiar, the concrete, and the simple and expanding gradually to the unfamiliar, the abstract, and the complex is not an accurate representation of how children learn. He suggests that children are in fact able to conceptualize, fantasize, and make mental models of what they may never have experienced before.

Disciplines-Based Approach

The disciplines-based approach to content organization is based on the recognition that each discipline has a basic structure composed of concepts and processes that should be adapted for study at all grade levels. As discussed earlier in this book, history is the social science discipline from which social studies content is most commonly drawn. Sometimes social studies programs are also organized like history programs, with students engaging in the chronological study of important people and events in the past and present. This approach is based on a belief that logic dictates that we know what came first before studying subsequent events. Critics of the disciplines-based approach contend that it is a very narrow and confining way of studying the world and that it ignores the holistic manner in which children observe their world. This approach to organizing content also ignores the interdisciplinary nature of social studies.

Concerns-Based Approach

The concerns-based approach to content organization usually takes one concern area as the organizer for the entire curriculum and revisits that concern at greater depth over subsequent years. Some of the more common examples of concerns-based organizers include environmental education, peace education, character education, human rights education, social activism education, and global education. A concerns-based framework for global education, for example, might include detailed study of systems (economic, political, ecological, and technological); universal and diverse human values; persistent issues and problems at the local, regional, national, and global levels; and global history. Learning about concepts such as interdependence, needs and wants, change, hunger, poverty, peace, and scarcity is central to the development of a global perspective and would be integral to this organizational framework.

While addressing global concerns and issues is acknowledged as being important to the study of social studies, a problem with the concerns-based approach to organizing curriculum is that its narrow focus tends to reflect only what is perceived to be the most current, high-priority issue. A more generic, concept-based approach takes a broader content focus, including studying problems and issues relevant to all of the concern areas mentioned above, as well as others. Using this approach, students apply reflective inquiry and higher order thinking to make reasoned judgments about diverse areas of local, national, and global concern.

Thematic/Cross-Curricular Approach

The teacher who uses a thematic/cross-curricular approach to organizing content is looking for a way to unify and coordinate similar aspects of all subject areas rather than focusing on small isolated segments across the subjects. In this approach, the boundaries between subjects are blurred and the content of each subject becomes subordinate to children coming to understand big ideas through in-depth exploration (see Figure 6.5 on the next page). Central to this organizational framework is an understanding and appreciation that much of what children learn should be interrelated rather than separated into a variety of discrete concepts and skills. Organizing content in this way allows for holistic skill development and for a cohesive, wide-ranging view of both the world and learning that address the whole before the parts.

Advocates of thematic/cross-curricular planning claim that it increases the relevance of the learning as well as children's motivation to learn. Further, the rapid increase in knowledge is better managed as it allows for more in-depth study and decreases the duplication of information and concepts. By choosing depth over breadth in its focus, a thematic/cross-curricular approach lessens the rush to cover *everything*, as more can be accomplished in less time. Also, we know that children learn best when they make connections between new material and their prior experiences and when there is time allowed for transference of knowledge from one area to another. As well, with the emphasis in schools on literacy and numeracy, the thematic/cross-curricular

FIGURE 6.5 ■ Sample Cross-Curricular Plan

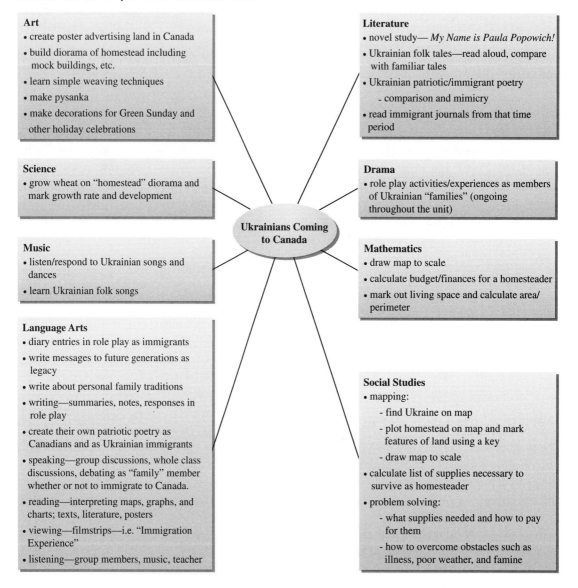

Art
- create poster advertising land in Canada
- build diorama of homestead including mock buildings, etc.
- learn simple weaving techniques
- make pysanka
- make decorations for Green Sunday and other holiday celebrations

Literature
- novel study— *My Name is Paula Popowich!*
- Ukrainian folk tales—read aloud, compare with familiar tales
- Ukrainian patriotic/immigrant poetry
    - comparison and mimicry
- read immigrant journals from that time period

Science
- grow wheat on "homestead" diorama and mark growth rate and development

Drama
- role play activities/experiences as members of Ukrainian "families" (ongoing throughout the unit)

Ukrainians Coming to Canada

Music
- listen/respond to Ukrainian songs and dances
- learn Ukrainian folk songs

Mathematics
- draw map to scale
- calculate budget/finances for a homesteader
- mark out living space and calculate area/perimeter

Language Arts
- diary entries in role play as immigrants
- write messages to future generations as legacy
- write about personal family traditions
- writing—summaries, notes, responses in role play
- create their own patriotic poetry as Canadians and as Ukrainian immigrants
- speaking—group discussions, whole class discussions, debating as "family" member whether or not to immigrate to Canada.
- reading—interpreting maps, graphs, and charts; texts, literature, posters
- viewing—filmstrips—i.e. "Immigration Experience"
- listening—group members, music, teacher

Social Studies
- mapping:
    - find Ukraine on map
    - plot homestead on map and mark features of land using a key
    - draw map to scale
- calculate list of supplies necessary to survive as homesteader
- problem solving:
    - what supplies needed and how to pay for them
    - how to overcome obstacles such as illness, poor weather, and famine

approach to organizing content for teaching provides a way to use social studies as the integrative subject and afford it greater prominence in an increasingly crowded curriculum. Teaching language arts and social studies together, for example, can allow students to develop better reading and writing skills through increased use of these skills. As well, Ehlers (1999) found that by teaching history in conjunction with literature, students grasped historical understanding as they began to acquire a deeper understanding of their role in constructing the past.

Critics of this organizational approach claim that it can result in a loss of academic rigor and in content distortion, which occurs when not all dimensions of a subject are covered. Care needs to be taken to ensure that the integrity of each subject area is maintained and that the activities planned are authentic; help to develop important knowledge, skills, and processes; and are at appropriate levels of ability.

Chapter Summary

In this chapter, we considered a number of factors that may influence what content you choose to focus on in your social studies program, as well as some ways to organize that content. First, we looked back at what you hope to accomplish in your teaching (your professional goals) as a way to help you to make decisions about what content is most important. While one of the main curriculum goals for social studies is citizenship education, we saw that there are a number of different ways of thinking about what that means and that each orientation represents differing views of what is important for children to learn in order to become effective citizens. We also examined the notion of pedagogical content knowledge and the importance of teachers knowing how to impart the ideas of social studies to their students in interesting and motivating ways. You were challenged to continue to grow in your understanding of both your social studies content knowledge and your pedagogical content knowledge.

Next, we looked at the children you are going to be teaching and their needs, interests, experiences, backgrounds, and views as influences on your content selection. Here, we looked at the theory of multiple intelligences as an example of the role that learning theory might have on your content selection. We also examined the importance of addressing the diverse makeup of your class when selecting content. Last, we explored the sociocultural context in which you are teaching as an influence when choosing content, including the selection of controversial issues. Controversial issues were identified as a critical part of your social studies program; you were encouraged to look for ways to bring them into your content and to think about what underlying biases you may be bringing to the issues selected. Whenever it comes to selecting content for teaching, it is important to consider what your purposes for selecting that content are and the value that it will have for your students. You will want to strive to select content in a way that fosters the kind of growth in your students to which you give highest priority.

At the end of the chapter, we examined a number of different ways of organizing the selected content for teaching in terms of the scope and sequence of that content. These organizational frameworks included the textbook as organizer, expanding horizons, disciplines-based, concerns-based, and thematic/cross-curricular approaches.

Part Three

Resources

How Do You Locate and Select Resources to Assist in Teaching Social Studies Content?

In the first two parts of this book, we have examined how to go about selecting goals for your social studies program and deciding on what content to teach. Part Three takes a step further to investigate what to take into account in order to choose resources that will best enable your students to learn the important social studies content identified in Part Two. To address the question of how to locate and select appropriate and effective resources that will assist in teaching social studies content, this part of the book is divided into three chapters, each with its own sub-question related to resource selection. Chapter 7 asks, What factors might influence your selection of resources for your social studies program? Here, we begin our investigation of the resource selection process by distinguishing between single authority and multiple authorities approaches to the use of resources as learning tools. Resources including textbooks, the news media, artifacts, the community, and students and teachers themselves are examined for their possible benefits as learning tools. Chapter 8 then asks, Why use children's literature in social studies? Children's fiction and non-fiction books and poetry as social studies resources are the focus of this chapter. Lastly, Chapter 9 asks, How can computer technologies be used as social studies resources? Here, a variety of web- and software-based resources are examined for their potential as social studies resources.

Chapter 7

What Factors Might Influence Your Selection of Resources for Your Social Studies Program?

Children today need the ability to work with, think critically about, and make meaning using multiple literacies. They need to engage with a variety of genres of text, in both print and electronic formats, to develop skills in listening, speaking, reading, viewing, writing, and representing. The resources that you select for your social studies program will be integral to helping your students develop these and other skills and understandings. While there are a wide variety of readily available resources to choose from, not every resource is necessarily useful or appropriate. The main focus of this chapter is on deciding what qualities make a resource appropriate for helping to develop your students' literacy skills and social studies content knowledge while adding to their enjoyment of their social studies learning experiences.

We begin our investigation of resource selection by once again looking back at your own personal goals for your social studies program and the needs, interests, backgrounds, and abilities of your students.

Your Goals as Influences on Resource Selection

As with the other components of the planning process we have studied so far, the approach that you will take to resource selection and use is embedded in your beliefs about teaching and learning. What you believe is important for your students to know to become good citizens of the twenty-first century and what you believe about how they can best learn that knowledge will influence the approach you take toward resource selection. When thinking about matching your resources to your goals, it is helpful to consider what purpose you have for using a particular resource.

The following sections describe two different approaches that teachers can have to resourcing their social studies program—one a "single authority" approach and the other a "multiple authorities" approach. Each is based on different teaching and learning goals.

ACTIVE ENGAGEMENT

As you examine the following two approaches to resourcing, think back to the earlier discussion (in Chapter 3) about hidden curriculum. What hidden curriculum would be at work in a classroom in which a single authority approach is used and in another using a multiple authorities approach? What norms and expectations would there be in each case? What is valued about knowledge, teaching, and learning in these two approaches? What roles would students be assuming in each classroom?

A Single Authority Approach to Resource Selection

A single authority approach to resource selection is typical of a more traditional view of social studies for citizenship education. A teacher using this approach believes that there is an official, predetermined, objective body of knowledge that students need to learn in order to become effective citizens and that this body of information can be adequately represented by one authority, usually a textbook. That single authority then becomes the students' main source of information about the topics being studied in social studies.

The content of the single resource is believed by the teacher and the students to be an accurate and adequate representation of the important knowledge about the topic to be learned. A teacher who holds this view of resourcing often teaches the content in the same order that it has been organized in the resource. Coverage of content and students' acquisition of knowledge as taught are the teacher's primary goals. Most of the students' learning experiences revolve around working with that one resource.

CLASSROOM APPLICATION

What can go wrong when a single authority view of resourcing is used in a social studies program is demonstrated in the mapping unit on Oxfam's Cool Planet website (www.oxfam.org.uk/coolplanet/mappingourworld). This unit presents a series of lessons that involve children in examining different map projections to learn how they can distort our sense of the world. For example, the Chat Show activity in Lesson 2 helps children to see that different map projections focus on different parts of the world. The Peters projection map, for example, stretches countries east to west near the poles and north to south near the equator (see Figure 7.1), while the Mercator projection has extreme horizontal exaggeration along lines of latitude (see Figure 7.2).

Also in Lesson 3, the How Many Times? activity demonstrates that the same information about the world can be presented in different ways, each providing differing degrees of accuracy in the way they depict the size of the countries and continents. The culminating activity, Walk the Plank, is a fun way of showing what can happen if an inaccurate map projection is used to solve a problem.

FIGURE 7.1 ■ Peters Map Projection

FIGURE 7.2 ■ Mercator Map Projection

REFLECTION POINT

Mrs. White, a Grade 6 social studies teacher, had this to say about resourcing her program: "A resource should add to the teaching of a topic; it should never be the sole focus from which the subject is taught." How does this statement help you to think about resource selection?

A Multiple Authorities Approach to Resource Selection

A constructivist view of learning would favour a multiple authorities approach to resourcing a social studies program. Such an approach is based on the assumption that the resources, including textbooks and informational books, always reflect their authors' perspective.

What one source presents as both true and important knowledge might not be the same as what another source, representing different beliefs and biases, emphasizes. This view of multiple truths comes from the belief that humans construct knowledge, rather than it existing independent of human minds, and that each of these individual constructions is influenced by sociocultural context.

A multiple authorities approach to resource selection would support a teaching goal that aims to develop students' understanding that there are many ways of seeing the world. Since no one interpretation of an event represents everyone's understanding or experience, students need to develop critical viewing skills to make judgments about what they are reading (Seixas, 1999). These skills include knowing how to use a variety of sources in varied formats to gather information; how to analyze those texts, including sorting the sometimes conflicting information collected, interpreting it, critiquing it for its authenticity and accuracy, and synthesizing it; and how to use it to assist in making thoughtful and reasoned decisions.

Teachers who take a multiple authorities approach to resource selection understand that their role is not just to provide access to more than one resource in their social studies program but also to select resources that provide differing viewpoints on the content represented in those resources. Resources that represent a particular historical event from a number of different perspectives, including those of women and children, are important in helping students to understand that there is no one way of interpreting the past (Levstik & Barton, 2005). For example, when examining the early history of Canada, rather than focusing solely on European male explorers and their experiences of "discovering" the "new land," differing interpretations of that history from the perspective of the Native peoples who were already living on that land must be included in the selection of resources. This would involve engaging students in an examination of different interpretations of how the Native peoples came to be there—including Native legends about creation, as well as scientific explanations such as the Pangaea and Beringia theories.

The purpose for taking a multiple authorities approach to resourcing is to provide ongoing opportunities for children to develop their critical literacy skills, as they can gather and critique information from multiple viewpoints, make sense of the information collected, and share their ideas with others. That information then becomes part of the total bank of information, which the entire class can use in their knowledge construction. Having a flexible classroom that addresses children's individual learning preferences and special learning needs through the available resources is important for them to feel successful as learners.

 Technology Connection One historical event that has generated a great deal of controversy in Canada is the North-West Rebellion and the role played in it by Louis Riel. The Canadian Broadcasting Corporation's (CBC's) History website offers a section about Louis Riel that contains over 20 clips, including reenactments of the history of the Riel Rebellion as well as modern-day perspectives on his demise. These varying interpretations can be used to help children to understand the importance of considering multiple viewpoints on any issue.

See the book's companion website for the link to this page on the CBC History website: http://history.cbc.ca. The book's companion website also provides links to pages on the following websites containing audio, visual, and print materials that could be used to show differing perspectives on the Northwest Rebellion and Louis Riel:

- Louis Riel page in the Historica Minutes section and First Nations page in the Radio Minutes section of the Historica website: http://www.histori.ca
- Louis Riel page of *The Canadian Encyclopedia* website: http://www.thecanadianencyclopedia.com
- "History Revisited: Louis Riel Letter Unveiled," article on *Indian Country Today* website: http://www.indiancountry.com
- Louis Riel Project page of the McCord Museum website: http://www.musee-mccord.qc.ca

A multiple authorities approach to resource selection ensures that students have opportunities to compare one resource to another and to look for author viewpoint and bias. Teachers using this approach encourage student debate of these competing versions of knowledge and truth. Such teachers have confidence in their students' ability to grow more capable of constructing their own knowledge and more independent in assessing competing knowledge claims.

These Grade 4 students have been consulting several books on the topic of study, and then synthesizing the information collected.

ACTIVE ENGAGEMENT

One limiting factor regarding resource selection can be the teacher's lack of knowledge about what resources are available. Another can be the limited budget that teachers have allocated to purchase resources. A third can be lack of time to search out all that is available. In groups, brainstorm some ideas about where to go to find the latest resources and how to stay within a limited budget when selecting resources—i.e., consider some of the free and inexpensive resources that are available to you through places like government agencies and public libraries.

Students' Needs, Interests, Abilities, and Backgrounds as Influences on Resource Selection

Teaching never takes place in a vacuum but instead is always carried out in the context of specific children. Unless you know something about your students' backgrounds, you cannot realistically decide on the resources that might be successfully used to achieve your goals for their growth. Therefore, you need to choose resources with the developmental needs, abilities, backgrounds, and interests of your students in mind. We have already looked at brain research and multiple intelligences theory to assist you in thinking about children's developmental needs and abilities, and at their diverse backgrounds and upbringing as influences on their interests and abilities (see Chapter 6).

Another way of thinking about your students' abilities when you are selecting resources is to examine their learning style preferences. Learning style theory is based on the premise that learning is the result of a personal, individualized act of thought and feeling and that each child has his or her own unique way of receiving information (Silver, Strong, & Perini, 1997). One model for thinking about the differences in how children take in and process information is in terms of perceptual modalities, or ways in which individuals take in information through their senses. Learners can be categorized into four different styles, based on which sense is dominant in their learning process. An auditory learner who learns best from listening and speaking would benefit most from different resources than a visual learner who responds to visual representations such as pictures, charts, maps, and graphs; and that learner in turn has different resource needs than a child who learns best from tactile, hands on experiences and from children who retain information best when they read it.

Children are not often aware that they have a particular way of learning. Helping them to come to know their own style and think about their own learning allows them to use a variety of resources to learn in a way that feels successful for them and develops a positive self-image. They also learn to respect that other people in the classroom have different ways of learning. While students each have a dominant learning style, they can still be provided with experiences that allow them to try out their ability to work in other styles, thereby encouraging them to learn to be more flexible in how they approach learning experiences and the use of learning resources. Figure 7.3 presents a number of possible resource formats that could be used to address the learning style preferences and needs of your students.

 Technology Connection The web provides a number of tools for determining an individual's learning style. See for example the link on the book's companion website to the page on the Ageless Learner website (www.agelesslearner.com) that provides a guide to determine your own dominant style.

FIGURE 7.3 ■ Resource Choices for Different Learning Preferences

READING	VIEWING
newspapers	art
brochures	photographs
children's literature	interactive computer programs
non-fiction books—biographies,	films/videos
informational books, how-to books	television
journals	slides
dictionaries	graphs
CD-ROMs	models diagrams
primary source documents	charts
diary entries	maps, globes
biographies	spreadsheets
poetry	magazines
textbooks	databases
websites	internet
letters	cartoons
blog entries	pictorial representations
case studies	artifacts
	overheads
	murals
	flow charts
	diagrams
	mind maps
	bulletin board displays

SPEAKING/LISTENING	DOING
peer teaching	field trips
guest speakers	puppetry
reader's theatre	models
audiotapes	scrapbooking
radio music	experiments
panel discussion	diorama
telephone conversation	dance
presentations	scavenger hunts
videoconferencing	demonstrations
debates	mobiles
choral speech	artifacts
dialogue	museokits
personal interviews	games
discussion	collections
the teacher	CD-ROMs
	role play
	first person experiences
	simulations, virtual and live
	community resources

Which of the types of resources shown in Figure 7.3 help you to learn better? Can you add anything to the chart? How might this chart help you to consider what resources to select for your social studies program? What resources do you think would be most effective in helping your students to develop critical literacy skills while engaging with the content?

While providing variety in the format of the resources used in your social studies program (i.e., audio, visual, and text-based) is important, you will also need to help your students understand that all types of resources, regardless of format, can be biased and that sources of information can provide differing and often conflicting interpretations of the past.

Technology Connection The Media Awareness Network (http://www.media-awareness.ca) offers a number of lesson plans that can be used to address biases in media such as stereotyping, racial profiling, and gender portrayal. See the book's companion website for links to articles on the site related to stereotyping in female action heroes, stereotyping on television, and media portrayals of ethnic and visible minorities.

Considering Students' Special Needs

When selecting resources, you will also need to consider specific learning challenges that the children in your classroom might have. It is important to ensure that you gather a variety of materials that cover a range of reading and vocabulary levels, from easy to difficult, and that have varied print size and wide-ranging levels of comprehensibility. Care is needed to ensure that text-based resources aimed at lower reading levels contain the same treatment of concepts as those of higher levels to avoid "dumbing down" of the content.

Students who have reading difficulties can also have a great deal of success with audio-recorded and electronic books. Audio books allow children to enjoy the stories that others in the class are getting to read. As well, the teacher, a parent volunteer, a peer, or a student from an older grade can audio-record information relevant to the topic of study so that students experiencing reading or language difficulties can have the opportunity to engage in information gathering. Electronic books can provide both audio and visual cues for readers so that a nonreader or limited reader need not be deprived of the opportunity to contribute to class discussions and participate fully in classroom experiences. As well, audio and video recordings of information collected during a field trip or when a guest speaker comes to the classroom can become a reservoir to which the class may return as often as is necessary.

A listening centre in the classroom could be equipped with CDs of music, poetry, and stories for all children to enjoy. Equipping this listening centre with music and songs related to the topic of study adds appeal and is especially useful for developing children's musical intelligence.

Technology Connection Visit the book's companion website for links to the relevant pages of the following websites, which provide examples and lesson plans for using songs and music to support your teaching of social studies.

- For an example of a project that a Grade 2/3 class undertook to look into the role of music in the cowboy culture, see the History of Cowboy Culture page on the Galileo Network: http://www.galileo.org
- Page on songs about Canada at the Songs for Teaching website: http://www.songsforteaching.com (provides songs about Canada)
- Inuit Throat Singing page at the Stuff Media Interactive Education website: http://www.stuff.co.uk
- Au Coeur du Vent: French and Francophone Songs page at the University of Tennessee at Martin website: http://www.utm.edu/staff/globeg/atelmusique.shtml
- Elementary Songs & Poems page and African Songs, Chants, and Games page on the CanTeach website: http://www.canteach.ca
- Traditional Song page on the Newfoundland and Labrador Heritage website: http://www.heritage.nf.ca
- Native Drums (website on Native music and culture in Canada): http://nativedrums.ca

Artifacts can be added to a resource center to offer another level of engagement with resources. Hands-on manipulation of real-life objects can heighten children's interest in a topic as they work with and interrogate these objects. These primary resource materials allow children to use their own background knowledge and experiences to try to figure out what the object is and how it works as they construct meaning for themselves, rather than having it presented to them from a secondary source perspective, such as reading about the object in a textbook.

CLASSROOM APPLICATION

At the beginning of the study of the topic "Our Community in the Past," the children in Ms. Klein's Grade 3 class come in from recess to find a table containing a number of artifacts set up in the middle of the classroom. The artifacts include toys and games,

(Continued)

books, utensils, clothing and accessories, musical instruments, and tools. The children are invited to examine the objects and talk with each other about what they think each object is, what it might have been used for, who might have used it, and where and when it might have been used. After the children have had sufficient time to play with and discuss the objects, Ms. Klein asks the class to write in their learning logs how they think the various artifacts are connected to each other and then orally share their idea with the class. When the oral sharing is complete, Mrs. Klein explains that all of the objects belonged to her great grandmother and that the class is going to be learning more about what life was like when her great grandmother was a child. She asks the boys and girls what else they would like to know about the objects and her great grandmother and writes their questions on the whiteboard.

 Technology Connection The Centre for Applied Special Technology's (CAST's) Teaching Every Student website (http://www.cast.org/teachingeverystudent) provides a case study entitled "Reading Challenges in Social Studies" that explores how Mrs. Jones, a Grade 4 teacher who is concerned about her students' widely diverse reading abilities, addresses those skills while attempting to achieve her social studies lesson goals. Although the case study takes place in an American setting, it provides universally applicable information about the classroom context, the teacher's and curricular objectives, the students' needs and abilities, the resources available, and the teaching approaches and assessment techniques used. Visit the book's companion website for a link to this case study, as well as links to pages on the teaching of reading comprehension strategies at the following websites:

- The Teachers' Cafe: http://www.theteacherscafe.com
- Reading Quest.org: http://www.readingquest.org

Criteria for Selecting Resources

When choosing resources for your social studies program, there are some important considerations to keep in mind regarding what makes a resource (regardless of its format) effective for supporting and enhancing your students' learning.

Age Appropriateness

One aspect to consider when selecting a resource for use in your social studies program is its age appropriateness. Factors that need to be considered include the reading and vocabulary levels, the use of abstract terms, and the print size, as well as the relevance of the information presented to both the topic being investigated and to the lives of your students. Having numerous and varied materials on the same topic at a range of reading levels and allowing the child to select the ones that he or she feels most successful using is recommended. The currentness of the information provided in the resource will also need to be considered, especially when dealing with a time-sensitive topic.

Effectiveness of Presentation

Another aspect to consider when selecting a resource is how effectively the material is presented. Assessing this aspect involves making judgments about economy, thoroughness, and appeal. Lengthy, convoluted text can be challenging for young readers and can cause them to lose interest quickly, while colourful, multidimensional pages with short text segments are more pleasing. The pictures and illustrations also should be carefully examined for their visual appeal, for the match between them and the text, and for their helpfulness in assisting the reader to understand the information being presented. Pictures of substance covering a range of circumstances can be used to teach the skill of picture reading, while contributing to other objectives at the same time. For example, illustrations and photos that show children engaged in talk with adults and other children or in creating charts, lists, posters, maps, and other representations demonstrate important social studies skills.

When considering how economically the information in the resource is presented to the student, look at whether some of the written information may be handled more effectively in charts, graphs, or tables. Also, regarding thoroughness, look for whether the information presented is both accurate and representative of the topic, as the resources used will need to assist your students in finding the information they are looking for.

Level of Engagement

When deciding on resources, also consider whether they encourage student engagement. Resources that present information in a way that children can identify with are the most engaging for them. Information presented in a personalized way, such as through a story populated with authentic and vivid characters engaged in storylines that are applicable to the children's lives, can pique their interest. As well, telling stories and sharing experiences through a child's eyes adds relevance, particularly for young readers. Resources that are written from an adult perspective are not as authentic and appealing for young children as those that attempt to reach the child at his or her level.

The best resources generate discussion, enrich social studies understandings, and enhance meaning. They allow students themselves to process the information presented—for example, by comparing and contrasting as they actively construct their own meaning. Books composed mainly of generalizations, or those in which video narration does the thinking for the reader by drawing conclusions, limit the number of opportunities the children have for thoughtful consideration of the information being presented. For the teacher, having the children interpret materials for themselves and then listening to how they are interpreting what they are seeing, hearing, and reading provides some insight into the shape of the children's thinking. The most meaningful text-based resources are those that present inquiry questions and challenge readers to think about how these questions apply to their own lives. The use of the inquiry questions also encourages the development of fundamental social studies skills such as critical and creative thinking, problem solving, decision making, and action taking. This approach ensures that the children are not only learning social studies content through the introduction of the knowledge concepts in the resource but are also addressing important social studies skill and attitudinal objectives that are critical aspects of effective citizenship education.

Attention to Social Studies Concepts

Another criterion to consider when selecting resources is whether the resource supports and enhances the teaching of social studies concepts and terminology. If we consider the overall purpose of social studies to be citizenship education, the most effective resources demonstrate democratic citizenship and engage children in thinking about democratic citizenship in relation to their own lives. In order for a deeper understanding of social studies concepts to be acquired, children need to see adults and peers being good, responsible citizens in a variety of settings that are relevant to their lives. They also need to see examples of children making decisions that balance rights and responsibilities. As well, children need to see examples of social participation in depictions of children engaged in real-life citizenship activities both inside and outside of the classroom, and they need to be encouraged to think about what they could do to participate in their social environment. At times, these initiatives need to be shown as being child-generated actions so that children don't get the message that only adults can make change.

Resources that make use of storylines portraying caring, responsible behaviours provide an effective beginning for children to learn to be good citizens. The most effective resources highlight the values and expectations of people in their relations within their social groups and within their neighbourhood groups through descriptions of them acting and speaking. Resources also need to show peoples' conflicting views on issues and decision making and to demonstrate that at times there are disagreements among people at home, in school, in the community, in the country, and in the world that cause feelings of anger or frustration—but that there are ways to resolve such conflict. Ultimately, resources should help children to make sense of their world.

Range of Perspectives

Another characteristic of resources that should be considered is their thoroughness of the information in terms of the range of viewpoints represented. Students' views need to be challenged if they are going to shift their thinking about the information being presented. For example, when examining the concept of citizenship in Canada, multiple ways of thinking about what it means to be a Canadian should be embedded in the text and in illustrations and photos. Also, when a viewpoint is stated in a resource, the teacher needs to caution that this is just one person's view and that it does not necessarily represent the views of all people of that particular racial, cultural, religious, or social group.

Resources can be used to demonstrate the diverse nature of Canadian society and expose students to previously neglected groups through inclusive storylines, illustrations, and photos. This exploration of diversity in Canada needs to focus on the lives of diverse people within the Canadian context, not on their lives in their countries of origin—i.e., it is more important in the context of this line of study for children to come to an understanding and appreciation of the lives of Chinese Canadians than to study life in China. It is also essential that this focus on diversity move beyond superficial, lower-level differences among people, such as food, clothing, and celebrations, in order to help children understand that while there are needs common among all societies, these can be met in different ways—i.e., choices about foods are based on cultural, social, and environmental factors.

FIGURE 7.4 ■ Criteria for Selecting Resources

Name of Resource: _____

CRITERIA	PERSONAL NOTES
Age appropriateness Effectiveness of presentation Level of engagement Attention to social studies concepts Range of perspectives Respect for people and places	

Respect for People and Places

Ultimately, the resources you select should help to develop children's respect for people and places. All resources need to be carefully examined in terms of the messages that they give to students, especially regarding stereotyping, racism, ageism, and sexism. Caution must be taken that the material used does not subtly reinforce stereotypes—e.g., Mexicans wearing sombreros, Native peoples living in teepees, or Chinese people eating with chopsticks. Such stereotypes must be avoided in both storylines and illustrations. Resources also should represent men and women in a diversity of roles across time, cultures, and contexts.

Some pictures in resources can present a very narrow or negative view of places, people, and events. For example, many historical pictures used to represent Native cultures depict Natives posing for the camera in ceremonial dress and in very stereotypical poses rather than representing them in a way that accurately depicts their daily lives. The language used to describe Native lifestyles in resources can also be problematic—especially such terms as "massacred," "warlike Indian," "redskins," "fierce tribe," "squaws," and "savages," or misleading references to Native "people" whereas there are in fact a multitude of diverse Native cultures and peoples, each with their own uniqueness.

Children need to see themselves in what they are experiencing in the classroom for the learning to be truly meaningful. One way of making their learning more relevant is by providing a wide variety of resources that take into account the heritage, life experiences, and interests of all of the students in your classroom. (See Figure 7.4 above for a summary of such criteria to consider when selecting resources.)

Examining the Various Types of Available Resources

Social Studies Textbooks as a Resource

Textbooks are the most commonly used resource in social studies classrooms. They are usually readily available and, in most provinces and territories, have been authorized by the respective ministry of education as best addressing the objectives of the social studies curriculum. These textbooks

Textbooks can provide some of the foundational information on social studies topics, but sole reliance on one text should be discouraged.

usually have been put through a screening process to determine not only their fit with the curriculum and their user-friendliness, readability, and age appropriateness but also their adherence to requirements regarding equity issues such as gender and minority representation.

While a textbook can be a very helpful resource for a teacher because of the vast amount of information provided, you will still need to peruse it for its usefulness in meeting your particular goals. Be aware that the content coverage in a textbook can vary significantly among topics, and carefully consider how appropriate the textbook is for conveying the content you have chosen to focus on in your social studies unit, both in terms of what the book covers and what is left out.

As well, some textbooks can tend to be outdated, especially when it comes to dealing with current issues and events. You will also need to consider the relevance and immediacy of the content presented in the book since there can be a considerable time lapse between curriculum revisions (sometimes as long as 20 years). This is not to say that the entire book is unusable, but you will need to be careful to be selective about what aspects of outdated texts you include in your social studies program, as well as to put any information that is no longer current in the proper context for students. This can be particularly important when dealing with concepts that have undergone radical change over the last two decades—for example, the concept "family" is defined very differently today than it was 20 years ago.

The presentation of the information in a textbook can vary widely, too. One criticism of textbooks is that some authors tend to try to put too much information into the book, resulting in thin coverage of a large number of topics. Readers can therefore experience texts as a confusing collection of unrelated facts, which can be particularly difficult for weaker readers and for English as a Second Language (ESL) students. As well, ESL students usually are unable to situate what they are reading about in the textbook pages within a context from their own personal experiences, as they lack the background assumed by the textbook author.

The best textbooks have text interspersed with photographs, tables, graphs, charts, primary documents, examples, narrative accounts, and stories and are written from the perspective of the child reader (Parker, 2001). All of the factors discussed here need to be considered when making the decision to use a textbook in your social studies program.

Select a textbook that has been suggested for elementary social studies in your province or territory, and then examine it in order to answer these questions: What is your opinion of the text? How appealing would this book be for your students? Does the way the text is structured support the view that content is something students acquire or that it is something they explore, debate, and use to construct meaning? How is diversity addressed? How sound is the history that is presented? Would this text enhance your students' skills of historical understanding? How might you use this resource in your teaching of social studies?

The News Media as a Resource

Using the news media and the study of current events as a resource in social studies has numerous benefits for your students, including increased relevance, interest, authenticity, and immediacy. If your goal is to prepare children in classrooms for their future roles as effective citizens and knowledgeable decision makers, then the study of current problems, issues, and controversies at the local, national, and global levels needs to be a part of the focus of their studies. Central to being a critically literate citizen is being an aware and informed citizen. This means that children need to know what is happening around them and to understand how the decisions made at the local, provincial, national, and international levels directly affect their lives. They need to learn that having an understanding of current affairs and keeping up with news are necessary before they as citizens can take action to bring about change. Such an emphasis in social studies has the potential to develop in children a lifelong habit of being informed about what is in the news. Studying issues in the news makes resourcing fairly simple, too, as both newspapers and online news sources are readily available and easily accessed.

The study of current events can also offer excellent opportunities for the stimulation of creative thinking skills through analysis of relevant contemporary issues. At the same time, critical reading, research, and evaluative skills, oral communication and participation skills, and cooperative learning skills can be enhanced (Pages, 2007). Newspapers, magazines, radio programs, television documentaries, and news-related websites are just a few of the media resources at hand. When using current affairs, it is important to collect a variety of news-related source material and to teach children to be able to distinguish between fact and opinion, identify bias and misconceptions, and look for inconsistency in argument. By drawing on a variety of news sources, you are also providing your students with opportunities to consider other views on events being portrayed in the news. This variety is necessary to conduct effective inquiry and to ensure that children are being provided ample opportunity to consider other perspectives on the issues and topics being studied.

Careful consideration has to be given to the best way to enhance children's learning through the use of current events in your social studies program. Students can be easily bored with the news if your program entails simply having them read the newspaper and cut out an article to be presented to the class during "current events time." A daily exposure to the outside world is preferable to a once-a-week current events session added on to the regular social studies program, as important events are occurring on a daily basis. Current events is therefore best taught as an integrated part of your social studies program, and the more importance that is attached to the study of current affairs in the classroom, the more it will be perceived by the children as being an important part of their learning. A "news centre" could be set up in the classroom to provide students with access to the news on an ongoing basis. Here, an up-to-date collection of local, national, and international newspapers and news magazines could be made available for your students to peruse at their leisure, in addition to a television with recorded documentaries and news broadcasts and a computer with access to news websites and online newspapers.

CLASSROOM APPLICATION

Mr. Wheeler likes to introduce his unit on Nova Scotia by having his class engage in a newspaper hunt. He divides his class into groups and each group is given an envelope with the following directions on the front:

NOVA SCOTIA NEWSPAPER HUNT

You will need newspapers, glue sticks, scissors, and a large sheet of art paper.
Begin by each person in your group drawing a card from the envelope and following the directions on the card.
Continue until all of the cards in the envelope are gone.
As a group, make a collage in the shape of Nova Scotia using all the news pieces that you have collected.

The activity cards in the envelope are made in the shape of Nova Scotia and contain tasks such as

- Find pictures of two animals found in Nova Scotia.
- Find a picture of the premier of Nova Scotia.
- Find an article about something interesting happening in Halifax.
- Cut out a headline that has the name "Nova Scotia" in it.
- Find pictures or words describing natural resources in Nova Scotia.
- Find a weather map for Nova Scotia.
- Find a news article about Nova Scotia.
- Find a photo of an athlete from Nova Scotia.
- Find a photograph or news story about community helpers in a Nova Scotia town.
- Find an article about a Nova Scotia–based environmental issue.

Children also need to become critical readers and viewers of media, and therefore to be taught important media literacy skills. To become effective citizens, they will need to learn how to analyze, evaluate, understand, and use mass media. When studying the news, they should learn about the nature of mass media and the techniques used to persuade. They need to be taught to think about the point of view of the teller, about what might be influencing the teller's story, and about whose viewpoint is not being heard. Engaging children in studying the events and issues being reported from a number of varying perspectives and then holding a class debate can be an effective method of both incorporating current events into your program and teaching critical viewing and thinking skills.

Technology Connection

- The CBC Archives website (http://archives.cbc.ca) provides teachers with invaluable news-related resources, such as access to daily national and international news and an archive of video and audio clips that address issues including religion in the classroom, clothing workers fighting for better conditions, and what has happened to the family farm (all in the Life and Society section) as well as a section on great Canadians (see the People section).

- The Newspapers in Education website (http://www.newspapersineducation.ca) provides sample lessons for addressing social studies topics using newspapers. See, for example, a lesson on Canadian political leaders and parties for the Grade 5 level. (Follow the link to this lesson on the book's companion website.)

- The Newspaper in the Classroom: Elementary Themes web page (on the Centre for Distance Learning & Innovation website: http://www.cdli.ca) by Jim Cornish, a Grade 5 teacher in Newfoundland, offers newspaper and media lesson ideas as well as lists of online newspapers. (Follow the link to this lesson on the book's companion website.)

Links to other lesson plans using various components of newspapers can be found on the companion website. Topics include political cartoons, latitude and longitude, character education, and how to write letters to the editor.

Using Primary Source Materials as Resources

Primary source materials are firsthand accounts from people who were actually engaged in a particular event or time and provided their own personal perspective on what occurred. These resources can include photographs, audio recordings, documents such as letters and journal or diary entries, and objects (artifacts). Using a variety of primary documents about any one event or time period in history can lend an air of authenticity to that study and provide a wide range of interpretations of that event. The use of such sources can help to reinforce for your students that history is not a static truth but rather is based on individual interpretations (Barton, 2005). Students' historical thinking skills are thus developed as they engage with resources that have historical relevance (Hicks, Doolittle, & Lee, 2004). Primary sources can be used not only to increase students' knowledge but also to develop analytical skills, such as questioning, thinking critically, and inference making (Edinger, 2001).

Oral accounts of the past can range from stories told by parents, grandparents, and other elders as they recall their various life experiences, to purposefully recorded speeches delivered by famous figures in history. For younger children, asking their elders about experiences of the past can be particularly powerful, especially in helping the young to understand the concept of change over time (Barton & Levstik, 1996). Further, listening to audio recordings of events from the past from the perspectives of a various participants in that event can show that not everyone alive at a given time had the same experience.

CLASSROOM APPLICATION

Miss Baker, a Grade 6 teacher, was studying the concept of immigration to Canada in her social studies class. She wanted to develop her students' ability to read and interpret visuals using primary source materials. After displaying three historic posters around the classroom, she gave her students the following assignment: Imagine that you are a person living in Europe in the late 1800s and are considering emigrating to Canada. You see posters such as those on the classroom walls. How might these posters influence your decision making? What do you see in these posters? What are some of the visual details in each poster? What do they tell you? What does the caption or other text on each poster tell you? What promises do they make to you as an immigrant? What do these posters make you believe? Do these posters make you want to come to Canada? What makes the image appealing? Is a one-sided point of view represented? (Think about who created the posters and why, when, and where they were created.)

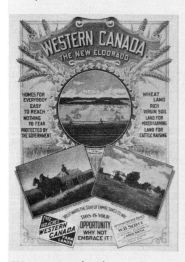

"Western Canada: The New Eldorado"

"Build Your Nest in Western Canada"

"Free Farms for the Million"

Technology Connection See http://www.galileo.org/projects/rural_roots/spirit_river for a project in which Grade 5 and 6 students in Alberta investigated the changes in the family farm using primary source materials.

The book's companion website provides links to other websites that students can use to find primary source documents including photos, letters, audio recordings, journals, newspapers, reports, and stories.

The School Community as a Resource

Another important resource for use in social studies is the child's own community. Guest speakers, including parents, from the community can be asked to come to the classroom to contribute to the study of a particular topic. A local government representative, for example, could be asked to come and explain why a particular decision was made regarding the community. Field trips to sites in the community can also add to the active engagement of the learners in the topic study. Many of these sites also have educational programs designed for specific topics in the provincial or territorial curriculum and often have resource kits that can be borrowed and taken back to the classroom for further study. For example, "museokits" can be borrowed, containing artifacts, historical documents, pictures, and other manipulatives that make history come alive. Resources that can help the child to see the connection between what is being learned in social studies and their lives at home add relevance to the learning. Further, the schoolyard itself can be an effective site for fieldwork.

Trips to local businesses, museums, government buildings, historical sites, and other locations provide opportunities for hands-on learning.

Teachers and Students as Resources

Both the teacher and the children in the classroom have much to offer as sources of information. They bring a very diverse range of experiences with them to the learning environment, which can be shared. But students can also contribute to the resource base by gathering information from resources such as non-fiction books, websites, and children's literature, which will offer differing and often conflicting viewpoints, and then presenting these viewpoints to others in the class and to peers in other schools around the world (see Chapter 12 for information about telecollaborative learning ideas). As students exchange information and share their understandings of these varying viewpoints, they are co-constructing meaning.

Chapter Summary

In this chapter, we started by looking at the important critical literacy skills today's children need in order to be able to use and interpret the variety of information sources available to them. Keeping the goal of developing these skills in mind when selecting the types of resources and resource-based experiences that you will use in your social studies program was stated to be essential. Next, two approaches to thinking about resourcing—the single authority approach and the multiple authorities approach—were examined to find the best fit with what we know about students' learning needs. A variety of resources for assisting the auditory, print, visual, and kinesthetic learner, as well as for meeting the special learning needs that children bring to the classroom, including difficulties with reading, were examined.

The next step in considering the resource selection process involved laying out some generic criteria for identifying resources that would add the most value to your social studies program. These included age appropriateness, effectiveness of presentation, level of engagement, attention to social studies concepts, range of perspectives, and respect for people and places. You learned that it is very important that you take an active role in carefully scrutinizing any resource before using it in your classroom. Ultimately, you as the teacher will need to make decisions about resources based on their overall appropriateness as a medium for conveying the particular content that you have selected for your social studies program.

In the last part of this chapter, we considered some of the specific types of resources that you can use in your social studies program, including textbooks, the news media, primary source materials, the school community, and you and your students. In the next two chapters, we will examine children's fiction and non-fiction books and electronic resources as other resource possibilities.

Chapter 8

Why Use Children's Literature in Social Studies?

In the previous chapter, we began an investigation into the selection of resources to support your social studies program. The initial step was to look at the influences of your social studies program goals and your students' learning needs on the resource selection process. Two distinct approaches to resource selection, informed by differing beliefs about teaching and learning, were examined: the single authority approach and the multiple authorities approach. We then looked at some of the resources available for use in social studies, including textbooks, the news media, primary source materials, and the school community, as well as your students themselves and you as the teacher.

In this second chapter on resource selection, we look at children's literature, including non-fiction informational and biographical books, fictional picture books and novels, and poetry, as other resource possibilities. Children's literature has a great deal to offer as a resource for enhancing learning in social studies. These benefits will be explored, as will suggestions for selecting and using various types of children's literature.

LOOKING BACK

What do you recall about the presence or absence of children's literature as a learning resource when you were a child in elementary school? If children's literature was present, how did it help you to learn? If it was absent, what might children's literature have added to the learning experience for you?

Using Children's Non-fiction Books to Teach Social Studies

Children's non-fiction books can be particularly powerful social studies learning tools, as they provide detailed information that is often missing in textbooks. Real-world information in non-fiction literature can help to expand children's knowledge and understanding about a particular phenomenon, event, or person. For instance, when studying about children's rights, the book *Stand Up, Speak Out* by Peace Child International (2001), composed of children's poems, reports, and pictures, can be used to explain the Convention on the Rights of the Child. Another selection, *For Every Child* by Caroline Castle (2000) highlights some of those rights through the use of words and pictures.

Young readers usually find stories based on real-life experiences more pleasurable and aesthetically pleasing than the content of textbooks. In Ted Harrison's book *O Canada* (1992), for example, the author uses art to take the reader on a colourful cross-Canada journey that depicts the rich ethnic diversity of the country. A similar book, focused on Canada's North, is *My Arctic 1, 2, 3* by Michael Kusugak (2001). Another example is *Fort Chipewyan Homecoming: A Journey to Native Canada* by Morningstar Mercredi (1997), a photo essay told from the perspective of a 12-year-old boy who learns about his Native ancestry while on a trip to Fort Chipewyan.

Real-life stories can be particularly helpful in social studies when children see average human beings being good citizens and taking action on issues. This is especially true when the main characters are children of their own age who are making a difference in others' lives. For instance, the autobiography of Craig Kielburger, *Free the Children* (1998), tells the story of a young Canadian who began an organization to fight the injustice of child labour when he was 12 years old.

Non-fiction books can also inspire children to think about possible career paths and life choices. *Marvelous Mattie* by Emily Arnold McCully (2006), for instance, is a non-fiction picture story about a young girl who loves to invent things and who grows up to be the designer of the modern-day paper bag. And *Supermarket* by Kathleen Krull (2001) presents an extensive amount of information about all aspects of the supermarket industry in a creative and colourful format. Literature that depicts people of both genders, from different socioeconomic levels and cultural backgrounds and engaged in a variety of occupations, can be particularly useful for influencing children's career and life aspirations. *Against the Odds* by Joe Layden (1998), for example, tells the stories of several basketball players who overcame challenges to become successful in professional sports.

Children's interest in and engagement with social studies can be enhanced by using non-fiction, informational texts.

Strategies for Effective Content Area Reading

Many non-fiction books are formatted differently than fictional storybooks. Therefore, when non-fiction informational books are used as resources in your social studies program, it is important to help your students to develop skills for effective content area reading. The same strategies as those for using textbooks with young children apply here, including using tools such as the glossary, index, table of contents, and chapter headings and subheadings to learn about the contents of the book. Since all informational books are written from a particular perspective, students will also need to be taught to be alert for the author's point of view.

As with any new learning, begin with what the children think they know about a topic by examining the title of the book and discussing what they think the book is about, what information they think it might contain, and what they think they know about the topic already. This also helps to uncover any biases and/or misconceptions that the learners may be bringing to the reading. Concept maps can be a very helpful learning tool in this regard (see Chapter 2).

CLASSROOM APPLICATION

To help her Grade 4 students develop strategies for reading social studies materials effectively, Mrs. Olsen uses the five-part SQ3R strategy developed by Robinson (1970). The first step she teaches is how to *survey* a book by examining the title, table of contents, and index to get an idea of what the book is about. She also checks to see how much of the vocabulary being introduced in the glossary is new to her students. She then shows them how to scan the material in the book to get a sense of what it is about by looking at headings and subheadings, introductions and conclusions, the first line in each paragraph, highlighted terms, and margin notes. In the second step, she asks students to look back at the *questions* they are working on to remind themselves what information they are looking for and decide if they feel the resource is going to be helpful. In the third phase—*read, reflect, and review*—she teaches the children as they *read* to look for the main ideas in the text, to distinguish main ideas from supporting details, and to examine the information provided in pictures, diagrams, illustrations, charts, and graphs, and in these images' captions; to stop frequently to *reflect* on what they are reading and try to make sense of it; and to *review* what they read by jotting down outline and summary notes and recording any questions they have about what they are reading. (See http://www.pgcps.org/~elc/readingacross1.html for more information on this reading technique).

www **Technology Connection** For more strategies and information on reading in the content area, follow the links on the book's companion website to pages on the following sites.

- Content Area Literacy page on the SCORE History/Social Science website: http://score.rims.k12.ca.us
- ReadingQuest: Making Sense in Social Studies: http://www.readingquest.org
- Social Studies page on the Literacy Matters website: http://www.literacymatters.org

Using a Combination of Non-fiction and Fiction Books to Teach Social Studies

Substantial learning benefits can result from the use of children's storybooks (whether fiction or non-fiction) as resources to support and enhance a social studies program. Teachers can encourage a love of reading by providing access to both fiction and non-fiction books that cover a wide range of topics and reading levels. The school's teacher librarian can be particularly invaluable for assisting you in keeping up on what is new and appropriate for your in-class collection. If your school is not so fortunate as to have a teacher librarian, then the local public librarians can be very helpful.

The benefits for young readers that emerge when non-fiction books and fiction books are used together include increased engagement; the development of historical understanding; opportunities to explore self, character, and identity; chances to investigate social and cultural issues and see examples of problem solving and decision making; and possibilities for active engagement with other cultures. Each of these benefits will be explored in further detail here, along with examples of appropriate fiction and non-fiction books for each area.

Using Stories to Promote Engaged Learning

By reading children's stories, students can learn the selected social studies content in a way that is meaningful and relevant to them. When children are allowed to choose literature that is of particular interest to them, reading becomes an exciting process. Stories can also personalize learning for young children by reflecting their own lived experience. While characters and settings that are familiar and recognizable to children can immediately capture the children's attention, the unfamiliar can be equally as engaging, particularly when children's imaginations are inspired by a story. One such example is Roch Carrier's *The Flying Canoe* (2004), a rendition of a French-Canadian folktale about an 11-year-old boy who goes to live with lumberjacks and gets involved in an exciting adventure.

Several selections that offer personalized perspectives can help you to teach geographical understanding and terminology in an engaging way. *Can You Catch Josephine* by Stephane Poulin (1987), a story about a young girl chasing her cat through her school, could be used to enhance a unit on developing an understanding of aerial perspective and other mapping skills in the early grades. Jan Brett's *Town Mouse, Country Mouse* (1994), which tells the story of two mice who change places and learn about the influence of location on lifestyle, could be used to introduce the concepts of rural and urban. *Niki's Walk* by Jane Tanner (1987), a picture book without text that follows a young girl as she walks through her neighbourhood, could be used to teach young children about what makes up a community and how communities meet people's needs. The pictures in the book could be used to create a map of Niki's community and introduce the features of maps, including scale, legend, and direction. This mapping activity could also help children to come

The story format is a powerful vehicle for teaching and learning because children are drawn to stories and find them engaging.

to understand that flat maps represent a bird's-eye view. Scott O'Dell's *Island of the Blue Dolphins* (1960), a novel about exploration and survival, is useful for teaching mapping skills to upper-elementary students. While reading this book, children could be encouraged to create more sophisticated maps illustrating advanced geographical concepts such as elevation. They could also learn about contour by designing three-dimensional models of the island. (See http://score .rims.k12.ca.us/score_lessons/dolphin/ for more lesson ideas based on O'Dell's novel.)

Using Stories to Develop Children's Historical Understanding

Stories about the past can make history come alive for young readers. These stories can add both breadth and depth to children's knowledge about past events and people and can also be used to present multiple perspectives on historical events. For example, the study of the history of slavery in Canada can be enhanced through the sharing of stories about this topic. By reading Barbara Smucker's *Underground to Canada* (1978), a historical novel set in the mid-1800s about the suffering and courage of two young girls who travelled a route from Virginia to Ontario in order to escape slavery, children can not only learn about the nature of slavery and about Canada's role as a safe haven for escaped slaves, but can also learn to develop empathy for others as they read about the young girls' suffering and courage. Another fiction book that presents a similar storyline about a young girl escaping slavery from the United States using the Underground Railroad is *Stealing Freedom* by Elisa Lynn Carbone (1998). The non-fiction picture book *Get on Board: The Story of The Underground Railroad* by Jim Haskins tells the story of the Underground Railroad through personal stories, historical material, and letters written by people who helped the slaves escape to freedom. A similar book about the role of Canadians in the Underground Railroad is *The Last Safe House: A Story of the Underground Railroad* by Barbara Greenwood (1998).

Caution is recommended, however, with regard to using books that depict only the positive role that Canadians played in any set of historical events, as children need to develop a balanced view of the past. For example, in the case of the subject of slavery, they need to be helped to understand that the owning of slaves was not a practice limited to the United States. You can add to your own background knowledge about the role of slavery in Canada's history by reading a book such as *The Hanging of Angelique: The Untold Story of Canadian Slavery and the Burning of Old Montreal* by Afua Cooper (2006). Further, the inclusion of children's non-fiction books such as *The Kids' Book of Black Canadian History* by Rosemary Sadler (2003) provides students with a broader, more well-rounded understanding of the roles that black Canadians have played throughout the country's history.

It is important as well that children are helped to see that many social problems that began in the past still exist in some form today. For example, teachers could select a work of children's fiction that addresses a more contemporary black issue in Canada, such as *Last Days in Africville* by Dorothy Perkyns (2003), about a 12-year-old girl growing up in a black community in Halifax. A follow-up discussion with the class about what students can do to help to address issues such as those presented in Perkyns's book would go a long way in assisting children to see themselves as possible agents of change, beginning with how they treat others.

Children's stories can also be used to demonstrate historical agency. Children need to understand that all actions and events in the past were a result of decisions made by people and that those decisions were influenced by the contexts in which those people lived. A useful novel in this regard is *A Proper Acadian* by Mary Alice Downie (1980), about a 12-year-old boy from Boston who goes to live with his mother's family in Acadia in 1754 and becomes embroiled in the events leading up to the War of 1812 between England and France. Another selection, *Goodbye Sarah* by Geoffrey Bilson (1981), tells the story of two young girls caught in the middle of the Winnipeg General Strike of 1919.

Children also need to understand that a similar dynamic applies today: people make decisions that influence the way events unfold. Stories can be used to help young children to see themselves as potential agents of change instead of being resigned to passively accepting and reinforcing what has always been. For example, in *Just a Dream* by Chris VanAllsburg (1990), a young boy who considers himself too busy to properly separate out garbage in order to recycle appropriate items dreams about what will happen in the future if he continues to live the way he has been living. He has a nightmare about piles of garbage mounting up around him and wakes up with new priorities and an understanding of the importance of environmental stewardship.

Stories can also provide a more personalized approach to learning about a historical event, especially when students have an opportunity to identify with a character close to their own age. Two such books that can help children to think about historical events, and that could be used as a starting point for discussions about the impact of these events today, are *A Child in Prison Camp* by Shizuye Takashima (1971), which tells the true story of the author's experiences as an 11-year-old child during the internment of Japanese Canadians on Canada's west coast in 1942, and *Naomi's Road* by Joy Kogawa (2005), which tells a similar but fictitious story. In *An Ocean Apart: The Gold Mountain Diary of Chin Mei-Ling* by Gillian Chan (2004), a 12-year-old girl and her father struggle to pay the required head tax so that the rest of their family can immigrate to

Canada from China. Another story with whose main character children can identify is *Sparks Fly Upward* by Carol Matas (2002), about the life of a young Jewish girl living in Winnipeg in the early 1900s.

Fiction and non-fiction books can also help children to explore topics, questions, and issues from a variety of perspectives. For example, when studying heroes, a book such as *Run* by Eric Walters, which is a fictional story of a boy who spends time with Terry Fox during his run across the country, could be used in conjunction with the non-fiction book *The Value of Facing a Challenge: The Story of Terry Fox* by Ann Donegan Johnson (1983). Similarly, while exploring the topic of the Holocaust, the non-fiction book *Hana's Suitcase* by Karen Levine (2002), which retraces the life of a real child who lived during the Holocaust, could be paired with the fiction book *Anna Is Still Here* by Ida Vos (1995), which tells the fictional story of a young Holocaust survivor named Anna who finally finds her parents after a long separation. Another selection, *A Picture Book of Anne Frank* by David Adler (1993), which is a non-fiction book based on the diary of Anne Frank, tells about the experiences of the young author's family as they attempt to hide from the Nazis in Amsterdam during World War Two. Lois Lowry's *Number the Stars* (1989), a fictionalized account of the experiences of a Jewish family in Denmark who were helped by their neighbours during World War Two, could be used to add another perspective to the study of the Holocaust. However, although such combinations can be effective, when using fictional and non-fictional accounts concurrently, it is important that children be taught to distinguish fact from fiction. In particular, children need to understand that fictional books are not factual, and that they therefore should not be used as a source of information.

 Technology Connection Some children's books have websites that have been developed as extensions to the reading of the book. For example, follow the links on the book's companion website for ideas on how to extend children's learning about the Holocaust while they read *Hana's Suitcase*.

Using Stories to Promote the Exploration of Self, Character, and Identity

Through the use of children's stories, students can be exposed to three-dimensional characters (whether fictional or non-fictional) that can evoke personal responses in children and lead them to a deeper human understanding of the types of experiences portrayed in the stories. Such stories thus help to develop empathy and understanding, as well as attitudes of compassion, caring, and concern, in young learners. Children can be encouraged to try to relate to the characters' struggles for identity and belonging. Examples of books illustrating such struggles are *The Hockey Sweater* by Roch Carrier (1984), which tells the story of a boy who faces discrimination because of the colour of his hockey sweater; *The Moccasin Goalie* by W. Brownridge (1995), a true story based on the author's childhood experiences with discrimination because of physical difference; and *Shabash!* by Ann Walsh (1994), about an 11-year-old Sikh Canadian boy's experience of dealing with prejudice, both his own and others', when he joins a minor hockey team in a small B.C. town.

Shel Silverstein's *The Missing Piece* (1976) and *The Missing Piece Meets The Big O* (1981) are examples of read-aloud books that can be used with young children to explore questions of developing individual identity and dealing with being different. *Tess* by Hazel Hutchins (1995) tells the story of a young girl living on the Prairies who is ashamed of how poor her family is, and who ends up helping and being helped by a neighbour. *Prairie Willow* by Maxine Trottier (1998) is also about the struggles of a family homesteading on the Prairies. Three stories with themes related to Aboriginal identity are *Knots on a Counting Rope* by Bill Martin (1987), about a First Nations boy's wish to be an eagle dancer and how he is able to overcome his self-consciousness; Sylvia Olsen's *Catching Spring,* (2004) about a First Nations boy living on Vancouver Island who looks for a way to enter a fishing derby from which Aboriginals are excluded; and *Thomas and the Metis Sash* by Bonnie Murray (2004), the story of a boy who learns something about the Metis culture when he has to bring something to talk about at school.

A story can also portray people's values and expectations in their relations within their social group and within their neighbourhood groups. For example, *The Polar Bear Son: An Inuit Tale* by Lydia Dabcovich (1997) tells the story of an Inuit woman who must make a decision between meeting either her own personal needs or the wishes of her community. There is added benefit when students are introduced to characters that model the values of good citizenship.

CLASSROOM APPLICATION

Select a children's non-fiction or fiction book that you could use in order to focus on a particular character trait. What questions and follow-up activities would you have students participate in when using this book in your social studies program?

Using Stories to Explore Social and Cultural Issues

Children's stories can allow young readers to explore various social and cultural issues within Canadian society. An example of an age-appropriate social issue that primary-grade children could tackle through the use of children's stories is bullying. The fictional book *The Ant Bully* by Jon Nickle (1999), for example, tells the story of a young boy who is forced to face the ramifications of his bullying behaviours.

Children's stories can be particularly powerful for directing young learners' attention to the lives of individuals within a culture, thus discouraging them from seeing only a mass of people belonging to that culture. These experiences of coming to understand and empathize with individuals can help to avoid stereotyping. Some examples of useful books in this regard are as follows. *From Far Away* by Robert Munsch (1995) tells the true story of a young Lebanese girl whose family immigrates to Canada, and *The Cat From Kosovo* by Mary-Jane Hampton (2001) tells the true story of a cat named Mishka who came to Canada from Albania with his refugee owners during the 1999 civil unrest in that country. Another selection, *From Far and Wide: A Canadian Citizenship Scrapbook* by Jo Bannatyne-Cugnet (2000), is about a 6-year-old girl who becomes a Canadian citizen and decides to keep a scrapbook about the experience for her unborn baby brother. The reader learns about the process involved in becoming a citizen and is then walked through the actual citizenship ceremony. *Petranella* by Betty Waterton (1980) and *Josepha: A Prairie Boy's Story* by Jim McGugan (1994) also describe the experiences of young immigrants, in the context of homesteading in western Canada. *The Sandwich* by Ian Wallace (1975) is a more contemporary story of an immigrant boy's experiences with discrimination at school. *The Sugaring Off Party* by Jonathan London (1995) tells the story of a young French-Canadian boy and his family's traditions. *Mary of Mile 18* by Ann Blades (2001) portrays a young Mennonite girl growing up in a tiny northern community in British Columbia, who finds a part-wolf pup and tries to convince her family to keep it. *The Sky is Falling* by Kit Pearson (2000) portrays the experiences of a young British girl and her brother, who are sent to live in Canada during World War Two. *The Water of Possibility* by Hiromi Goto (2002) tells the story of a 12-year-old Japanese-Canadian girl and her brother, living in Alberta, who learn about Japanese folklore. Stories such as these can also help children to become conscious of the idea of perspective, as they come to understand that not everyone sees the world the same way they do. Further, themes such as those presented in these books can encourage students to take pride in their own heritage. These types of books are best used at an early point in the learners' introduction to a particular culture or ethnic group, once again so that children learn to see the individuals within a culture instead of developing stereotypical ideas about all members of a culture being the same. Other examples of books that can help young children to see the world through different eyes are *Ghost Train* by Paul Yee (1996), which portrays the hardships faced by the Chinese immigrants who built the Trans-Canada Railway and *Kiss the Dust* by Elizabeth Laird (1991), which recounts the experiences of a young girl living in Iraq during the Iraq/Iran conflict of the 1980s.

Stories can be powerful learning tools for dealing with issues of power, race, class, culture, and gender. A book such as *The Giver* by Lois Lowry (1993), for example, about a society of people who have decisions made for them about time of death and birth and what profession to pursue, can be used to help older children to understand and question the idea of giving in to a dominant power.

Using Stories to Model Problem Solving and Decision Making

Children's literature can provide an excellent introduction to the skills of problem solving and decision making. Using children's stories that address problems and issues relevant to students can help to develop their critical thinking skills as well as their ability to see things from others' perspectives. Children can also learn about the importance of taking action on important issues. These types of stories are particularly beneficial when they help students to see themselves as citizens and stewards of the world.

Many children's books, for example, have a survival-related theme. *Lost in the Barrens* (1956) is an adventure story set in the Northwest Territories, about two boys who become separated from their hunting party and have to spend the winter alone in the wilderness. Readers learn how the boys solve the problem of how to survive on their own in Canada's North. *Hatchet* by Gary Paulsen (1987) is a similar survival story of a 13-year-old boy who has to survive in the Canadian wilderness after the plane he is travelling on to meet his father crashes and the pilot dies. *Julie of the Wolves* by Jean Craighead George (1972) tells the story of a young girl who survives by living with wolves in Alaska, and *The Killick: A Newfoundland Story* by Geoff Butler 1995 is about the experience of a young boy and his grandfather surviving a severe storm in a boat.

Heroism is another common theme in children's literature that can help to develop problem-solving skills. *Delores and the Big Fire* by Andrew Clements (2002), for example, is a true story about a cat that saves her owner from a deadly fire. Another selection, *Horace Splattly, the Cupcaked Crusader* by Lawrence David (2003) tells about the adventures of a 10 year old who becomes a hero by eating magic cookies. One of the boy's adventures involves confronting a monster in the school playground. Another similar story about heroism and being willing to stand up to unfairness is *Shredderman: Secret Identity* by Wendelin Van Draanen (2004).

Using Stories to Allow Readers to Experience Other Cultures

Children's stories can help readers to develop awareness of and respect for cultures other than their own. By reading *Hide and Sneak* by Michael Arvaarluk Kusugak (1992), for example, children can learn about culture and life on the Arctic tundra through the story of a young Inuit girl who plays hide-and-seek with a mythical creature called ijirac. *Raven: A Trickster's Tale of the Pacific Northwest* by Gerald McDermott (1993) engages readers in a story from the perspective of Aboriginals from Canada's northwest coast. And *The Song within My Heart* by Dave Bouchard (2002) tells the story of a Cree boy getting ready for his first powwow. Using a wide range of stories about different groups can help to prevent the stereotyping of all Aboriginals as being the same. A window into another culture is provided in Na'ima Bint Robert's *The Swirling Hijab* (2002), in which a young Muslim girl lets her imagination run free as she plays with her mother's hijab.

Not all children's books about other cultures are effective for developing respect for these cultures, however. For example, the picture book *Ten Little Rabbits* by Virginia Grossman (1991) is an example of a book that has the potential to be controversial as it can promote stereotyping of Aboriginals. This counting book shows rabbits dressed in traditional Aboriginal blankets and wearing feathers and masks as they engage in activities such as dancing, playing hide-and-seek, sitting on a travois, sending smoke signals, fishing, and beating on drums. Problems with this book include the representation of Aboriginal peoples as rabbits (McCarty, 1995) and the potential for young children to be misled into thinking that the practices depicted are typical of all Aboriginal peoples and in modern Aboriginal society, thereby leading to stereotyping. Other books, such as *Sign of the Beaver* by Elizabeth George Spears (1983), have been criticized for objectifying Aboriginals by not allowing them to speak in their own voices. In the case of Spears's book, the lives of the Aboriginal characters are described through the eyes of a non-Aboriginal boy. This is not to suggest that such books should be avoided altogether, but rather that they would be better used as a starting point for a discussion about the issue of the objectifying and stereotyping of Aboriginal cultures. Such discussions could also help to uncover misconceptions students may have, which is always an important first step when children are reading any novel or picture book, as such misconceptions will affect the way the children read the book and can potentially reinforce stereotypes.

In David J. Smith's *If The World Were a Village: A Book About the World's People* (2002), the author considers culture on a more global scale, depicting the human population of the

Paired reading can help children to engage with books and develop literacy skills as they share their thoughts while reading the material together.

world as a small village of 100 people and examining, among other aspects, what percentage of that population speak various languages, are literate, use varying amounts of energy, and produce certain percentages of waste. The book ends by offering projections of future human lifestyles based on today's practices. Such books can help children to construct knowledge about the human condition. Smith's book is also an excellent example of how children's literature can help to integrate other subject areas with social studies—in this case, math, by incorporating lessons on understanding percentages and creating and interpreting bar graphs. However, other books with a similar global focus have faced criticism. For example, *People* by Peter Spiar (1980), which depicts numerous cultures around the world through illustrations of people in traditional dress, has been criticized as mis-educative because of the cultural distortion it engages in. Readers could erroneously assume that the clothing shown—which is usually worn only for festive occasions, and belongs to the culture's history—in fact represents what is worn in daily modern lives. Thus, it is important to always exercise caution when you are selecting books to represent other cultures.

CLASSROOM APPLICATION

Ms. Stanovich used the children's book *Flat Stanley* by Jeff Brown (1996) with her Grade 3 social studies class as an opener for her unit on people around the world. She was hoping to capture her students' interest in the topic and to motivate them to want to learn more about other cultures and communities through the eyes of Stanley, the main character in

(Continued)

the book. Stanley is a young boy who is flattened when a bulletin board lands on him. In his flattened state he is able to visit many places and engage in adventures.

Ms. Stanovich began the unit by reading the book to the class and discussing the many adventures of Flat Stanley. Using the Flat Stanley template available at http://www.flatstanley.com/template.htm, Ms. Stanovich had her students each make a replica of Flat Stanley and then choose a place outside of their own community—anywhere in the world—where they had a relative or an acquaintance to send their Flat Stanley for a visit. A letter crafted by the children explained the purpose for sending Flat Stanley and asked for information about Flat Stanley's trip. The children brainstormed a list of information that they wanted to obtain about the place that each Flat Stanley visited, including location of community—i.e., name of city/town, province/state, country, and continent; size of community; language(s) spoken; typical seasons; current weather; etc. The letter recipients were also asked to take their Flat Stanleys on excursions with them over a two-week period and to write a return letter to the Grade 3 class about what Stanley saw and did while on his trip. The information was then collected by the class and became the basis of a study of communities around the world.

For examples of ways in which other Grade 3 social studies teachers have used this book, see http://www.flatstanley.com/curriculum_rubric.htm. Lessons include using Flat Stanley to explore historical understanding by having him travel back to pioneer days; to explore the similarities and differences between rural and urban communities; and to explore the concepts of similarities and differences of peoples, places, and environments. The site also provides suggestions for using Flat Stanley in Grade 1 social studies in order to explore relationships in families.

The Flat Stanley Project website (http://www.flatstanleyproject.com) provides other telecollaborative options for teachers, including keeping Flat Stanley journals and sharing them with other classrooms. (See Chapter 12 for more information on the use of telecollaborative projects in the social studies classroom.) Have a look at this website and decide how you might be able to use a book like *Flat Stanley* in creative ways to teach specific social studies outcomes.

Finding Appropriate Children's Fiction and Non-fiction Books

As a teacher, you will need to carefully select good books—both fiction and non-fiction—to support and enhance your social studies program. A teacher librarian and other teachers in your school who teach the same grade as you can be very helpful during the selection process. You will also want to check for any sets of books that may have been purchased as resources for your school's language arts program, as these may be also appropriate for use in social studies. Figure 8.1 offers a set of guidelines that can help you in your decision making about appropriate fiction and non-fiction resources. Perhaps the most important of these guidelines are those that ensure that the pieces of literature you choose support your social studies learning outcomes.

FIGURE 8.1 ■ A Checklist of Selection Criteria for Children's Literature

Here are some criteria to consider when selecting appropriate children's literature to support your social studies program:

- uses social studies related terminology
- matches your social studies goals
- enriches social studies understandings
- addresses social studies content knowledge
- presents authentic storyline and characters
- is free from bias and stereotyping
- has three-dimensional characters who create empathy
- has complementary text and illustrations
- is clear and understandable
- is at appropriate reading levels
- helps to enhance students' understanding of the topic
- others?

This 'others' bullet applies to the third stop in the Active Engagement box below.

ACTIVE ENGAGEMENT

1. Working in groups, select a topic from the social studies curriculum guide for your province or territory.

2. Use the links provided on the companion website to help you to locate children's fiction and non-fiction books to address your chosen topic.

3. Once you have located some books that look interesting and appropriate, use the list of criteria for selecting children's literature provided in Figure 8.1 to make judgments about which book(s) might be best for enhancing your teaching of that topic. Are there any criteria that you would add to or remove from the list? Why? Share your selections with the rest of the class and begin to compile a list of appropriate social studies–related children's literature.

REFLECTION POINT

Not all books are recognized as effective teaching tools; in fact, some have been challenged and at times banned for use in classrooms by schools and school districts. Usually the content of these books is deemed to be controversial. For example, in the

(Continued)

late 1990s, books about same-sex parents, including *Asha's Mums* by Rosamund Elwin (1990) and *One Dad, Two Dads, Brown Dad, Blue Dads* by Johnny Valentine (1994) were banned for use in schools in Surrey, B.C., because they addressed the topic of homosexuality. However, the B.C. Supreme Court overturned the school district's decision. Books such as these provide an excellent opportunity to help children to understand that, at times, societal norms need to be challenged.

Many other books have been considered contentious as resources in schools at various times in our history, mostly because of what was perceived to be either inappropriate language or sensitive content. For more information on censorship of children's literature in Canada, follow the links to relevant web resources on the book's companion website. How might these resources help you if you were challenged by parents about the use of a particular piece of children's literature as a resource in your social studies program?

 Technology Connection Engaging children in critiquing books can be an excellent way to develop critical literacy skills. Further, collaborative skills can be developed by having your class share their thoughts on books with others. The Young Readers' Choice Award (YRCA)— www.pnla.org/yrca—has a forum that your class can join to discuss books being considered for the annual critics' choice awards. Visit the book's companion website to link to this forum, where you can see what books are currently being recommended and learn more about the YRCA and about how the selections of books are made.

Using Poetry to Teach Social Studies

Children's literature in the form of poems and rhymes is another resource available for helping children to learn important social studies content knowledge in an engaging way. A study of Canada's geography, for example, could be enhanced through the use of Robert Heidbreder's book of poetry *Eenie, Meenie Manitoba* (1996). The action poems in this book tell stories about all parts of Canada, including various locations, animal life, and weather. Similarly, in *The Elders Are Watching*, Dave Bouchard (1997) uses poetry to describe life on Canada's west coast. *If You're Not from the Prairie* by David Bouchard (1999) is a book-length poem about the unique experience of life on the prairies as told from the perspective of a young boy. Different parts of the poem address geographical concepts such as the weather, the seasons, and the landscape. *Winter Eyes* by Douglas Florian is a collection of poetry with a winter theme; the poem "Sugaring Time" is particularly useful for teaching about the production of Canadian maple syrup. *Winter: An Alphabet Acrostic* by Steven Schnur is a book-length poem about the seasons. It contains acrostics about winter such as the following one entitled "Cold" (p. 3).

Cold

Crystals
Of ice as delicate as
Lace ring the
Duck pond.

All of these poems can help children from various parts of Canada understand what influences weather has on our lives and lifestyle choices.

Using poetry can make social studies fun and engaging and can also help to impart a message to young readers. Dr. Seuss's poetry, for example, is excellent for appealing to a child's imagination. Seuss's *The Lorax* (1971), for example, is useful for raising environmental issues with primary-age children. In the story, a young boy cuts down all the trees in his town despite the warnings of the Lorax and learns about the effects of his actions on the environment.

Shel Silverstein's *A Light in the Attic* (1981) and *Where the Sidewalk Ends* (1974) are two examples of collections of children's poetry that can be used to address specific social studies objectives. For example, the poem "The Oak and the Rose" (p. 165) in *A Light in the Attic* is particularly powerful for discussing personal growth and change. Another selection, *Muslim Child: A Collection of Short Stories and Poems* by Rukhsana Khan (1999), could be used to develop children's understanding of multiple viewpoints, as it shows the world as seen through the eyes of Muslim children. *Peace Crane* by Sheila Hamanaka (1995) could be used to educate children about peace as a complement to *Sadako and the Thousand Paper Cranes* by Eleanor Coerr (1981), which is the story of a young Japanese girl who is afflicted by leukemia as a result of the bombing of Hiroshima and Nagasaki, and the action she takes to try to bring about world peace.

CLASSROOM APPLICATION

Mr. Craig read Shel Silverstein's poem "Colors" (in Silverstein, 1974, p. 24) to his Grade 1 class and then asked the children to paint a profile picture of the person depicted in the poem. The pictures were displayed around the classroom, as in an art gallery, and the students went on a "gallery walk" to compare and contrast them. A discussion ensued about the concepts of similarities and differences. Next, Mr. Craig displayed a second poem by Silverstein entitled "No Difference"—about how people's appearances may differ on the outside in terms of the colour of their eyes, hair, and skin, but when the lights are turned out everyone is the same (p. 81)—and had the class read the poem aloud together. The children were then asked to put on blindfolds and, without speaking, find a partner and try to identify that person by gently feeling his or her facial features. Following the activity, through discussion, the students came up with the generalization, "We each have our own ways of being unique, but as humans we are all basically the same."

Another benefit of using poetry in social studies is that it can allow for children to participate in shared reading, in which they take on the different roles of the characters in the poem. A follow-up discussion after this type of activity could include talking about what it was like to see the world from the different points of view in the poem and to come to understand that not everyone sees the world the same way.

 Technology Connection For other examples of poetry, and lesson plans for teaching it, follow the links provided on the book's companion website.

Added Benefits of Using Children's Literature

Some of the added benefits of using children's literature in your social studies program are the accessibility of resources and the wide variety of available options that can appeal to all interests and developmental levels. As well, the use of non-fiction informational and biographical books, picture books, novels, and poetry can encourage children's love of reading, boost their reading comprehension, and expand the size and depth of their vocabulary. Additionally, children's literature can be used as a way to develop critical thinking and literacy skills and to generate discussion about topics being addressed in social studies. Finally, the use of children's literature can provide opportunities for the integration of many of the language arts learning outcomes into the teaching of social studies. Considering all of the benefits discussed in this chapter, it is highly recommended that you look for ways to incorporate good children's literature into your social studies lessons whenever possible.

Chapter Summary

This second chapter on resource selection focused on the use of children's literature, including non-fiction and fiction books, picture books, and poetry, to provide a child-friendly, multiple resource approach.

The appeal of children's literature for young learners is manyfold. Stories can engage children in their learning as they identify with characters and unleash their imaginations. Children's literature can also develop young learners' historical understanding, promote the exploration of identity, allow for exploration of social issues, show problem solving in action, and provide insights into other cultures. In addition, children's literature is readily available, inexpensive, and comes in a wide variety of genres that can appeal to all interests and developmental levels. Taking the time to select pieces of literature that address social studies concepts and understandings will ensure that these selections support the development of social studies learning outcomes.

Chapter 9, the third and final chapter on resource selection, will examine the possibilities for enhancing your social studies program through the use of electronic resources.

Chapter 9

How Can Electronic Resources Be Used for Information Gathering in Social Studies?

In the last chapter on resource selection, we investigated the use of children's literature as a way to increase the appeal of social studies and further engage young children in their learning. This third and final chapter on selecting resources examines electronic resources that can augment your social studies program.

Using computers as learning resources has become much easier over the last decade as their availability has increased in schools. According to Statistics Canada (2004), in 2003–2004, over 97 percent of all elementary schools were connected to the internet and 93 percent of all school computers provided internet access. Most provincial and territorial education ministries and/or school districts have developed lists of suggested media education learning outcomes to help teachers in envisioning the use of computers in teaching and learning.

 Technology Connection Have a look at the document *Media Education in Canada: An Overview* at http://www.media-awareness.ca and find out what the policy on media outcomes is for your province or territory. How does this help you to think about the role of technology in your teaching of social studies? How do technology learning outcomes compare across the provinces?

Educators across Canada recognize that our children are the digital citizens of the future. Creating digitally literate citizens is therefore an important goal for both our schools in general and for our social studies programs in particular. Being a digitally literate citizen means being knowledgeable about and skilled not only in using digital technology to find and apply information, but also in problem solving and decision making, creating, and collaborating and communicating with the help of electronic tools. Equally as important is coming to understand the importance of using technology respectfully and responsibly, and having a critical attitude toward the role of computer technologies in society.

REFLECTION POINT

What does digital literacy mean to you? Do you see addressing digital literacy as (a) very important, (b) somewhat important, or (c) unimportant to your teaching of social studies? Why? What have you done to prepare yourself for this responsibility? How can you better prepare yourself?

Defining Digital Literacy

The term "digital literacy" is one of the latest catch phrases in educational circles. The overall focus of this type of literacy is on developing knowledgeable, skilled, and responsible users of computer technologies. Included under the umbrella of digital literacy are such skills as understanding how to operate a particular technology, knowing how it can be used, and recognizing the effects of its use.

Developing the skills of information location and application is one important aspect of digital literacy. These skills include the ability to find, evaluate, synthesize, and use information to make informed decisions. Digitized information comes in text-based, audio, and visual forms, and children need to acquire the ability to read, interpret, understand, and use all of these media forms. Critical literacy skills are also needed so that learners can recognize and act on the fact that everything on the web, for example, represents an individual's point of view. An important skill that children need to develop in social studies is the ability to recognize that all information must be carefully and critically examined for bias, and that no single source should be used as the sole reference

Collaboration and communication skills, both within the classroom and beyond the classroom walls, can be enhanced through the use of computers in social studies.

about a particular topic. A second component of digital literacy requires that children develop an understanding that computers can be valuable resources for assisting in problem solving and decision making. Children need to learn how to engage in inquiry into important problems and issues that have no clear answers and to come to conclusions or make decisions about those issues based on the available evidence.

A third component of digital literacy is creative use of computer technologies. Included here is children's ability to see themselves as producers of knowledge and to use electronic resources in a way that advances thinking rather than simply consuming what someone else has produced. Digital creativity skills include being able to contribute original ideas, design web pages and multimedia presentations, and produce digital images and video.

A fourth aspect of digital literacy is the ability to use electronic resources as collaborative and communicative tools. Skills in this area include the ability to use videoconferencing, blogging, and other telecollaborative tools in order to learn with and from others.

Finally, digital literacy includes the development of a critical attitude toward computer technology in our society in terms of its present and future impact on humanity. This ability to ask questions and critically examine issues is also a central goal of social studies.

 Technology Connection For more information on digital literacy and the skills needed by citizens of the twenty-first century, visit the 21st Century Skills page on the North Central Regional Educational Laboratory (NCREL) website: http://www.ncrel.org/engauge/skills/agelit.htm.

Addressing all of these components of digital literacy is a major undertaking for schools and teachers, and all subject areas have a role to play. Social studies is a particularly effective context for developing digital literacy because of the emphasis the discipline places on conducting research.

In this chapter on resource selection, we begin to uncover what social studies teachers can do to help to develop the information location and application skills necessary for digital literacy, specifically through the ways in which they employ computers as resources to enhance student research. Later, in Chapter 12, we will examine the remaining digital literacy skills presented above as we look at ways to enhance the social studies learning environment by using computer technologies to develop the skills of higher-level thinking, decision making and problem solving, producing and sharing, and collaborating, as well as the ability to be critical users of technology.

Using Electronic Resources to Enhance Social Studies Research

LOOKING BACK

What experiences have you had with teaching and learning using computers? What uses of computers do you feel would be most effective for enhancing children's learning? What concerns do you have about integrating computers into your social studies program?

Searching for, understanding, evaluating, synthesizing, and applying information to a question or problem are all components of a social studies program that is research based. Computers can be effective tools for helping to develop these information literacy skills in children and for facilitating their social studies research. Computer technologies can provide students with quicker and easier access to more extensive and current information, and the breadth and depth of this available information can be used to encourage students to learn to manage information rather than simply memorize it. Information on the computer is presented in a variety of forms (e.g., graphs, pictures, text) and through multiple modalities (e.g., auditory, visual), which make the information appealing to learners with diverse learning styles and intelligences. With the assistance of computers, students are able to further develop their own unique strengths by accessing information through their preferred modality and by having opportunities to present their learning in a variety of ways. Providing students with alternative ways to learn, including both audio and visual, can be particularly helpful for students who have learning challenges.

Another benefit of electronic technologies is that children tend to be more motivated to explore ideas further when using them. As well, the use of computers can allow children to exercise more control over the direction of their learning, which can increase feelings of independence and empowerment, promote creativity, and encourage active involvement in their learning. These aspects of using computer technologies help to make children's learning experiences more personally relevant.

The most common use of computer technologies in social studies is for searching for information on topics. Two of the most used electronic sources for information retrieval are the World Wide Web (the web) and educational software. In the following sections, we will look first at web resources and consider some ways to develop children's skills for accessing, evaluating, and synthesizing online information. Next, we will examine computer software for its potential as an information retrieval source.

Using the Internet as a Social Studies Resource

The internet is a vast repository of resources that can support and expand your social studies program. Not only does it provide abundant topic-related sites that your students can access to find information as a part of their investigations, but it is also a cornucopia of resources that you as the teacher can use for your own professional development.

Teachers' Use of the Internet

The internet provides teachers with opportunities to e-mail, blog, and chat with fellow teachers about professional development matters. It also provides access to the web's expansive and readily available resources for both lesson plan ideas and content-related information. Most subject areas have discipline-specific professional development websites that provide collections of teacher-vetted weblinks related to the particular discipline. When the internet first became popular, teachers spent a great deal of time trying to locate these useful information sources to support their content selection. However, there are now some well-known excellent educational websites on which educators have created databases of available resources and websites that best address a variety of topics of study from the curriculum. These databases are categorized by subject area, grade, and topic to make it easier for teachers to locate exactly what they are looking for. One such website is the 2Learn Education Society portal (www.2learn.ca), which provides sample projects by grade level and access to online tools for each grade level, as well as articles on classroom-based research and opportunities to connect with other teachers. Another similar site is the Community Learning Network (www.cln.org), created by Open School BC.

ACTIVE ENGAGEMENT

Search the web for other databases of teacher professional development resources that could be used to enhance your social studies program, and share your findings with your classmates. Beware that the greatest majority of the sites that you will find originate in the United States and therefore won't necessarily address the social studies curriculum requirements of your province or territory; nor will they contain topics and information to support research on topics from a Canadian perspective. When searching, look for Universal Resource Locators (URLs)—more commonly known as website addresses—that have .ca in the domain address, as this usually indicates that the site host is Canadian. Other domain suffixes include .com (which is an abbreviation of "commercial" and often denotes a for-profit site), .edu (which is most commonly used by schools and post-secondary institutions), .gov (which is used by U.S. federal government departments), and .net or .org (which tend to be used for most other purposes beyond those already listed.)

One place to start to look for Canadian-generated sites is on your teacher institution's library website, as most online education libraries have links to peer-reviewed teacher resource sites that have been vetted by the librarians. Another helpful resource is the teachers' association website for your province or territory.

When deciding on a lesson plan from the web to use in your teaching, a good rule of thumb is to *adapt* that plan for your use, not *adopt* it as is. Why do you think that this would be important? Find one online lesson plan that would be appropriate for a particular grade and topic in social studies, and decide how you might need to adapt it for use in your teaching.

In addition to using these teacher resource websites for professional development and for identifying topic-related sites, teachers can also direct students to the same sites to conduct their research investigations. For example, the Learning Resources section of the Statistics Canada website (http://www.statcan.ca/english/edu) offers numerous online statistical databases in both English and French that can assist you in designing lessons that make use of the available Canadian-generated statistics and can provide resources to support your students' research on Canadian trends. Similarly, the Country Reports website (www.countryreports.org) provides statistics on global trends, which can help both teachers and students to do country-by-country comparisons.

CLASSROOM APPLICATION

The Statistics Canada website (www.statcan.ca) offers many useful research resources for social studies students. For example, during a unit on "People in My Community," students could begin by using the 2006 Community Profiles section to find information about the diverse cultural, religious, and linguistic makeup of their community and the level and type of immigration to their community. Comparisons could then be made with other communities in Canada. The Thematic Maps section could be used to compare population distributions across the country and to track the movement of Canadians from province to province. Students could then visit the Kids Zone section, to access numerous maps of Canada that show distribution by population, language, religion, and culture; plus, there are puzzles and a quiz about Canada.

Also at the Statistics Canada site, lesson plans are available to assist elementary teachers in teaching children how to collect and work with statistics. Have a look at these lessons and decide how you might use them to develop your students' information literacy skills. What else can you find at the Statistics Canada website that would assist you in your teaching of social studies? (The book's companion website provides direct links to all of the sections discussed here.)

Developing Students' Information Retrieval Skills Using the Web

Students today may be proficient at downloading music videos, text messaging, and playing digital games, but this does not mean that they are effective searchers of the Web. In fact, locating useful and accurate information on the Web can be difficult for them. The sheer volume of information available can cause students to be easily sidetracked and to spend a great deal of time off task. Information gathering can easily become a mindless exercise in which quantity overrides quality and which does little to promote deeper thinking and understanding. There is also a large amount of moving text and advertising on most websites, which can be highly distracting for young users. Therefore, when you make the decision to have your students conduct online research, you will need to be cognizant of these concerns.

Using Web Hunts to Introduce Students to Web Searching

When first engaging their students in using the web as a resource, teachers often opt to pre-select sites for them to access. Teacher-designed online web hunts (or alternatively called scavenger hunts and treasure hunts) are good starting points for children who lack web searching skills. Web hunts are inquiry-oriented activities that actively engage students in locating information on the web. They are useful activities for developing students' navigational skills, including how to access information, how to move around within a website and among different websites, and how to read efficiently online in order to locate specific information.

Here is an example of a web-based treasure hunt that was prepared by a Grade 4 teacher as an introductory activity to her unit on Canada's Aboriginal peoples. Her students worked in pairs and alternated the responsibilities of reading and recording.

FIGURE 9.1 ■ A Treasure Hunt about Canada's Aboriginal Peoples

Use the websites provided to answer the questions. Scan the text at each site and study the pictures and other information sources before responding:

How are the terms Aboriginal, Indian, and First Nations different?
http://www.ainc-inac.gc.ca/pr/info/tln_e.html

Which province or territory has the greatest number of Aboriginal peoples?
http://www.ainc-inac.gc.ca/ks/pdf/fnpc_e.pdf

In your own words, retell the story of the Inuksuk.
http://www.ainc-inac.gc.ca/ks/inuks_e.html

What does the name of your province or territory mean?
http://www.ainc-inac.gc.ca/pr/info/info106_e.html

Examine the work of several Native artists and tell which one is your favourite and why.
http://www.ainc-inac.gc.ca/ks/3040_e.html

How many Aboriginal languages are there in Canada? Find out how to say your name in several of them.
http://www.ainc-inac.gc.ca/ks/5000_e.html

Read the story "Claire and Her Grandfather" and tell something about Aboriginal peoples that you learned from this story.
http://www.ainc-inac.gc.ca/ks/cgf/story-text_e.html

Why do you think the eagle feather is an important Aboriginal cultural symbol?
http://www.aaanativearts.com/article360.html

Pretend you traveled back in time to a buffalo hunt. Describe your experiences.
http://www.saskstories.ca/ (click on First Peoples)

Go on this virtual tour from the Head Smashed In historical site then tell one additional thing that you learned about the buffalo jump.
http://www.head-smashed-in.com/

Listen to the audio clip and explain the origin of the Iroquois Confederacy. How has this Confederacy influenced our modern day government?
http://www.histori.ca/minutes/minute.do?id=13575

Web hunts often provide a specific challenge to students in the form of questions or clues that they need to use in order to find answers to assigned questions or to solve a problem. Children can be engaged in searching and scanning sites for textual information, in examining photos and illustrations, and in watching and listening to video and audio clips to retrieve information.

Web hunts can be paper based, requiring students to type in the provided URLs to find answers to questions, or they can be created online, in which case students need only click on the weblink provided to direct them to the site where they are to search for the requested information. In most cases, young learners should not be required to type in URLs, as many are very long, which can result in children making spelling and keyboarding errors that prevent access and cause frustration. If you do use a paper-based hunt with young children, it is a good idea to have an older student from a higher grade buddy up with a younger one to assist with the typing. The buddies can also help younger children with reading the information on the websites and defining challenging vocabulary they encounter, as well as helping to keep the younger children on task.

Numerous sites provide web hunts appropriate for addressing social studies curricular topics. Some of these hunts require students to use only one site to search for answers to questions. For example, the "Holiday" Treasure Hunt (at www.museummania.com) links only to the archives at the Museum Educational Foundation. Other hunts make use of a variety of websites that focus on one topic. One example is The Hockey Quiz (available from Laurier University at http://www.swlauriersb.qc.ca/english/edservices/pedresources/webquest/hockeyquiz.htm), in which students can research Canada's national sport as they learn to navigate among and locate information on numerous websites. A third variety of web hunts do not take a specific content focus but rather are designed solely to help students develop their web searching skills.

 Technology Connection If you prefer, you can design your own web hunt using an online template. The book's companion website provides links to some sites offering guidelines and tools to help you get started.

 ## ACTIVE ENGAGEMENT

1. Follow this link to a scavenger hunt designed to teach searchers how to make use of the Worldbook Online Reference Centre: www.worldbookonline.com/training/assets/ CanadianScavengerHunt.pdf. Try the hunt to see what it teaches about effective web-searching skills. How might you adapt a hunt like this for use with children?

2. Have a look at some other online encyclopedias such as *The Canadian Encyclopedia* (www.thecanadianencyclopedia.com), *Encyclopœdia Britannica* (www.britannica .com), and Wikipedia (http://wikipedia.org). Which of these resources do you feel would be the most effective for assisting young children with their research? Why?

3. Using the suggestions and templates referred to in the Technology Connection above, try designing a scavenger hunt to introduce students to the use of this online encyclopedia.

Enhancing Students' Online Reading Skills

Reading online is a different task than reading a textbook or other traditional forms of print text. Students will need to acquire particular skills in order to achieve the maximum benefit from the sites they are researching. Using a lighted computer screen and dealing with differences in font sizes, varying background colours, lengthy running text, having to scroll to find information, distracters such as advertising and moving text, and the temptation to follow numerous links to other sites are all factors with which children need time and experience in order to become proficient in researching online. They also need time to practise examining all of the different types of information that are available on many websites and time to reflect on how to go about accessing and processing web-based information. Reflection can be used to assist students in thinking about their impressions of what they are seeing on a website, including what information is most helpful, what they feel makes a site effective, and how the use of web-based information contributes to their overall understanding of the topic under study.

As the teacher, you could begin by selecting one website for everyone in the class to examine that has topic-related information in a variety of media formats and at an appropriate reading level. While exploring the site, the children could be asked to respond to questions such as those in Figure 9.2. A follow-up discussion could be used to encourage students to share their ideas about what features of a website make it most effective as a resource.

FIGURE 9.2 ■ Reflecting on My Online Experience

My initial impression of this website is . . .

The static images (pictures, photos, illustrations) are . . .

The moving images (video clips) are . . .

The text size and type (font) are . . .

The information provided is . . .

The colors are . . .

The advertising is . . .

To move around the site I . . .

When I think about how reading this website was different from reading a book I realize . . .

From exploring this website I learned . . .

Teaching Students to Locate and Think Critically about Online Information Sources

Students can be given pre-selected hyperlinks to relevant sites on which they have to locate the necessary information to answer the questions, or they can be challenged to further advance their searching skills by finding their own topic-specific, appropriate websites. The latter approach also can be used to increase students' awareness of the various search engines and to teach critical viewing skills such as determining the reliability, accuracy, currency, comprehensiveness, bias, and trustworthiness of a web-based information source.

As the teacher, you need to be aware that finding quality information can be difficult for students because information on the web is not regulated in any standard manner and individuals are free to post almost anything they want. Another challenge for you is addressing the danger of students' stumbling on inappropriate content. Most schools have opted to install filtering software such as "Net Nanny" and other protective website blockers to institute some level of control over what students can access.

Views differ regarding the effectiveness of limiting student access to the web. One criticism is that when students are rendered less involved in the process of selecting resources to support their research, they are also denied a chance to develop their critical analysis skills. The use of such filtering tools can also cause problems in accessing important authentic information sources, as many sites that would be relevant to the study of a topic such as war and conflict, for example, might be rendered inaccessible to students. As well, the use of blocking software does not necessarily guarantee that unwanted sites will be inaccessible. Therefore, instead of relying on filtering software to protect children, teachers would do better to focus on teaching them critical viewing skills so that they can learn to make their own informed decisions and judgments about the information they encounter on the web. Children will also need to be taught what to do if they find themselves accidentally on an inappropriate website.

CLASSROOM APPLICATION

Canada's Media Awareness Network's website (www.media-awareness.ca) offers helpful information for educators on how to teach children to protect themselves when they are online. Interactive safety games can be accessed on the site, such as *Privacy Playground: First Adventure of the Three Little Cyberpigs,* which teaches children ages 8 to 10 how to safeguard their identity, avoid online predators, and recognize advertising ploys. The MNet site also offers a variety of other resources to help teachers facilitate media literacy education. Alberta Children's Services' *Bad Guy Patrol,* a similar game designed for children ages 5 to 10, is available at www.badguypatrol.ca. How might you integrate such websites into your social studies program?

Another concern about young students' use of online information sources is that children are inclined to accept what they read, hear, and see on the web as coming from a reliable authority and to view the information accessed online as the truth. Since the web is a self-publishing medium filled with data generated by anyone who wishes to post it, it is imperative that children be taught how to distinguish fact from opinion in what they read online. One important critical literacy skill young students will need is the ability to recognize that the information on a website represents a particular viewpoint and that it is therefore important to always examine several sites in order to obtain varied points of view on any issue. Further, students need to be made aware that much of the content on the web originates in the United States and that the majority of sites are created for commercial use while only a very small portion of all the accessible sites are designed for educational use. Critical literacy skills such as these need to be carefully taught and monitored to ensure that your students are developing proficiency in their use.

Children need instruction in, and opportunities to practise, how to critically examine and make informed choices about the information they access on the web.

Judging the Appropriateness of Websites for Young Students

As a teacher, you also need to ask questions about the websites that you are considering for use in your social studies program. The following is a list of some of the types of factors you might want to consider when deciding on which websites to select. Your students could also use the first five questions as guidelines to help them decide on the usefulness of websites they may be considering.

- Who is providing the information on the website?
- Is the information presented objectively without an obvious bias?
- How accurate is the information presented on the website?
- How reliable is the source of the information?
- How current is the information and how often is it updated?
- How comprehensive is the coverage of the topic on the website?
- How easy is the website to use?
- Is the information at an appropriate reading level for your students?
- Will the website be interesting and motivating for your students to use?

ACTIVE ENGAGEMENT

Based on your experience with searching the web, what other criteria for judging the appropriateness of websites could you add to this list?

FIGURE 9.3 ■ **Sample Boolean Logic and Other Search Strategies**

> Enter no more than two or three keywords connected by Boolean operators.
>
> Using AND between two keywords narrows the search results by finding sites containing both search terms—e.g., social studies AND technology.
>
> Using OR between two keywords increases the search results by looking for either one term or the other—e.g., social studies OR technology.
>
> Using AND NOT between terms narrows the search by finding records with the first term but not the second—e.g., social studies AND NOT technology.
>
> Quotation marks (" ") around search terms are used when referring to a term or concept that is normally made up of two words—e.g., "social studies."
>
> Using the asterisk at the end of a term, a method known as truncation (*), retrieves all alternate endings of the word including plurals and variations on spelling—e.g., comput* will find records containing *computer, computers, computing,* and *compute.*

Teaching Students to Use Search Engines

When students begin to do their own online research, not only should they be taught how to view sites with a critical eye, but they also need to know how to find sites that provide the information they are seeking. Locating possible information sources online also requires the use of retrieval skills that are unique to researching on the web, including how to use search engines and subject directories.

When your students are looking for a specific tool, site, or subject, a useful place for them to start is with a search engine such as Google, AltaVista, Lycos, or HotBot. However, keyword searches on these engines often return thousands of sites, and young learners tend to open only the first few to look for the information they need. Although some search engines are continually being redesigned to make searching with them easier—with some now allowing users to enter searches in question format—children still need to have a working knowledge of how to enter search terms to make the outcome of their search most effective.

Before your students conduct searches for websites to support their research in social studies, they need to be taught some basic web searching strategies such as using Boolean logic and truncation to narrow the parameters of a search. Figure 9.3 presents some of the more common search strategies that students can use to make their web searches more efficient and effective.

 Technology Connection Some of the more commonly used search engines for young children are:

- Ask for Kids, which allows users to enter a search in the form of a question: www.askforkids.com

- Yahoo! Kids, for ages 7 to 12: http://kids.yahoo.com
- Awesome Library: www.awesomelibrary.org
- KidsClick!, a search engine created by librarians: www.kidsclick.org

Choose a social studies topic from your elementary program of studies and come up with some search terms to use based on the information above on searching strategies. Try entering the same search terms in each of these engines and compare the results. What does this exercise tell you about having young children use these search engines?

Most search engines allow users to refine their web searches to images, news, or people, which can help to narrow search results significantly. A subject directory (e.g., Yahoo! Canada Directory, Google Directory), which is a catalogue of sites collected and organized into categories by humans instead of by automated programs, is an alternative for conducting narrower searches. Subject directories are often called subject "trees" because they start with a few main categories and then branch out into subcategories, topics, and subtopics. Many large directories, such as the Look Smart directory (http://search.looksmart.com), include a keyword search option that allows users to search categories such as health, food, cities, music, travel, sports, games, and education. Because directories cover only a small fraction of the sites and pages available on the web, they are most effective for finding general information on a given topic.

Teaching Students to Use Digitized Primary Sources

One of the greatest advantages of the web is that it provides easy access to primary sources so that students can engage with authentic materials such as diaries, artifacts, letters, photographs, speeches, maps, audio and video recordings, newspapers, art work, and posters. Using these historical records can enrich children's experiences of social studies by bringing history to life in the classroom. For example, children can learn to have empathy for others as they "live" the experiences of the past through the eyes of the person who created the primary source. Children also can be assisted in understanding that history is ongoing and that primary sources are not necessarily from a long time ago but rather can be things from their own short past. However, the proliferation of online primary sources now available on the web makes it increasingly important that children are engaged in activities with these resources that help to develop their critical viewing skills. Learning about point of view can be particularly effective when the children begin to interrogate these sources as records that reflect an individual's perspective. By looking at a variety of primary sources about the same event or time period, children can discover that people did not all necessarily perceive a particular event the same way. Therefore, digital primary sources need to be interrogated just like all of the other resources we have examined so far. The Do History website's Using Primary Sources page (http://dohistory.org/on_your_own/toolkit/primarySources.html) suggests that the following questions be used to interrogate primary sources:

- What is it?
- Who wrote or made it?
- When was it written or made?

- Where was it written or made?
- How was it written or made?
- What evidence does this source contribute to my research?
- Why was this document/object written or made?
- Who was the intended audience/user?
- What questions does this source raise? What don't we know about this source?
- What other information do we have about this document or object?
- What other sources are similar to this one?
- What other sources might help to answer our questions about this source?
- What else do we need to know in order to understand the evidence in this source?
- What have others said about this or similar sources?
- How does this source help me to answer my research question?
- How does evidence from this source alter or fit into existing interpretations of the past?

ACTIVE ENGAGEMENT

1. Go to the Historical Treasure Chests website (www.k12science.org/curriculum/treasure) to examine an integrated social studies and language arts activity for helping children to distinguish between primary and secondary sources. What would this site teach children about the use of photos and artifacts as information sources?

2. Try the primary source investigation activity at www.cyberbee.com/yesteryear/photo.html. How might a site such as this help children to collect data from historical photos?

3. For other ideas about using primary sources, read the article "Using Primary Sources in the Classroom" on the U.S. Library of Congress website: http://memory.loc.gov/ammem/ndlpedu/lessons/primary.html. Also visit the U.S. National Archives website (http://www.archives.gov/education/lessons), which offers suggestions for teaching with documents, artifacts, photographs, posters, and sound recordings, as well as worksheets on how to analyze the information collected from these sources. How do these sites help you to think about using online primary sources in your teaching of social studies?

4. The Histor!ca website is an example of a site offering primary source audio recordings. Visit the website and play the "History by the Minute" audio files at http://www.histori.ca/minutes. How might a site such as this be best used as a social studies resource?

Encouraging Students to Use Online Museums as Resources

Students can also access the collections of a number of museums that have been put on the web. One online museum, at www.civilisations.ca, provides access to the exhibitions and collections of the Canadian Museum of Civilization, the Canadian Children's Museum, the Canadian War Museum, the Canadian Postal Museum, and the Virtual Museum of New France, among other resources. Another Canadian museum site appropriate for younger children is the British Columbia Archives' Amazing Time Machine (http://www.bcarchives.gov.bc.ca/exhibits/timemach), which has 11 different galleries geared to young children, with minimal text and many archival photographs. Social studies–related topics addressed on this site include, among others, families and communities in B.C. history, First Nations peoples of B.C., multiculturalism, and the Cariboo Gold Rush. The Pier 21 website (www.pier21.ca) is another online museum offering a variety of resources about immigration to Canada, including some personal stories.

Using Computer Software as Social Studies Resources

Providing access to the web is just one way of using computers to support and enhance students' research. Computer software that encourages students to collect, organize, and analyze information can also assist with the development of important research skills. For instance, digitized encyclopedias are an excellent source of information. *World Book 2006*, the *Youth Encyclopedia of Canada, Encyclopædia Britannica,* and *Encarta* are all available in CD-ROM format, which teachers may choose to use in schools or classrooms where internet access is limited. Using the software version can also alleviate a teacher's concerns about students accessing non-approved sites when searching online. These encyclopedias are easier for children to use than the more cumbersome print versions, as they provide built-in search functions and other features to scaffold children's learning. They are also easier to store and to update than the hardcover print versions.

Using Simulation-Based Software

Most of the available educational software is simulation based. Electronic simulations are computerized re-creations of real-world situations that lack any of the limiting factors of danger, time, cost, or distance that can be a part of real-life learning environments. These simulations can be used to show cause and effect through real-life examples, rather than leaving students to try to visualize the consequences on their own. Simulations can also provide students opportunities to practise testing newly acquired concepts and skills, solving problems, and making decisions. Often, simulations allow students to manipulate and modify a situation and then receive feedback that shows the results of their decisions and actions. Such an environment allows abstract ideas to be transmuted into a form that is more meaningful and interactive for the learner. Different approaches can easily be taken with these manipulations in order that students can compare and contrast the results to find the best solution to a problem.

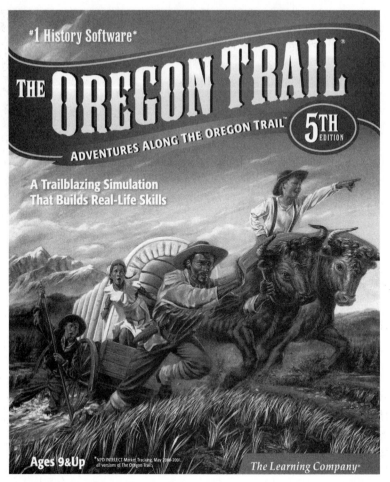

The Oregon Trail, 5th edition

One popular example of simulation software is the *SimCity* series by Electronic Arts Inc. (see http://simcity.ea.com). For example, *SIMCity 4* immerses students into the world of urban planning by having them take on the role of mayor to make decisions about how to build and control a city, make a budget and decide on resource allocation, and deal with factors such as natural disasters and citizens' concerns.

Other simulation software can be used to augment the teaching of historical and geographical understanding. Riverdeep Inc./The Learning Company, for example, has developed *The Yukon Trail,* which involves the user in the 1897 Klondike Gold Rush in the Yukon; the *Oregon Trail* 5th edition, which allows the user to lead a wagon train through the early American West; *Amazon Trail* 3rd edition, in which the user explores the Amazon rainforest; and *Africa Trail,* in which the user takes a modern-day bike trip across Africa. All of these pieces of software are appropriate for upper elementary–aged students. They provide some opportunity for students to engage not only in information collection but also in using that information to problem solve and make decisions. However, all of these software programs are very limited in the content they cover and, therefore, in their appropriateness for addressing social studies learning outcomes.

Several software programs created by Riverdeep Inc./The Learning Company are less topic-specific and could be used to cover a wider range of outcomes. For example, *Where in the World Is Carmen Sandiego?,* for ages 10 and up, involves the user in searching around the globe for clues about the whereabouts of the story's main characters while they acquire important geographical place and location information about 60 countries. Its companion piece, *Junior Detective,* for ages 5 to 8, allows nonreaders to travel the world looking for clues using the visuals and maps provided. A third selection, *Carmen Sandiego's Great Chase Through Time,* could be used to engage upper elementary–aged students in adventures during a variety of historical periods, ranging from ancient Egypt to the present day. However, while these software programs teach some knowledge about world geography and history respectively, they are also very game-like and might be best used as part of "free time" or in a learning centre.

While designed mainly for English as a Second Language (ESL) learners, the CD-ROM *Explore Canada: Canada's History and Geography in Plain Language,* created by the Department of Canadian Heritage: Parks Canada (www.newlanguage .ca), contains very useful information on Canada that could be used to support students' research. Also for new immigrants to Canada and ESL learners, NAS Software Inc.'s program My *Canada* (www.nas.ca/mycanada/new .htm) covers topics in Canadian history, government, and culture and would be useful for all elementary-aged learners.

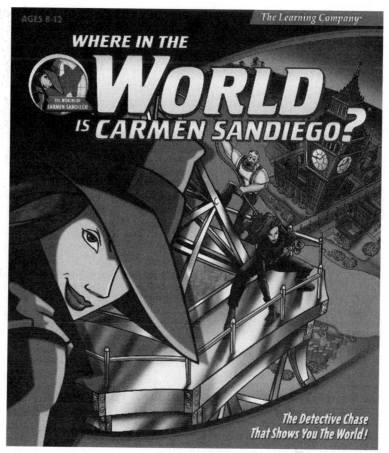

Where in the World Is Carmen Sandiego?

Explore Canada

Computer software programs can be highly motivating resources for helping children to explore social studies concepts.

Numerous other pieces of educational software are available to support and enhance the teaching of geographic skills. Tom Snyder Productions (http://www.tomsnyder.com), for example, has created the following programs. In *Geography Search*, students learn about latitude, longitude, the earth's rotation, weather, and wind patterns through a simulated ocean voyage to the New World during the age of exploration. The *Inspirer Geography Series: International Inspirer 4.0* engages students in Grade 4 and above in collaboratively investigating issues related to geography in countries around the world. Other programs in this series focus specifically on Europe, Africa, and Asia. *Neighbourhood MapMachine 2.0* involves students in constructing maps to learn about directional terms. Edmark (http://www.synapseadaptive.com/edmark) has created *Trudy's Time and Place House,* which develops primary-aged learners' understanding of directions, and *Travel the World with Timmy*, which allows the K–2 student to explore Russia, France, Argentina, Japan, and Kenya. *My First Amazing World Explorer* by DK Multimedia (http://learnatglobal.com) helps young children to compare and contrast various locations around the globe.

Tom Snyder Productions has also designed other software that promotes higher-level thinking and decision-making skills. *Decisions, Decisions 5.0,* for example, engages older elementary students (ages 10 and above) in collaboratively and interactively investigating issues such as prejudice, violence in the media, lying and cheating, and saving the environment. Two programs based on children's books are *If the World Were a Village,* which provides K–6 learners with opportunities for hands-on exploration of the storybook by David Smith (see Chapter 8 of this text), and *How Would You Survive?,* based on the series of print books of the same title, about the worlds of the ancient Egyptians, Vikings, and Aztecs.

Deciding What Simulation-Based Software Will Best Meet the Needs of Your Social Studies Program

Careful perusal of all software selections prior to use with children is crucial, and is important to the development of a quality social studies program. As with any other resource, before you use any piece of software you will need to be sure that you are very familiar with its contents. One aspect of careful selection is determining whether the piece of software represents your curriculum in an accurate and sufficiently detailed way. Some software programs cover only a very narrow slice of a topic and can also deal with content that is extra to the curriculum. Further, you need to be aware of the level of interactivity that the software promotes. Software that has a drill-and-practice format tends to emphasize the transmittal of information followed by the testing of students' recall of that information through lower-level questioning and drills. As with textbooks, instructional

FIGURE 9.4 ■ Suggested Criteria for Selecting Software

Encourages active and collaborative learning

Accuracy of information

Adds to user's knowledge about the topic

Appropriateness of reading level and vocabulary

Developmental appropriateness

Logically sequenced

Relevant to the topic and the curriculum

Up-to-date information

Interesting and visually appealing

Able to work independently with ease

Allows for child interactivity and control

Aesthetically pleasing

Represents diverse groups and gender balance

Free of bias, stereotyping

Based in concrete experience

Encourages critical thinking

outcomes of software programs are strongly influenced by the goals and tasks in the programs—both by what is included and by what isn't. Consequently, you will need to think through your own curriculum first and then find ways to integrate technology so that it meets your curricular needs. Figure 9.4 presents some recommended criteria to consider when deciding on what software to select to complement your social studies program.

ACTIVE ENGAGEMENT

Choose one of the pieces of software presented in this chapter or locate a new piece in your institution's library and critique it using the criteria presented in Figure 9.4. How useful is the list of criteria? Are there any other criteria that you would add to the list? With which grade level would you use this software? What topic from the social studies curriculum might this software program help you to address, and how might you use the software in your teaching of this topic?

Using Information Organization Software

Other software-based resources that can be used to support students' research are database programs. A few of the programs more commonly used in schools are Apple Works, Microsoft Access, and FileMaker Pro (which has both Windows and Mac platforms). Databases are particularly helpful for providing students with opportunities to access, store, and organize data. These resources allow not only for manipulation of information during research but also for analysis of that information. Perhaps their most important function is that they can help students to make meaning from raw data. Databases can be effective for stimulating higher-level thinking, and for enabling the visualization of complex historical relationships, the integration of information from a variety of sources, and the learning of facts as well as concepts. They can also assist students in making predictions and comparisons, observing trends, drawing conclusions, and formulating generalizations.

Databases can be loosely structured by the teacher so that the students can select the information they wish to present and design their own way of presenting it. For example, as part of a unit on "Canada in the World," students could collect and record data from databases for use in comparing and contrasting the geography of cities, communities, and countries, or the lifestyles of individuals in the class, the community, and around the world. The class could begin by brainstorming a list of things that they would like to know about other countries. For example, categories of information collected might include, among others, name of country, population, land dimensions, capital city, latitude, longitude, continent, major water bodies, climate, industry, and resources. A generalization emerging from the use of this database might be: People's needs vary according to where they live.

Another software tool, the spreadsheet, provides an alternative structure for organizing the data students collect. Using a spreadsheet can allow students to sort data in a variety of ways so that it can be analyzed from a number of different perspectives. This organized data can then be analyzed more easily for the purpose of problem solving and decision making. Microsoft Office Suite (for both Windows and Mac) and AppleWorks are application software packages that combine word processor, database, and spreadsheet programs.

CLASSROOM APPLICATION

When teaching his Grade 5 students about Canadian geography, Mr. Bandy began by having the class use the graphic organizer software program *Inspiration 8* by Inspiration Software (www.inspiration.com) to generate a brainstorm web of what they already knew about the various regions of Canada. For an opener to the unit, Mr. Bandy decided to use *Cross Country Canada 2*, designed for ages 9 and above by Ingenuity Works Inc., to actively engage his students in learning about the regions of Canada. Using this program, students experience driving an 18-wheel truck across Canada, picking up and delivering a variety of commodities in 70 Canadian cities, and facing many problem-solving situations along the way. Mr. Bandy felt that this piece of software would pique his students' interest in the topic and act as a motivator to want to learn more. At the midpoint of the unit, while the students were engaged in research projects about the various regions of Canada, Mr. Bandy used the CD-ROM *The Great Canadian Adventure* by Micro-Intel Educational Software (http://www.innovativeeducation.com/microintel) to help his students to learn specific content knowledge by actively involving them in an exploration of the culture, people, and history of their region and others. Students created a spreadsheet to keep track of the information they gathered about each region. At the end of the unit, students checked back with their initial brainstorm webs to see in what areas their ideas had changed.

Chapter Summary

The focus of this final chapter on resource selection has been on the electronic resources available to support your social studies program. We began by defining the term "digital literacy" and identifying some of the skills crucial for digitally literate citizens. The emphasis of the remainder of the chapter was on those electronic resources that are available to support students' research and information gathering. We looked at the potential of the web as a source of information for both teachers' professional development and students' online social studies research. Some of the information sources available in audio, video, graphic, and text formats that were examined included primary source materials, museum collections, and online encyclopedias. We also examined some of the information retrieval skills that students need in order to efficiently and effectively make use of these web-based resources. In particular, we explored ways to develop students' searching skills and their critical viewing skills. Finally, we looked at educational software—specifically databases, spreadsheets, and other content-specific educational software—for its potential to assist students in information collection and organization. You were cautioned once again that, as a teacher, you would need to view these software programs with a critical eye in terms of how they would help to develop your students' understanding of the social studies content being taught before deciding how to use them in your social studies program.

Ultimately, resource selection will be one of the important responsibilities you will have as a teacher. Whether you decide to use a textbook, media source, primary resource, artifact, children's non-fiction or fiction literature, website, or piece of computer software, your resources will need to address the children's needs and interests as well as your province or territory's curricular learning outcomes and your overall program goals. It is never too early to start a collection of resources for use in your future teaching.

Part Four

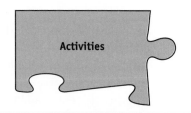

Activities

What Activities Would Help You to Meet the Goals of Your Social Studies Program?

In the three previous parts of this book, we have explored the process of defining your goals for your social studies program and then selecting content and resources to match those goals as well as the needs and interests of the children in your classroom. In Part Four, our area of inquiry will involve you in investigating the question of how to teach. The chapters in this part of the book each address a sub-question that helps to answer the larger question of what activities would help you to meet your goals for your social studies program. Chapter 10 asks, What approach to teaching would best meet your goals for your social studies program? Three approaches to teaching, each with differing goals and beliefs about learning—and the types of activities that support such learning—are examined in this chapter. What we know about children's learning needs is also reviewed, to help you in your decision making about what approach to teaching you will adopt. Chapter 11 asks, How can learning activities help you to meet your goals for your social studies program? Differing approaches to student research are presented here, as are activities for developing the skills of higher-level thinking collaboration and cooperation, and participation. Chapter 12 asks, How can online learning activities be used to develop students' higher-level skills? Multiple examples of ways to use the web as a pedagogical tool to enhance your social studies program and support your students' learning are provided in this chapter.

Chapter 10

What Approach to Teaching Would Best Meet Your Goals for Your Social Studies Program?

When deciding how to teach the content you have chosen using the selected resources, it is important to look for an approach that addresses your beliefs about the most beneficial learning experiences for your students. To guide you in determining your preferred teaching method, this chapter begins by exploring three different approaches to teaching, each based on differing views of the roles and responsibilities of the teacher and the learner. A review of what we know about how children learn follows, to assist you in making decisions about what approach to teaching you will adopt.

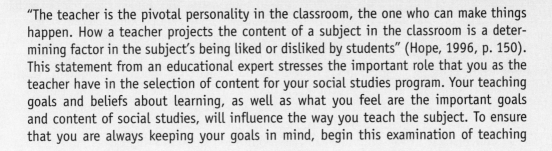

LOOKING BACK

"The teacher is the pivotal personality in the classroom, the one who can make things happen. How a teacher projects the content of a subject in the classroom is a determining factor in the subject's being liked or disliked by students" (Hope, 1996, p. 150). This statement from an educational expert stresses the important role that you as the teacher have in the selection of content for your social studies program. Your teaching goals and beliefs about learning, as well as what you feel are the important goals and content of social studies, will influence the way you teach the subject. To ensure that you are always keeping your goals in mind, begin this examination of teaching approaches by looking back at the orientations to social studies as citizenship education in Chapter 4 that seemed to fit best with your beliefs about what type of learning is most important in the development of good citizens. How might these beliefs affect the way you teach in the future? Have your ideas changed in any way since reading Chapter 4?

Three Approaches to Teaching Based on Different Teacher Beliefs and Goals

Three differing approaches to teaching—teacher directed, shared direction, and student directed—are discussed in the following sections. Each of these approaches is driven by specific beliefs about what students need to learn, how best to ensure that students learn it, and who is in charge of the learning. The main difference among the three methods lies in their views about the locus of authority, or who controls decisions about what and how to learn.

Teacher-Directed Classrooms

A teacher-directed approach to instruction places the teacher in the position of being the sole authority in the classroom and assuming total control over all teaching and learning decisions. This approach is informed by the belief that the teacher holds the vital knowledge about the content and skills to be learned and must impart that knowledge to the students.

Advocates of teacher-directed classrooms see the process of learning as both logical and sequential, so that students must be carefully directed into activity sequences that best ensure maximum cognitive, skill, and affective growth. These sequenced activities are believed to result in cumulative learning, as activity number one builds a foundation and prepares students for the experiences to follow in activity two, and so on. Topics are broken down into smaller components, and then sequenced from simple to complex and taught to the students in small steps. For example, history's chronological sequencing or geography's whole-to-parts study of a country may dictate a particular sequence of activities.

In this approach, the teacher is the focal point in the preparation and carrying out of all activities. The teacher (with the guidance of the curriculum and the authorized textbook) sets the objectives for activities, as well as the content, type and sequencing, pacing, resources to be used, and assessment plan. The students are guided through the instructions for activities by the teacher, who determines the best use of class time, and the students are dependent on the teacher for direction, motivation, and assessment. Lessons are usually taught didactically and tend to be textbook, lecture, worksheet, and fixed-response driven. Instruction is teacher centred and occurs frequently with the whole class, while small-group or individual instruction is much less common. Teacher talk exceeds student talk during instruction, and limited student-to-student and student-to-teacher interaction takes place. In this approach to teaching, all aspects of the classroom environment are carefully managed and controlled by the teacher.

The students' role in a teacher-directed classroom is to respond to the teacher's questions and directions and to assimilate the knowledge imparted to them by the teacher to ensure that their understanding mirrors that of the teacher. It is further assumed that all students learn the same way. "What [the student] should learn is decided for her and neatly packaged into student-sized chunks. How to learn is a pre-ordained pathway consisting of recording and organizing information into categories and compartments that can be reproduced at will, in as near-perfect a form as possible, whenever required for the purposes of 'assessment'" (Pike & Selby, 1988, p. 50).

A teacher-directed approach leads to students assuming a passive role toward authority.

Paulo Freire (1970) called this approach to teaching "banking education," which he described as education "where the teacher leads the students to memorize mechanically the narrated content. Worse yet, it turns them into 'containers,' into 'receptacles' to be 'filled' by the teacher. The more completely he fills the receptacles, the better a teacher he is" (p. 58). According to Freire (p. 54), banking education has the following characteristics:

- The teacher teaches and the students are taught.
- The teacher knows everything and the students know nothing.
- The teacher thinks and the students are thought about.
- The teacher talks and the students listen meekly.
- The teacher disciplines and the students are disciplined.
- The teacher chooses the program content, and the students adapt to it.
- The teacher is the subject of the learning process, while the pupils are mere objects.

REFLECTION POINT

Which view of social studies as citizenship education does the teacher-directed approach to teaching exemplify? What kind of citizenship qualities would be promoted by the hidden curriculum that underlies this approach? What rules, norms, and self-concepts are students learning? What effect might these roles have on the development of independence, self-direction, and responsibility? What are students learning about their own power and influence?

Michael, a Grade 3 student, was directed to read a passage in his social studies textbook on the Inuit, write down five things about them, and then draw a picture showing their food, clothing, and shelter. Looking at his answers, below, what do you think that he learned from this exercise?

Early Inuit People

① The Inuit struggled to eat and keep warm

② Inuits have light brown skin. ③ Inuit live together.

④ Iniit live in a place called the Arctic. ⑤ The Inuit don't like to be called Eskimo.

Shared Direction Classrooms

Brooks and Brooks (1993) argue, "Current impediments to student understanding include lessons dominated by 'teacher-talk,' lessons that are predominantly textbook oriented, the devaluing of students' thinking, and overemphasis of curriculum mastery" (p. v). They contend that teachers can "begin to make a difference in how students learn by encouraging student-to-student interaction, initiating lessons that foster cooperative learning . . . [and] making students responsible for their own learning" (p. v). Teachers who adopt a shared direction approach to teaching are attempting to address some of these concerns by shifting the focus of authority in their classrooms so that students share in making decisions about their learning. When this type of approach is used, students are given a degree of autonomy to plan jointly with the teacher the goals, pace, method, and assessment of their learning.

Advocates of a shared direction approach to teaching see each student as a unique individual capable of his or her own meaning making. They view knowledge not as something predetermined by the teacher or another authority, but rather as something that each individual constructs based on his or her experiences. Rather than pre-designing a unit in a lock-step sequence to develop a particular main idea, as the teacher-directed approach dictates, teachers who believe in shared decision making draw on their students' prior experiences and ideas to decide on the direction that the teaching of a particular unit will take. The teacher recognizes that knowledge is shared among teachers and students and that it is important to build on the personal experiences, strategies, and existing knowledge patterns and constructs that children bring to the classroom. The students therefore help to choose and organize the content to be learned and are also invited to set their own personal learning goals within the framework of what is to be learned. The teacher provides options for activities that are of interest to students and that meet their varied developmental needs and interests. Students are also directly involved in assessing what they are learning in the light of their goals. In this way, the teacher acts more as a facilitator of the learning than as the sole director, and the process of learning becomes the important focus of classroom activities.

Within a shared direction approach, social studies classroom work is often done in a collaborative and cooperative fashion through activities such as student-designed projects, open-ended inquiries, and learning centres and stations. Most instruction occurs with either individuals or groups instead of with the whole class, and the

In a shared direction classroom, the teacher's role is to probe student answers with further questions to reveal their thinking and uncover any misconceptions.

amount of student talk about learning tasks is at least equal to, if not greater than, the amount of teacher talk. Children are challenged to ask their own questions and to apply critical thinking skills through the use of higher-level questioning. They are encouraged to construct and use their own knowledge and to share that knowledge with others.

A shared direction classroom is usually arranged in a manner that encourages students to work together as a whole class, or in small groups, or an individual workspace; much movement of desks, tables, and chairs occurs in the realigning of the classroom workspace on a regular basis. Varied instructional resources, including computers, are available in the classroom so that students can use them independently or in small groups; the teacher and the students jointly determine the use of these resources.

REFLECTION POINT

How might students learn to see themselves differently through experiencing a shared direction approach? What roles are they expected to take within this approach? What roles and relationships to authority would students learn? What hidden curriculum underlies this approach?

The intentional sharing of control with the students that is central to a shared direction approach changes the roles that students become accustomed to taking in the classroom, and therefore also changes the self-concepts they develop from the learning experiences. Using learning centres (sometimes referred to as learning stations) in the classroom is one way of shifting the locus of authority away from the teacher and toward students. Learning centres contain collections of different types of activities and resources at varied difficulty levels that address a particular theme or topic and allow for student decision making and self-pacing. Some activities can be completed independently; others call for working with a partner or in small groups. Students take on the responsibility of choosing from a large selection of activities the ones they prefer, completing them in the sequence they prefer and in group sizes they prefer, using resources they prefer, and generating products they prefer and at a rate at which they can succeed.

Using learning centres is particularly effective when you are planning for a hidden curriculum that seeks to develop students into independent and responsible learners. To increase the level of shared direction in the classroom, the students can share in jointly creating a learning centre with the teacher by identifying areas of interest to extend and reinforce their learning about the topic under study, by suggesting ideas for activities, by designing and constructing parts of the centre, and by bringing in materials. Clear goals for the use of the learning centres need to be set, and the activities in the centres should be focused on achieving those goals. The children need to be made aware of the goals so that they understand the purpose behind the activities available at the centres. Learning centres are more satisfying for both the students and the teacher if the intended outcomes are clearly understood and both parties can observe the learning that is happening. One of the added benefits of using learning centres is that the teacher is freed up to do more small-group and one-on-one instruction where it is most needed.

The following is a sample selection of the learning centre activities that Ms. Best used with her Grade 5 social studies class to supplement the teaching of a unit on Canada's physical regions and political divisions. Her students were encouraged to select at least six of the available activities. When an activity was completed, they were to bring their work to Ms. Best for discussion. Each student then received one of the letters in the word "Canada" to place next to his or her name on a tracking board. When all six activities had been completed, the students all had the word C-A-N-A-D-A spelled out next to their names.

1. Games: Complete a jigsaw puzzle of Canada's provinces and territories. Play a matching game that challenges players to connect physical regions by shape and to identify their location on a map of Canada. Play a trivia board game that has questions about the physical regions and political divisions of Canada.

2. Bulletin Board Display: Cut out magazine pictures of various parts of Canada and place them on a large map of Canada displayed on the classroom bulletin board. Come up with several adjectives to describe what the pictures tell about each region and use these adjectives to write a poem.

3. Letters Home: Choose a region of Canada to explore; then keep a scrapbook of an imaginary journey around the region and write letters home to provide details about the trip.

4. Travel Pamphlet: Choose a province or territory of Canada and design a travel brochure that will entice tourists to visit.

5. Art Activities: Learn about provincial flower emblems and pick one to draw in abstract form. Study the paintings of the Group of Seven; then produce a landscape painting of a specific region in Canada using some of their techniques. (See www .groupofsevenart.com for images of Group of Seven paintings).

6. Current Events: Study an issue of importance to the residents of one of the regions of Canada. Using the Internet, research various viewpoints on the issue and propose a solution to the problem in a letter to the editor of a local newspaper.

7. Computers: Test your knowledge of Canada's geography by using the map games available on the Social Studies page of the iKnowthat.com website http://www .iknowthat.com). Play the *Cross Canada 2* software simulation game and tell about your adventures.

Here is a sample of an activity card for Ms. Best's learning centre on Canada's regions. What do you notice about the various components of this task card?

(Continued)

Task #5 – The Group of Seven

Purpose of Activity:

To be able to describe the techniques of a group of famous Canadian landscape painters.

To depict personal knowledge about the regions of Canada through painting.

Materials:

For this activity you will need:

- a sheet of black construction paper
- oil pastels
- a piece of white chalk
- a piece of newspaper to lay underneath the construction paper while you work

Background Information:

In 1920 a group of adventurous Canadian artists got together to paint the land of Canada in a new way. They called themselves the Group of Seven. Most paintings in their time in Canada were about gentle farmland, but the Group of Seven wanted to paint Canada wild and untamed. They decided to paint how Canada made them feel inside, not only how Canada looked. The Group of Seven should actually be called the Group of Nine because one of the original members died and one member left and was replaced.

Activity:

1. Look at all of the painting cards. The title of the painting and the name of the artist are on the back of each card.

2. Pick the painting that makes you feel best. Do you think the Group of Seven succeeded in painting how Canada feels and looks? Why or why not?

3. Create your own unique version of your favourite Group of Seven painting. What will you do differently to make it yours?

Assessment:

In your journal, reflect on the experience of trying to represent what you have learned about a region of Canada in a pictorial format.

LOOKING BACK

Here is Ms. Best's reaction to using the learning centre on Canada's regions in her classroom for the first time: "In spite of my personal approval of learning centres, I have to admit [I had] a certain amount of skepticism. As it turned out, the children were focused and self-motivated and my uncertainty was unfounded. I was surprised by the fact that they did not just go for the enticing puzzle and trivia game but also chose the other activities as well, which just goes to show that kids really do have varied interests and preferences. They actually did read directions for the most part and even commented on the clarity of the task cards, but the biggest surprise for me was the focus and effort they immediately brought to the tasks. The kids really demonstrated that they like having choices and taking some control and responsibility for what they produce. They obviously would rather get busy and get their hands dirty so to speak than sit and listen. And for me this clearly has implications for teaching and planning activities that meet this preference."

What does Ms. Best's reflection suggest to you about the shared direction approach to teaching? Discuss with a classmate any experience you have had with learning centres as a student or teacher.

Technology Connection

1. The following two websites provide examples of learning centre activities, as well as strategies for setting up and managing the use of centres in the elementary classroom:

   - The TeacherVision website offers ideas for scheduling, grouping, and rotating students through centres. On the home page (www.teachervision.fen.com), enter "learning centers" in the search tool and scroll down to the article "The Basics of Centers."

   - Visit Kathy Schrock's Guide for Educators (http://school.discovery.com/schrockguide/edlearn.html) to choose among a number of links to resources on learning centres.

2. The Classroom Centers Chatboard (http://teachers.net/projects/centers/posts.html) is a good place to engage in discussion with other teachers or read the interchange among teachers regarding the use of learning centres. Think of a question that you have about using learning centres and post it to this chatboard. How do the responses help you to think about using centres in your future teaching?

3. For more information on learning centres and examples of various types of centres, follow the link on the book's companion website to the Learning Centres page on the Regina Public Schools and Saskatchewan Learning website.

The shared direction approach to education, when it is authentically implemented, enhances students' creativity, self-concept, cooperation, responsibility, positive attitude toward school, curiosity, and independence. The approach also promotes a positive student–teacher relationship through the shared responsibility for the learning that takes place. However, critics caution that such an approach to teaching is more difficult to manage and that it can make less efficient use of class time, as encouraging children to share in the decision making about what they want to learn, and how they will go about learning it, takes significantly more time to orchestrate than having the teacher make these decisions for everyone. This approach can also make students' learning more difficult to assess, as each child could potentially be producing something very different to demonstrate what they have learned—e.g., a poem, a model, a slide show, a written report, etc. Another criticism is that this approach often focuses less on content coverage and more on skill development. While skill development is an important goal of social studies—some would say the most important goal—there is a concern on the part of more traditional teachers that learning and recalling a common body of content is of primary importance. Lastly, one of the greatest challenges for most teachers who adopt this approach is being willing to relinquish some of the power over the decision making in the classroom.

Student-Directed Classrooms

A third method of teaching is the student-directed approach. This approach shifts the focus of authority in the classroom almost entirely to the students by envisioning the class as a community of researchers. The focus of the social studies program becomes the learners instead of the teacher or the curriculum. The teacher's role is that of a consultant who systematically encourages students to take more and more responsibility for planning their own learning activities. Students are encouraged to make personal educational choices, as they are put in control of many decisions about their own learning. The objective is for students to set goals for their learning, determine what they would like to learn and how they wish to go about learning it, decide on what resources they would like to use, demonstrate their learning in a way that best fits with their preferred learning style, and decide on the best way to to go about assessing their own learning. Developing in students a sense of pride in their ability to teach themselves and investigate and find answers to their own questions is a key outcome of this approach.

By giving students control over decisions about the activities they engage in, the teacher's intention is to increase students' sense of control, ownership, and responsibility for their own learning while ensuring the growth of knowledge and skills. Intrinsic motivation, or self-motivation, is central to the student-directed approach. Students are provided with opportunities to work in their own cognitive and learning styles and to assess their own work and learning processes in ways that encourage the kind of internal locus of control and intrinsic motivation that are needed to generate creativity and self-motivation.

Learning contracts or student plans for independent projects are commonly used to promote student-directed learning. These contracts or work plans are negotiated between the teacher and individuals or small groups of students. The learning is carefully tailored by the teacher to fit each student's unique learning needs and interests; the content and activities a particular student engages with depend upon the student's decision about what he or she wishes to learn and how he or she would like to go about learning it. The teacher has the important role of helping students to identify the gaps in their knowledge and of determining what they need to know. The teacher also needs to ensure that what a student plans to do is going to be sufficiently challenging but not too difficult.

CLASSROOM APPLICATION

Miss Singh uses the following contract with her Grade 6 class to negotiate their independent project work. The students fill in the contract and then meet with her to discuss their plan.

Learner Contract

Date _____

Name: _____

Focus Topic: _____

My Questions: _____

_____

My Research Plan and Timeline: _____

_____

_____

_____

I feel _____

_____

Fill in this part after teacher meeting:

My Comments: _____

_____

Teacher's Comments: _____

_____

Teacher's Signature: _____

Student's Signature: _____

Reflection is a critical part of these work plans. By engaging in exercises such as the one presented in Figure 10.1 on the next page, students are encouraged to pause at various points throughout their learning activities to look back at their work plan. They reflect on what they have been doing in order to determine what is working for them and what is not, as well as noting any unanticipated surprises that have arisen in their learning journey, and then reassess

FIGURE 10.1 ■ Reflective Exercise for Independent Projects

1. What steps have you gone through to complete your project?

2. What strategies and resources have you been using?

3. What difficulties have you experienced? How did you overcome them?

4. What is going well for you?

5. What have you been feeling over the course of this project?

6. What do you know now that you didn't before you started working on this project?

7. What will you do differently now?

8. What are your next steps? Does your work plan need to be revised?

their work plan accordingly. Frequent student–teacher conferences, in which teachers talk with children about what they are doing and why, can help the children to learn to be more reflective. Students using contracts or independent project plans are often engaged in integrated, cross-curricular projects that incorporate important content and skills from all of the subject areas. Instead of dividing class time into predetermined subject-area chunks, the teacher provides students with extended blocks of time to work on their independent projects.

ACTIVE ENGAGEMENT

Take a few moments to think about a project that you are currently working on. Use the questions in Figure 10.1 to help you reflect on your work to date. Does this reflective exercise help you in any way?

The project approach, as described by Lillian Katz and Sylvia Chard (2000), is an example of a student-directed approach that involves either whole classes or small groups in investigating things from the children's real world. For example, a combined class of Grade 1 and 2 children decided on the project of improving their school's playground area. They began their research by going on field trips to visit school playgrounds and interviewing children and teachers from other schools. They also conducted polls of students and teachers in their school to see what factors they felt would contribute to create the ideal playground space. Expert guests were also invited to come and speak to the class about what changes they would recommend (e.g., one student's parent was an engineer and another student had a relative who was an environmentalist). Once all of the data was collected, a design for the playground was drawn up, and the children then built features to include in their new playground, including benches, a compost area, and a sandbox.

See the Project Approach website (www.projectapproach.org) for examples of similar elementary-level projects. How might you use a project of this kind to achieve the outcomes of your social studies curriculum? What other subject areas might you be able to integrate into the project?

Two key factors in student learning that teachers who choose a more student-directed teaching style need to consider are the varying abilities of students to work independently and the diverse learning needs of individuals. Some students are very teacher-dependent and, if expected to take full responsibility for planning their own learning, will be off-task much of the time. They have not had enough previous opportunities to accept responsibility, structure their own time use, or work cooperatively and productively in small groups. The teacher needs to take a more active role in helping to ensure that such students have adequate structure in their learning process in order to promote successful learning as well as growth in responsibility, independence, and self-direction. A more structured, short-term contract accompanied by frequent teacher checkpoints during which the student confers with the teacher about his or her progress is necessary for a dependent learner. However, the intention of the student-directed teacher is to consistently encourage all students to take greater levels of initiative. To the extent that growth in independence occurs, teachers need to gradually reduce their own control over the sequencing, pacing, group size, materials used, and other learning activity components.

 Technology Connection Follow the link on the book's companion website to the Learning Contracts page on the Regina Public Schools and Saskatchewan Learning website. This resource provides an in-depth look at learning contracts, including the theory behind these contracts, teacher and student responsibilities, starting points, organizational tips, common questions, sample contracts, and student and teacher assessment of contracts. According to this website, what information about the independent project or work to be completed should be included in a learning contract? Is there anything that you would add to the sample contract in the Classroom Application box on page 207 after examining this website?

The student-directed approach to teaching has a hidden curriculum that emphasizes growth in independence, responsibility, and initiative. However, this approach has been criticized for the high level of individualism that it promotes. The classroom, according to critics, becomes less about developing a community of learners and more about each student "doing his or her own thing." The teacher has the difficult task of orchestrating all of the individual plans and ensuring that students are meeting not only their own learning goals but also those of the required curriculum. Consequently, a teacher using a student-directed approach needs to be very knowledgeable about all of the curricular requirements for each subject area. Another criticism pertains to student resistance to the approach (Woods, 1994). Since the student-directed approach is relatively uncommon, most students, especially older ones, likely have not encountered it in their experience in school and therefore will need to be convinced of its legitimacy. The same holds true for many parents. As well, students unfamiliar with the approach will need to be taught the skills for working independently, and a supportive learning environment will need to be created—i.e., the teacher will need to have strategies for controlling factors such as noise level, movement in and out of the classroom, use of resources, and interaction among students.

REFLECTION POINT

Have you had any experience with the student-directed approach? If yes, how did you like it? If not, what do you think it might have been like if you had experienced this approach as a student? How might it work best?

The major difference among the three approaches to teaching discussed here is who holds the power to make decisions about what and how to learn (see Table 10.1). The teacher-directed approach prescribes a program to students, and the locus of control over the learning is therefore external to students. The students learn to be dependent on the teacher because they are being taught in a way that is teacher directed and teacher centred. In the shared direction approach, authority over the learning is shared by the teacher and students, who together determine what and how the students should learn. The student-directed approach sees the locus of authority over learning as being internal to the individual student, who formulates his or her own program of study for the most part. In each of these approaches, students learn to take on certain roles but not others, depending on how the teacher shares control over decisions. Thus, the degree of teacher–student sharing of control over decisions shapes a program's hidden curriculum.

TABLE 10.1 ■ Three Approaches to Teaching

MODE	TEACHER-DIRECTED	SHARED DIRECTION	STUDENT-DIRECTED
Learner Role	Dependent	Interdependent	Independent
Objectives	Predetermined	Jointly determined	Self-determined
Content	Disciplines or subjects	Problems or themes	Interests or concerns
Teacher Role	Director	Facilitator	Consultant
Methods	Teacher centred	Group centred	Individual centred
Outcome	Product oriented	Process oriented	Performance oriented
Focus	Doing things to the learner	Doing things for the group	Doing things with resources

ACTIVE ENGAGEMENT

Use the following questions to help you think about the hidden curriculum that under-pins each of the three approaches to teaching discussed in this chapter.

1. Who controls the decisions in the classroom in each approach?

2. What roles are students learning to take in each approach?

3. What kinds of self-concepts are encouraged by each approach?

4. Which approach to selecting activities would best promote the kinds of growth to which you gave highest priority in Part One?

In the following chart, under each approach, write either "teacher" or "student" in each box to indicate who has control over the factors shown in the first column.

FACTORS ABOUT WHICH DECISIONS ARE MADE	TEACHER-DIRECTED	SHARED DIRECTION	STUDENT-DIRECTED
Goals			
Content			
Materials			
Sequencing			
Pacing			
Activities			
Grouping			
Products			
Assessment			

What does this exercise tell you about the hidden curriculum underlying each approach? Which hidden curriculum best matches your goals and your conception of a good citizen? How do these hidden curricula influence your thinking about the goals you have set for your social studies teaching? Do they change your ideas in any way?

The hidden curriculum that underlies a teacher's preferred approach to teaching is important to consider because it can affect students' self-concepts and the roles and responsibilities they learn to take. The approach you decide to adopt in your social studies program can have powerful ramifications for your students not only in the present but also in their future lives as citizens. Students carry into their adult lives the self-concepts and role expectations developed during their schooling, which can influence the extent and nature of their participation in civic affairs such as voting, campaigning, letter writing, demonstrating, and organizing group actions.

Children's Learning Needs as an Influence on Choosing an Approach to Teaching

LOOKING BACK

Here is what Monica, a student teacher, recalled about her memories of school: "When I was a student of social studies all of my teachers taught the subject quite differently. I remember that in the lower grades a lot of worksheets and colouring was involved. Then as we got older we spent a lot of time studying maps, atlases, and encyclopedias to receive our information. My favourite memory of social studies included the study of China. In this unit our Grade 6 class built a replica of a city in China near the Great Wall of China. For this project we had to build the houses the people lived in (and thus had to research their architecture), their crops (and there found out that the rice plantation needed to be built on a slope), and had to build the Wall of China proportionate in size to the other structures. This hands-on activity taught us much more than all the worksheets and definitions we memorized. We had to find the information so that we could apply it to the project and as a result we remembered it."

What does Monica's experience suggest about what makes an effective approach to teaching from a child's perspective? Recall your own experiences in social studies classes from primary school through high school. How would you describe the way your teachers taught? How were their approaches similar and different? Which method did you prefer and why? How might these experiences influence your thinking about the most effective way(s) to teach?

When choosing an approach to use in your teaching, it is important to consider what we know about children's learning needs. Recall that, according to the principles of social constructivism, students learn best when (a) the content is relevant and the learning experience takes place in a context that is meaningful, (b) they are encouraged to engage in inquiry by asking questions and seeking answers, (c) their ideas are invited and acknowledged as being important, (d) learning new knowledge is viewed as a process of building on and revising previous knowledge and experiences, (e) they are afforded opportunities to examine their ideas, seek out patterns, and construct relationships between the new learning and their prior learning, and (f) they are encouraged to elaborate on their initial ideas and seek clarification through dialogue with the teacher and their peers, and with other experts and learners.

Our understanding of children's learning needs is also enhanced by what we know about the role of the brain in learning. You may recall from our discussion of brain research in Chapters 5 and 6 that a hands-on approach to learning increases what students remember about a learning experience. When students are actively and concretely involved in their learning and in putting what they learn to immediate use, and when they can see real-world applications for it, they retain more knowledge. As well, they are better able to transfer what they have learned to other learning situations and to apply it to new situations.

Activities that do not encourage students' active involvement in the learning process—such as listening to a lecture or presentation, reading about something, or looking at an audiovisual or a demonstration—are not as effective in the transfer, application, and retention of what is learned. Enriching and challenging environments that offer varied resources and instructional strategies are essential to learning. The best learning occurs in a low-threat, supportive environ-

Young children need firsthand sensory experiences; play and active learning are essential to the development of the young brain.

ment in which natural curiosity is sparked, emotions are engaged, and student response drives lessons, alters content, and shifts instructional strategies. In such an environment, student choice and self-pacing are encouraged, as are student autonomy and initiative. Students also need to be provided with plenty of opportunities to seek out patterns and construct relationships between their prior learning and their new knowledge. In addition, they need to take frequent pauses that allow them to both check for understanding and take time to process what they have learned.

According to researchers at the Centre for Applied Special Technology (CAST), which is a branch of Universal Design for Learning group, all brains are unique not only in their physiological and chemical makeup but also in their recognition network (how we select and categorize the information we are exposed to), their affective network (what excites, interests, and challenges us), and their strategic network (how we organize and present our ideas). (See the accompanying Technology Connection for more information on these networks.) In order for teachers to address the vast differences among learners' brains, CAST researchers recommend an approach that accounts for individual differences by providing students with multiple means of engaging in learning, acquiring information, and demonstrating what has been learned (see http://www.cast.org/research/udl).

 Technology Connection The Centre for Applied Special Technology (CAST) provides an activity that demonstrates how the three brain networks work. Visit CAST's Teaching Every Student website (www.cast.org/teachingeverystudent), click on Tools and Activities, and then scroll down and click on the activity Your Three Brain Networks.

ACTIVE ENGAGEMENT

In *Brain Matters: Translating Research into Classroom Practice,* Patricia Wolfe (2001) states, "The more we understand about the brain, the better we'll be able to design instruction to match how it learns best" (p. 1). Which of the three approaches to teaching examined at the beginning of this chapter seems to fit best with what we know about the brain and learning? What would instruction in this brain research–based classroom look like?

What we know about children's diverse learning styles also contributes to our understanding of their learning needs. We looked at learning styles and their influences on students' learning in Chapter 7. However, this earlier discussion considered only the *cognitive* dimension of learning—i.e., the various ways in which learners perceive and order information and ideas. Other dimensions of students' learning styles include the *affective* (the social and emotional aspects that affect learning—level of responsibility, structure, motivation), the *physiological* (the senses and the learning environment—auditory/visual/kinesthetic/tactile), the *psychological* (how students feel about themselves— and whether they are analytical or global in their way of thinking or reflective versus impulsive), and the *sociological* (whether they like to learn alone, in pairs, or in groups). (Another way of thinking about the various learning styles is provided on the The 21 Elements web page: http://www.geocities.com/educationplace/element.html). The diversity of learning styles highlights the importance of having a flexible classroom that addresses students' individual needs by offering a variety of learning experiences and resources. The teacher who understands the implications of differing learning styles helps students to know their own style, think about their own learning, and develop a positive self-image by learning in the way that feels best for them. However, the teacher also encourages the students to be flexible by developing their ability to work in other styles. In this way, students learn to respect and look positively on others' preferences and also understand that it is all right to be different.

Gardner's theory of multiple intelligences also helps us to understand children's learning needs. As we saw in Chapter 6, Gardner has identified nine different intelligences that individuals use to interpret and understand the world. Your students' intelligences should have an influence on the approach to teaching that you adopt. The idea is not to create different lesson plans for each intelligence but instead to allow for variation in how children engage in the learning experiences and demonstrate what they have learned. Teaching to children's individual strengths can make the learning more enjoyable and motivating for them. It can also help children to develop a healthy self-image and a positive attitude toward their own uniqueness, especially when the teacher and their peers recognize that they are special. Figure 10.2 lists the types of activities most appropriate for stimulating various intelligences.

FIGURE 10.2 ■ Activities that Support Various Intelligences

VERBAL-LINGUISTIC INTELLIGENCE

Activities: choral reading, making speeches, debating, dramatizing, interviewing, teaching others, letter writing, researching, sharing time, story telling, brainstorming, creating a class newspaper, using word processors, reading to the class, journal writing

LOGICAL-MATHEMATICAL INTELLIGENCE

Activities: problem solving, classifying, analyzing, reasoning, using puzzles, patterning, research projects, making flow charts, graphing, making charts, computer work, creating codes, brain teasers

MUSICAL INTELLIGENCE

Activities: choral reading, raps, performances, singing, musical games, singing information to be learned, using music to enhance presentations, playing recorded music while leading, using environmental sounds, playing an instrument, composing songs

VISUAL-SPATIAL INTELLIGENCE

Activities: illustrating, sketching, visualizing, mapping, playing board games, using diagrams, mind mapping, creating models, computer work, cartooning, charting, graphing, photographing, picturing, visual arts, computer graphics software, draw and paint software, visual organizer software

BODILY KINESTHETIC INTELLIGENCE

Activities: touch/feel activities, constructions, dramatizing, experimenting, role playing, simulations, going on field tips, computer work, mime, cooking, crafts, virtual reality software, games, dancing

INTERPERSONAL INTELLIGENCE

Activities: discussion, peer teaching, group work, coaching, simulations, drama, current events, cooperative games, board games, peer sharing, interactive software

INTRAPERSONAL INTELLIGENCE

Activities: journals, goal setting, independent study contracts, mentoring, visualization, programmed instruction software, providing student choices, invoking personal feelings, self directed learning opportunities

NATURALIST INTELLIGENCE

Activities: field trips, exploring, environmental studies, field studies, experiments, collections

EXISTENTIAL INTELLIGENCE

Activities: examining spirituality, religions, and other belief systems; investigating questions about existence, life, and death; finding out about what life was like before they were born; exploring life on other planets

REFLECTION POINT

What do the suggestions in Figure 10.2 tell you about the best approach to take to your teaching of social studies?

Approaches that take into account the factors discussed here—brain-based research, children's learning styles, and multiple intelligences—share some similar objectives. They all advocate focusing on the uniqueness of the learning process for each individual in the classroom, and avoiding standardization (Guild, 1997).

ACTIVE ENGAGEMENT

Review the three approaches to teaching discussed earlier in this chapter. Which approach(es) do you feel would best address learners' needs, given what we have just reviewed about how children learn? In groups, discuss the question, What might the ideal enriched learning environment look like? Draw your ideal classroom on chart paper. Sketch out a floor plan of your unique classroom, including, for example, how desks would be clustered, where the teacher's desk would be located, what resources and equipment would be available for the children to use, whether there would be bulletin boards and/or a white board, and how many windows there would be, and share it with the rest of the class. Be prepared to defend your choices.

Chapter Summary

In this chapter, we began our exploration of how to teach social studies by considering what approach to teaching would best meet your goals for your social studies program. The importance of taking into account students' developmental learning needs as well as your beliefs and goals was considered in the light of three different approaches to teaching: teacher directed, shared direction, and student directed. We saw that each of these three approaches defines the roles of teacher and students differently, and that consequently each has a distinct hidden curriculum. The approaches are also driven by divergent ideas about the teacher's and students' control over factors such as the selection of goals, sequence of lessons, pace of learning, group size, what kinds of activities students should engage in, and what kinds of materials students should use.

Since it is important to consider what is known about how children learn when making decisions about what approach to teaching to adopt, we reviewed what we have learned so far regarding the principles of social constructivism, the recommendations that have been generated on the basis of brain-based research, learning style theory, and Gardner's theory of multiple intelligences. All of these views of learning recognize that each individual is unique in the way he or she learns. The most important factor to keep in mind is that no single instructional approach will be optimal for every teacher.

In Chapter 11, you will be introduced to several examples of learning activities that could be adapted for use within any of the three approaches to teaching.

Chapter 11

How Can Learning Activities Help You to Meet Your Goals for Your Social Studies Program?

In the previous chapter, you considered students' developmental learning needs, as well as your professional goals for your social studies teaching, in relation to three different approaches to teaching: teacher directed, shared direction, and student directed. Each of these three approaches presented different roles for the teacher and the students in shaping the learning experiences. You were challenged to decide on an approach to teaching that would work best for both you and your students. You are now ready to begin using the content and resources you selected in Parts Two and Three, and your chosen teaching approach from Chapter 10, to think about what learning activities would help you to meet your goals for your future social studies program.

LOOKING BACK

What were your social studies classes like as a child in school? What kinds of things did your best social studies teachers do? What activities in social studies do you remember as the ones from which you learned the most (or were the most fun or the most exciting)? What was missing from your social studies learning experiences?

In this chapter, you will be introduced to several examples of learning activities that could be adapted for use in any of the three approaches to teaching outlined in

Chapter 10. These activities have been designed to address the important social studies skills and processes of inquiry, higher-level thinking, collaboration and cooperation, and participation that are essential for children to develop into effective citizens (see discussion in Chapter 5). It is generally agreed among social studies educators that one of the most effective ways for students to learn these skills and processes is by engaging in inquiry. However, embedded in the approaches to inquiry taken by various teachers are differing views about who decides on what is inquired into, how the inquiry is undertaken, what resources are used to guide the inquiry, and what are the expected outcomes of the inquiry. These outcomes can vary along a continuum—from students finding the right answer to the teacher's question at the one end, all the way to arriving at a shared decision on an issue as a class and then taking action to bring about change based on that decision at the other end. These varying approaches to inquiry (which correspond to the three approaches to teaching discussed in Chapter 10) will be discussed in the first section of this chapter.

A number of social studies skills and processes can be developed through inquiry, but here too a teacher's goals can vary from students learning the basic procedural steps of a research plan to developing the more complex skills of higher-level thinking, cooperation and collaboration, and participation. The activities in this chapter are presented in terms of their use in teaching these latter types of skills.

REFLECTION POINT

As you read about the activities described throughout the rest of this chapter, think about how they might help you to teach social studies from the approach that you identified with in Chapter 10.

Sharpening Students' Research Skills through Three Approaches to Inquiry

Central to any research-oriented social studies program is students' learning how to access and use information. However, there can be varied levels of teacher and student control over the research process. What the teacher defines as research can vary significantly, from a teacher-controlled, fact-gathering exercise to an open-ended, loosely defined, problem-centered investigation driven by students' interests and concerns.

The approach you choose to take to research in your social studies classroom will depend on your purpose for doing the research. The difference lies in whether you are more interested in the acquisition of a pre-determined body of knowledge and the "discovery" of the right answers or in student exploration and shared meaning making about the content being examined. Another difference lies in the amount of student involvement in directing the research process that you wish to encourage.

Teacher-Directed Inquiry

A teacher who chooses a more teacher-directed approach to research has the goal of knowledge acquisition and recall of information about a specific teacher-selected topic. Such a teacher typically assumes complete control of the research process. This approach to research usually begins with the teacher selecting the topic to be studied and the important things to be learned about that topic based on the official curriculum and the textbook. The teacher then selects the process for teaching the important topic content or knowledge, which usually is revealed to the students through as a series of cumulative steps or sequenced lessons. Typically, students are directed to find information on specific aspects of a topic—i.e., when doing research on a country, they must find the location, population, languages, type of government, resources, industry, etc., and write a report. The teacher may also approach the topic to be studied in the form of a question that, when answered, ensures that the children have acquired the important content identified. The question is worded so that the series of lessons on the topic eventually point the children to the right answer. These types of questions tend to be fact oriented and directed at finding out the who, what, where, when, why, and how of the topic.

A teacher using such an approach chooses the resource (often only one source) that the children are to use (usually the official textbook or an encyclopedia) and decides on the type, length, and format of the product of the research (often a written report). The teacher also decides on the amount of time to be spent on the research, sets the pacing for the project, and directs all of the children in the classroom to use the same format. The students' information retrieval and use is thus highly teacher directed. The finished reports are then collected by the teacher and marked for completeness and neatness.

Shared Direction Inquiry

A less structured, shared direction approach to research encourages more open-ended inquiry and more student involvement in the selection of the research focus. Shared direction inquiry is based on the belief that children need to ask their own questions in order to develop their own ideas and their own unique perspectives on the topic under investigation. The emphasis in this approach is on students learning to use research as a way to explain and understand their world, rather than using it to get the "right answer." One variable in this approach is the amount of control the teacher has over the research process. While the teacher often engages all students in the same research activity, more opportunity is built in for the students to make choices about what resources to use, how to assemble what they find, and how to represent their new knowledge.

The first step in a shared direction approach to research usually consists of a decision-making process about what the topic of investigation will be. The teacher involves the children in generating the focus of the inquiry by having them help to select a problem or issue to investigate related to a limited set of ideas identified in the curriculum. In this exploration stage of the research, the children begin to identify with the topic by engaging in a variety of multisensory experiences to pique their curiosity and imagination, such as field trips, drama, art, children's literature, community walks, guest speakers, and web searches.

Prior to beginning their actual data collection, the students reflect on what they think they already know about the general topic to be researched. As a class, they may then brainstorm questions that they still have about the topic. These questions are then categorized and become the areas to be researched. Once the children have chosen a specific question to focus on, they begin to gather information in order to acquire a new understanding about their topic, using a wide array of resources. They are given mini-lessons as needed on how to select

In shared direction inquiry, students may choose to work in groups, pairs, or individually, depending on their preferred learning style.

important information from all of the available resources; how to choose and judge the appropriateness of those resources (including determining the authenticity, accuracy, quality, reliability, and relevance of that information); and how to identify opinion, bias, and inconsistencies in argument. The information collected is recorded and organized using retrieval charts, concept maps, databases, and/or spreadsheets. The students then synthesize the information and use it as evidence with which to develop an answer or solution to their initial question.

Collecting family stories is one example of a data-gathering strategy that engages young children in research while addressing both social studies and language arts learning outcomes, such as being able to produce pieces of writing using a variety of specific forms and learning to communicate orally. Through this activity, students learn important evidence-gathering skills such as interviewing and recording techniques, as well as how to ask appropriate questions that will elicit the information they are interested in. They also develop note-taking skills, synthesis skills such as connecting thoughts to tell a story, and oral storytelling skills. At the same time, children learn to place themselves in history and to understand the historical concepts of time and change.

As a culmination to their inquiry, students engage in some form of formal discussion in order to present their viewpoints in an organized manner. Activities might include debates, small-group and whole-class discussions, pair sharing, displays, walkabouts to view each other's work, forums, and presentations. Such activities can improve students' ability to articulate their ideas verbally, listen to others, and pay attention to all sides of an argument, and can develop higher-level thinking skills. These sharing activities can also be used to teach students how to arrive at an informed consensus on the best way to solve a problem or issue being investigated. The children can be given a choice as to how they wish to present what they have learned and should be encouraged to be creative in producing something novel; however, the learning process should always be presented to students as more important than the end product.

A shared direction approach to inquiry allows students to work in their preferred learning style on a topic of interest to them. Such an approach thus encourages students to build on their strengths, interests, and prior experiences. Allowing for more in-depth learning and flexibility in the pacing, resource selection, and reporting is particularly helpful for second language learners and those with other special learning needs. Throughout the inquiry process, students need to be encouraged to reflect on their learning about the question or problem under investigation and the research process they are engaged in. Frequent opportunities for children to reflect on their own work promote a more internal locus of authority as well as intrinsic motivation.

REFLECTION POINT

How is shared direction inquiry different from teacher-directed inquiry? What hidden curriculum is at work in this approach? What experiences related to doing research in social studies do you recall?

Student-Directed Inquiry

A student-directed approach to inquiry is similar to the shared direction approach. The main differences are in the degree to which the process is individualized and open-ended, and in the level of student directedness. In student-directed inquiry, students engage in negotiation with the teacher, with each individual setting out his or her own work plan to investigate a particular area of interest or concern broadly related to the curriculum. An

In student-directed inquiry, although students sometimes work alone, they can also work together on independent projects that are negotiated with the teacher.

integrated approach to the selection of the research focus is taken. For example, researching a topic such as "life in the Arctic" could involve children in investigating aspects of how people in the Arctic live, including their culture (music, dance, art, games and recreation, and stories), as well as the physical environment in which they live, including the climate, the land, and the plants and animals.

The student-directed research process unfolds according to the plan laid out by the learner, with the teacher requiring a number of checkpoints during the process, as determined by the child's level of independence. The approach emphasizes holistic skills instruction, in which the necessary skills are taught to an individual or a small group as needed. The results of a student's inquiry may or may not be shared with the whole class, depending on how disparate the students' topics are. Holding a Celebration of Research sharing time once a month is one way to showcase individuals' work.

Technology Connection To see some examples of humanities inquiry-based projects for elementary children, visit the What Is Inquiry? page on the Galileo Educational Network website: http://www.galileo.org/inquiry-what.html. Click on Selected On-line Resources, and then on Humanities. Choose one of the projects and consider how you might be able to adapt such a project for use in your teaching of social studies.

Promoting Higher-Level Thinking

Higher-level thinking skills such as critical and creative thinking are widely acknowledged as being essential for achieving the citizenship goals of social studies, as well as important literacy learning goals. These skills help students to make connections between new learning

FIGURE 11.1 ■ Higher-Level Thinking Skills

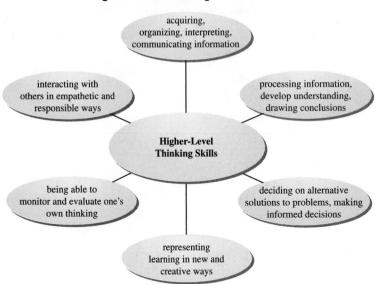

and what is already known, develop an understanding of what is being learned, and apply learning in new contexts. (See Figure 11.1 for a description of the skills that promote more complex thinking.)

Higher-level thinking is difficult to encourage within a teacher-directed approach to teaching and learning. In order to value higher-level thinking as a skills set, the teacher needs to hold the view that knowledge is not fixed, that all questions can and should be encouraged, that multiple perspectives are accepted, that ambiguity is a given, and that all information sources need to be viewed critically. Teachers need to model higher-level thinking in their own interactions with students. They need to be seen seeking clarification and being willing to reconsider their ideas on the basis of careful consideration of evidence before making up their mind. A positive, collaborative classroom environment is an important prerequisite for encouraging students to speak openly, ask questions, raise issues and problems, and engage in active learning, which are all important aspects of developing higher-level thinking skills. The development of attitudes such as open-mindedness, thoughtfulness, and a willingness to change one's ideas is crucial to the growth of these skills.

Developing students' higher-level thinking skills takes time and practice. Unfortunately, a curriculum that champions broad coverage of a multitude of topics rather than in-depth study of a few—which is true of most social studies curricula—does not allow for the promotion of genuine higher-level thinking. Teachers therefore need to make decisions about what the most powerful ideas in the curriculum are, and to focus on these in their social studies programs.

Using Questioning Strategies to Develop Higher-Level Thinking

Teachers' questioning of students is an important teaching and learning strategy for developing higher-level thinking skills. Questioning is also used to scaffold students' learning by challenging them to think about what they are learning in new and more cognitively challenging ways. The type and quality of questions used for stimulating this kind of thinking are critical. Teachers also use questioning as a scaffold to help students to focus and organize their research (McKenzie, 1999).

A half a century ago, Benjamin Bloom and his colleagues (1956) developed a taxonomy of various levels of cognitive processing intended as a framework of educational objectives for test developers to use in identifying what students should be expected to learn and do as a result of instruction. The original taxonomy presented a hierarchical scheme of six levels, ranging from simple factual recall to more complex analysis and evaluation. Table 11.1 shows the six levels of cognitive processing as identified by Bloom and provides an example of what the teacher could ask the students to do at each level to engage their cognitive processes.

TABLE 11.1 ■ Applying Bloom's Taxonomy

BLOOM'S LEVELS OF COGNITIVE PROCESSING	REPRESENTATIVE TEACHER/STUDENT ACTIONS
Knowledge	Ask the student to recall specific information
Comprehension	Have student put information into another form that shows they have grasped its meaning
Application	Invite student to make use of what s/he knows in a different situation or to solve a problem
Analysis	Encourage student to take ideas apart to explain what s/he knows by finding relationships, identifying causes, making inferences, supporting generalizations
Synthesis	Require student to produce something different by rearranging ideas in a new way
Evaluation	Challenge student to form an opinion about an issue, determine the validity of an idea, or judge the merit of a problem solution or decision based on criteria

This taxonomy is a tool that is still commonly used by educators to develop questioning strategies. These questions vary in complexity with those at the lower levels of the hierarchy tending to be closed-ended or right-answer kinds of questions. This type of questioning often is the focus of much classroom instruction, which is problematic as it fails to stimulate much student thinking about their knowledge. The higher-level questions are more open-ended and require students to use their knowledge to think and reason.

CLASSROOM APPLICATION

Mr. Booth is introducing the concept of community to his class using the levels of thinking in Bloom's taxonomy: He uses a series of pictures of various neighbourhoods and asks:

- What do you see in these pictures? (Knowledge)
- What do all of these pictures have in common? (Comprehension)
- What do the things in these pictures have to do with the concept of community? (Application)

(Continued)

- How do the communities in these pictures compare with yours? (Analysis)
- What would you predict that it would be like to live in these communities? (Synthesis)
- Explain which community you think is better, yours or one of the ones pictured? (Evaluation)

Bloom's taxonomy was recently revised to include not only the cognitive processes that learners draw on (using categories slightly different from those in the original taxonomy: remember, understand, apply, analyze, evaluate, and create) but also the knowledge to be learned (factual, conceptual, procedural, and metacognitive) in each of the cognitive process categories (Anderson & Krathwohl, 2001). One criticism of Bloom's taxonomy in both its earlier and later forms is that the hierarchical method of questioning it presents suggests that mastery of each level of questioning is a prerequisite for moving up to the next level. Critics argue that, in fact, children are capable of thinking that is not lock step. For example, they can make predictions about what might happen without having factual information first. Another concern is that the six levels of thinking have been tied to children's age and mental development, thus implying that younger children are incapable of thinking beyond the lower levels of the taxonomy. The latest brain research provides evidence to contradict this schema, as does research into young children's use of imagination and fantasy (Egan, 2006).

Another criticism of this taxonomy is directed at its lack of attention to creativity. Marks-Tarlow (1996) in *Creativity Inside Out* notes that the creative process involves lateral thinking, which includes flexibility, originality, expressiveness, openness, visualization, and imagination. Questions that encourage the imaginative process are particularly powerful for developing creative-thinking skills and for helping children to make suppositions and predict possible consequences for actions. For example, beginning questions with "Suppose …" or "What might happen if …," or "Imagine …" are all ways of engaging students' imaginations. Perspective-taking questions are also important for helping children to be able to see a problem from a variety of viewpoints and for developing empathy and altruism. For example, questions such as, "Can you tell about this event from _____ 's perspective?" or "If you were _____ how might you have felt?" can encourage perspective taking. Bloom's taxonomy does not encourage the use of any of these creativity-inducing types of questions.

w(w)w Technology Connection

- For more examples of how to develop higher-level thinking skills using Bloom's taxonomy, see the links provided on the companion website.

- Another excellent resource for developing questioning techniques is Jamie Mackenzie's "questioning toolkit," in which he proposes 17 types of questions that can be used as tools to develop children's higher-level thinking, along with lesson plans for their use in elementary schools (see http://questioning.org/Q7/toolkit.html).

Developing Collaborative Skills

What do you remember about the group work experiences that you had when you were in school? How useful were they for helping you to learn?

Collaborative skills, or the skills of working together, also can be enhanced as a part of the research process. However, the approach you decide to take to your teaching can promote distinct goals with regard to how your students interact with you and with each other. More individualistic and competitive goals tend to be set by teachers who assume that children work best alone and whose instruction is dominated by teacher talk, textbook reading, and worksheets. When this type of teacher asks questions, they are usually directed to one specific student at a time. In this context, students often feel pressured to have the right answer and to compete for both the teacher's attention and an opportunity to be called on to provide that answer.

Collaborative goals, on the other hand, have different purposes. According to Reid, Forrestal, and Cook (1989),

> For students to learn to use their own thinking and language to help them learn, the classroom should be a place where their language and ideas are valued, and are seen to be valued. This is why the idea of a small group of students as a basic unit of classroom organization is both useful and practical, as well as being theoretically sound. The classroom that asserts the value of social and collaborative interaction as fundamental to human learning is one where students are able to learn more easily using their expertise in making sense of the world and its ideas. (p. 8)

Teachers who emphasize collaborative goals structure in their classrooms believe that students need to participate actively as citizens in classrooms and schools in order to develop lifelong citizenship skills and attitudes. These teachers work hard to develop a supportive and emotionally safe classroom environment. Such classrooms encourage public talk, collective deliberation over shared problems, and the building of a classroom community through the sharing of ideas.

Teachers who use cooperative learning strategies to build collaborative skills believe that these strategies can engage active learning and creativity and that they can build a sense of community in the classroom by motivating students to help one another, value teamwork, develop leadership skills, improve social skills, increase self-esteem, and build an understanding and acceptance of differences. Working together can also help students who have difficulty listening or staying on task, as they become active group members with important roles to play, and students who in general prefer to work independently can learn about the value of working together. Cooperative learning strategies have also been found to be helpful for second language students, for students new to the Canadian school system, and for students with other special learning needs.

Using a cooperative learning strategy has been considered by many to be synonymous with group work, but although cooperative learning does take place within a group, by no means does this suggest that *all* group work is cooperative. The truth is that when students work in groups, the result is often that some students do not contribute while others do the majority of the work. In contrast, activities that are truly cooperative in nature are guided by a group goal that recognizes that success as a group depends on the individual efforts and accountability of every group member.

Working effectively as a group does not come naturally to most students, and they need to develop participation skills to enable the group to function more effectively. These skills include taking turns, listening to others' ideas, encouraging others, giving help, checking understanding of what was said, probing for clarification, building trust, managing conflict, making consensus decisions, and staying on task. For group work to be successful, students also need to learn to organize their efforts. One way of helping students to learn organizational skills is to have them take on different roles when they work in groups. (For examples of possible roles, see Figure 11.2.) These roles should be rotated each time there is a group activity so that students have opportunities to experience a variety of roles. Role rotation also prevents the natural leaders in the group from always taking over while the more reticent students hang back and remain uninvolved.

FIGURE 11.2 ■ Sample Roles for Cooperative Group Work

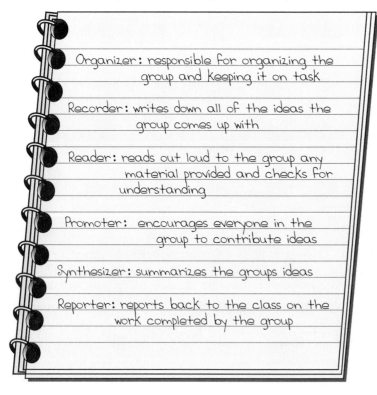

Organizer: responsible for organizing the group and keeping it on task

Recorder: writes down all of the ideas the group comes up with

Reader: reads out loud to the group any material provided and checks for understanding

Promoter: encourages everyone in the group to contribute ideas

Synthesizer: summarizes the groups ideas

Reporter: reports back to the class on the work completed by the group

There are a number of important steps that need to be taken to build successful groups in a classroom, such as getting acquainted, learning to take on various roles, understanding the importance of making a contribution to the group, and learning to listen to and respect others' ideas. The activity ideas presented here review some of these actions.

1. To function effectively, group members need to be familiar with one another and to feel comfortable working together. Here is a useful activity for the beginning of the school year, when children are not necessarily acquainted with each other, but it can also be effective for "breaking the ice" and helping to rid the group of feelings of discomfort that may exist at the beginning of any new cooperative task. Separate students into groups of four to six. Ask group members to introduce themselves and to include aspects such as name, hobbies and after school activities, interests, likes, dislikes, and so on. Once everyone has been introduced, start back at the first person and have each member go around the circle naming everyone and telling one thing they remember about each person in the group.

   An alternative activity requires the students in the group to come up with adjectives to describe themselves that begin with the first letter of their names— e.g., Jolly Janice. Again, the children go around the group and try to remember each person's name and adjective. Discuss the activities with the class when each group is finished. Talk about the importance of turn taking, encouraging, sharing, listening, and being supportive.

2. The following exercises provide each student with an opportunity to see how it feels to be the leader. Choose a different leader each time. In groups of four to six, have group members organize themselves by

   (a) Age from oldest to youngest
   (b) Size of family from smallest to largest
   (c) Distance of home from school—from farthest to nearest
   (d) Height from tallest to shortest
   (e) Number of pets from most to least
   (f) Farthest to nearest location of family relatives

   As a whole class, discuss any problems the groups encountered with these types of organization and come up with strategies for the most successful and efficient organizational strategies.

3. To teach the importance of contributing, in small groups have the children discuss a question such as, What is the best program on television? Challenge each group member to contribute to the discussion at least three times. Discuss the experience as a class.

   (Continued)

4. Here is a whole-class sharing activity that Miss Takats uses during discussions. The children are seated in a circle. Miss Takats explains the importance of showing respect by listening to others during a discussion. She shows them the talking stick and asks them to say what they think it is. She then explains that to ensure for all people an equal opportunity to be heard, an Aboriginal custom is to use the talking stick. At council meetings, the talking stick is passed around the circle and the bearer is given the attention of all others while talking. Miss Takats then passes the stick around the circle and invites each bearer to share his or her views on the topic under discussion. (To make your own class talking stick, see the Making Friends website: http://www.makingfriends.com/na/na_talking_stick.htm.)

Another important part of building cooperative learning skills is allowing for an assessment of the group's effort. The culmination of any group activity should include an opportunity for group members to discuss their collaborative efforts and suggest areas that can be improved on for the next group experience.

 Technology Connection For more information on the cooperative learning strategy, follow the weblinks provided on the book's companion website.

Using the Jigsaw Strategy to Promote Cooperative Learning

One cooperative learning strategy that works effectively for both developing students' social skills and ensuring individual accountability is the jigsaw strategy. This strategy is also an excellent way of dealing with a large amount of content in an efficient and engaging way while at the same time building essential research and participation skills. The jigsaw strategy allows everyone to contribute to group work by developing expertise in one area that is then shared with others. Large amounts of information can be relayed in a more interesting way by using this strategy. The Classroom Application box presents an example of an effective use of this strategy.

CLASSROOM APPLICATION

Students in Mrs. Baker's Grade 5 class are studying the regions of Canada using a jigsaw strategy. As an opener to her unit, Mrs. Baker has her students work in cooperative groups to try to sell their classmates on why they should want to live in a specific region of Canada. The class is divided into "expert" groups that are heterogeneous in terms of gender, ability, and learning style preferences, and each group is assigned a specific region of Canada to study. These expert groups meet to decide what they wish to learn about their region and how they want to go about accomplishing that learning. The members conduct their research and then come back together as an expert group to synthesize what they have learned. Each group member records the key points from this synthesis to present to the class. Next, the students are rearranged into "jigsaw" groups that have one member from each of the expert groups. Once the students are arranged in their jigsaw groups, they present what they have learned about their region. When all jigsaw group members have finished presenting, each student has collected similar information about the various regions of Canada on a retrieval chart. Mrs. Baker then has the class use the information collected to discuss what region they think would be the best to live in and why.

Enhancing Participation Skills through the Arts

Children come to understand their world in many ways. They also communicate that understanding in diverse ways—not only through talk and writing but also through such means as drawing, singing, and dancing. The arts provide numerous ways of increasing active participation in social studies. They also allow for the integration of social studies learning outcomes with language arts learning outcomes, such as exploring thought, ideas, feelings, and experiences by listening, speaking, reading, writing, and representing. Through the use of story, drama, visual arts, movement, and music, teachers can help children to create and express meaning and can enhance their understanding of important social studies concepts while developing critical literacy skills. Use of the arts adds relevance to students' learning by encouraging active participation and involvement, and activities using the arts can engage emotions, develop creativity, increase literacy, create historical empathy, develop higher-level thinking, and heighten student interest in social studies. Incorporating the arts in your social studies program can also help to promote students' social development and improve verbal and nonverbal communication and collaborative skills. As well, controversial topics and issues can be effectively dealt with in less threatening ways through recourse to the arts. The following sections focus on the particular effectiveness of drama and storytelling in social studies.

Dramatic Arts

Drama is particularly effective for encouraging participation in the social studies classroom, as it provides a forum in which students can be actively involved in experiencing problems, situations, and challenges, and can consider consequences of actions and decisions in a safe environment. One characteristic of dramatic activities that makes them appealing to use with young learners is their success in generating emotional responses to problems under investigation. Such responses help to develop research and perspective-taking skills, as dramatic play allows children to take on roles and investigate issues or problems from the standpoint of that role. An added benefit is that the opportunity to take on identities in a protected environment frees the shier, more reticent children. Using drama in the classroom can also develop language and oral presentation skills through children's expression of thoughts and ideas.

Not only can dramatic activities develop young learners' self-confidence and ability for self-expression; they can also spark children's imaginations and motivate them to want to learn. For example, children's excitement about about learning history can be encouraged by immersing them in a historical situation—that requires them to put themselves in someone else's shoes and imagine what a specific experience might have been like to live through (e.g., the experience of an immigrant child newly arriving in early Canada or a child during the Depression). Drama can also be used to help children learn about social behaviour in a group and about the importance of cooperation. Through dramatic activities, children can share their ideas and feelings, develop trust and sensitivity to the feelings of others, explore their own and others' values, and develop group cohesiveness. For young children, the most meaningful situations explored in such activities will be those derived from real or potential conflicts related to the students' own experiences. Further, when children see real-life connections to what they are learning, they are more apt to remember it.

All dramatic activities need to be followed by guided discussion in order to draw out children's thoughts and feelings about their experiences. These discussions need to address both the experience of engaging in the drama as well as what has been learned about the topic or problem under study.

The following are some dramatic techniques you may wish to try in your classroom.

Dramatic Free Play

Dramatic free play, a technique used with very young, kindergarten-aged children, involves the unstructured enactment of situations in which children assume real-life roles and improvise a dialogue as they engage in the play—e.g., a community is set up in the classroom with amenities such as a grocery store, a bank, a hospital, a veterinary clinic, etc., and students adopt the roles of the people involved in the community. The purpose of this kind of free play is for students to vicariously experience the lives of the people they play and to raise questions that lead to further investigation. Everyone is involved in this type of dramatic activity, and there is no audience.

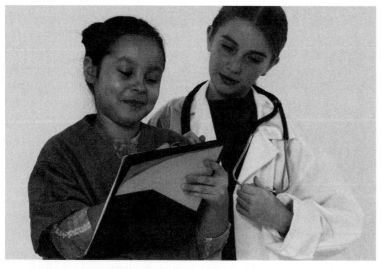

Engaging in role play can help children to develop new perspectives on subjects such as culture, lifestyle choices, and careers.

Role Play

Role play is a short-duration dramatization activity in which individuals or small groups assume roles within a particular real-life type of situation and are confronted with a problem that they must make a decision about. It is focused around one specific scenario and is not normally used with very young children. The purpose of this type of activity is to give students an opportunity to "feel" the experience of a particular situation from the perspective of one or more of the participants. For example, a group of students could brainstorm about the life of an individual living through the Depression or a war, or marching for women's rights, and then plan a multi-character dramatic episode in that person's life and act it out in front of classmates. Follow-up discussion questions with the whole class might include: What is happening here?; What time of day is this happening?; Where in the story are we starting?; What are the various people doing?; How does [a particular character] feel?; Could this really happen?; What will happen now?; What is [a particular character] like?; What is the situation (or problem)?; Why does [a particular character] behave the way he or she does?; Are there other ways this situation could end?; and, Is this a true-to-life situation? Role play can range along a continuum from completely structured to completely unstructured, depending on the level of improvisation and the amount of preplanning undertaken.

CLASSROOM APPLICATION

1. To spark his Grade 4 students' interest in a topic to be investigated and have them begin to generate questions about the topic, Mr. Sivak appears in class as a mystery guest representing a particular time period, event, or phenomenon being studied. The class asks him questions to try to figure out who the mystery guest is.

2. As a review technique after a current events session with her Grade 6 class, Mrs. Pelletier plays the role of someone in the recent news and has the students try to figure out whom she is representing. They can only ask questions to which she can answer yes or no. Sometimes Mrs. Pelletier has a student take her place as the role player.

Tableau

Tableau is a type of dramatic activity in which the "freeze" position is used to illustrate and provide an intense focus on the feelings of the people involved in a particular event. Using this strategy, students learn that facial and physical expressions are important ways to communicate ideas. For example, students could depict a scene from the life of an immigrant to Canada in which they are trying to show the difficulties that immigrants faced.

Simulation

Simulation involves the whole class in recreating real-world situations in the classroom for the purpose of gathering information, developing attitudes or values, or teaching certain skills. Simulation activities might include a mock trial, a deserted island scenario, simulated interactions among different cultural groups, or a recreated assembly line. Simulations are more structured than role play or dramatic free play activities in that all students in the class are given a task or a part to act out related to the scenario or phenomenon being enacted. This type of activity is useful for exploring cause and effect relationships as well as teaching decision making and problem solving. Since they normally represent real problems that can be encountered in life, simulations allow participants to experience a real-life sense of frustration in engaging with the problems. Having felt this frustration themselves, children are more likely to empathize with the people being studied and to be concerned about finding solutions to their problems; the learning experience thus becomes more emotionally meaningful and powerful for them.

CLASSROOM APPLICATION

1. When beginning her unit on people's interactions with their environment, Miss Bergum uses a simulation as an introductory activity to engage her Grade 5 students' interest in the topic. The simulation investigates alternative neighbourhood designs and the diverse population densities resulting from high-rise, duplex, condominium, and single-family dwelling patterns. Three areas in the classroom are blocked off to represent various population densities. One third of the students are directed to move their desks into the smallest area, another third to move theirs into an area about half again as large, and the remaining students' desks are distributed around the large remaining space (at least half of the classroom). The layout is left as is for the remainder of the simulation. The groups are rotated twice over the next two days so that all students experience the three degrees of density. Miss Bergum encourages the students to keep records of how frequently they are bumped into by someone, or are otherwise annoyed while working. At the end of the simulation, she asks the class which of the three settings they preferred and why, how the crowdedness affected how they felt about the people around them, and how it affected their work. She then shows pictures of neighborhoods with differing population densities and asks students to speculate about how it would be to live in each one based on their experience in the simulation.

2. When studying the causes of group conflict with her Grade 3 students, Mrs. Boora uses the following simulation. A series of 10 piles of paper are arranged in a row along the side of the classroom, each pile containing as many papers as there are class members. A stapler is placed at each end of the paper piles. The class is divided into two equal groups—Team A and Team B. Mrs. Boora explains that each person

is to make a booklet, and the group that finishes first will be rewarded. Team A is to make their booklets by picking up the papers starting at the front of the room and moving toward the back where they will staple them. Team B is to make their booklets by starting at the back of the room and picking up papers as they move to the front where they will staple them. After the activity has gone on long enough to build up a level of frustration, Mrs. Boora poses the following questions:

(a) What was this experience like for you?
(b) What problems did you run into?
(c) Which was the best way to pick up the papers?
(d) What words could be used to describe how you felt about the other group?
(e) How could the problem have been solved?
(f) Can you name grown-up groups in Canada that disagree about the way in which things should be done?
(g) How might problems between these groups be solved?

The Power of Story

Using story and narrative is a particularly effective way to incorporate the arts into your teaching of social studies content and skills. As we saw in Chapter 8, stories are meaningful for and appealing to young learners, and children are more engaged in social studies through stories about events, places, and people. As well, understanding and acceptance of others can be promoted through the use of personal stories, especially when those stories show characters overcoming hardships or obstacles, as students are drawn into the story and empathize with the characters. Values can also be effectively taught through the story format.

By way of example, storytelling has a particularly important place in the traditions of Aboriginal peoples. Myths and legends are told to explain natural phenomena, describe customs and religious rites, and tell about important events and heroes. Using mime in storytelling to convey ideas through gestures is a favourite pastime of the Blackfoot and Cree peoples.

Technology Connection

- Visit The Circle of Stories page at the PBS website (http://www.pbs.org/circleofstories/index.html) to listen to Aboriginal storytellers and learn about the history of Aboriginal storytelling.

- For life stories and lesson plans about Canadian people who have overcome disabilities and prejudices to become successful, visit the Elementary Teachers' Federation of Ontario's Resources for Teacher's page (http://www.etfo.ca/Resources/ForTeachers/Pages/default.aspx) and scroll down to "The Power of Story Volume 1—A K to Gr 8 Resource that Links the Experiences of Canadian Girls and Women to Curriculum."

The storyline strategy is another way to use the story format to teach children about social issues by immersing them in a situation that exemplifies the issue under study. The teacher sets a scenario that addresses the particular issue from the curriculum that is the focus of study. For example, the issue may be how to address global warming or the depletion of fish in the oceans. In groups, the children develop an appropriate setting for the study of the issue and then determine and create characters involved in the issue and write stories in which they flesh out details about the lives of their characters—i.e., their name, age, physical features, occupation, marital status if it applies, etc. The teacher then introduces a critical incident that the characters must confront (Fulwiler & McGuire, 1997).

CLASSROOM APPLICATION

Mr. Emme's class is exploring the environmental impact of landfills with his Grade 4 class, and he decides to use the storyline strategy to help to develop his students' understanding of this issue. Mr. Emme sets the scene by explaining that the students are all community members in a small mountain town with a river running through it, and that the town is located a one-and-a-half hour drive away from a major metropolitan area. Students then brainstorm what services and amenities they feel they would need in their town. They each take on the role of a community member who lives in or near the town. The students make up a life story about their character. The class then creates a map representing the set-up of their community—i.e., showing the mountains, the river, the streets, the location of services and other amenities, etc. Once the map is finished, Mr. Emme introduces a challenge that the townspeople have to face and reminds them about the importance of the community working together. A town meeting is called to alert the people that the town council has received a request to allow the nearby city to dump waste close to the town. A decision has to be made whether to allow the dumping and, if they do, where to locate the dump. The town stands to make a lot of money from the proposal. Mr. Emme directs the community members to research the effects of the dump's presence from the perspective of their various characters and to hold a town meeting to discuss their findings and make a decision regarding the proposal.

Readers' Theatre

Readers' Theatre is an activity that combines storytelling and drama by engaging children in writing plays and performing them for an audience. Scripts that depict specific historical times, events, and peoples can be used to develop children's historical thinking as they engage in research and then prepare a script to share what they have learned. Children can also develop respect for others' points of view as they listen to how and why the characters in the scripts made the choices that they did about incidents in their lives. Readers' Theatre can also be used to demonstrate creative problem solving and risk taking. For example, young children can be introduced to this type of activity by reading scripts out loud that are based on fables, legends, and fairy tales in which the characters confront and resolve conflicts.

 Technology Connection In your first uses of Readers' Theatre, you may want to try out some already existing plays. Visit the book's companion website for links to web resources that provide prepared Readers' Theatre scripts.

Chapter Summary

As a teacher, you may have clear-cut personal professional goals for your social studies program that are based on your beliefs about your students' learning and your role in that learning. You may have carefully selected content for your program that addresses both your goals and the students' learning needs. You may select resources that you feel will best support the teaching and learning of that content. And you may identify a teaching approach that matches your beliefs and goals. However, in order to teach in a way that meets your goals, you will need to ensure that the learning experiences that you plan for your students match the choices you have made. The intent of this chapter was to engage you in thinking about what learning activities would help you to meet your goals.

We began this chapter on choosing learning activities by examining three ways of approaching inquiry in the social studies classroom, each of which defined the roles of the teacher and students differently. You learned that your choice of approach to inquiry should reflect the goals that you set for your social studies program as well as your beliefs about how children learn best and the amount of control they should have over their learning. In the remainder of the chapter, you had the opportunity to examine a variety of activities for teaching the skills of higher-level thinking, collaboration and cooperation, and participation. We examined questioning strategies, the use of cooperative learning strategies such as the jigsaw, and a variety of arts-based activities including dramatic play, role play, simulation, tableau, story, and Readers' Theatre.

Whenever you are choosing an activity for your classroom, it is always important to ask yourself these three questions: Why am I choosing this activity?; Will it provide a genuine learning experience for my students?; and, Will it be enjoyable for my students?

Chapter 12, the final chapter on choosing activities, looks at the types of online learning activities that can enhance your teaching of social studies.

Chapter 12

How Can Online Learning Activities Be Used to Develop Students' Higher-Level Skills in Your Social Studies Program?

In Chapter 11, we examined a variety of learning activities you can use to engage students in inquiry that promotes higher-level thinking, supports collaboration and cooperation, and encourages active participation. In this final chapter on choosing an approach to teaching, and activities to support that approach, we will look at how computer technologies can be used to further augment students' social studies learning in these areas. We have already examined some of the computer-based resources available to support students' research and develop the information location and retrieval component of their digital literacy skills (see Chapter 9). In this chapter, we will focus on the use of online activities to develop in students the more complex skills of higher-level thinking, decision making and problem solving, collaboration, and producing and sharing. The chapter will conclude with a discussion of the importance of both teaching students' to be respectful, responsible, and critical users of online technologies, and enhancing their awareness of the impact of technology on society.

Based on your prior experience, what uses of computer technologies do you feel would be most effective for enhancing your social studies program? Why do you feel this way?

The Learning Benefits of Online Activities

Longitudinal research has shown that online activities can be highly beneficial for students' learning. However, while the possibilities for the use of online resources in teaching social studies are limitless, not all use of the internet and web provides the maximum benefit for learning. The greatest challenge for teachers when using online technologies with students lies in thinking differently about teaching and learning. These technologies have the potential to be a catalyst for change in the learning environment by altering traditional student–teacher relationships, but teachers need also to shift from viewing themselves as transmitters of knowledge to seeing their students as constructors of knowledge. As well, the use of online technologies needs to go beyond students being able to demonstrate an understanding of how to operate them proficiently. The merging of technology and constructivism offers many possibilities for designing and directing innovative online learning environments.

Technology use that is shaped by constructivist learning principles supports a more student-centred, inquiry-oriented approach to teaching that encourages students' independent exploration of ideas. Taking such an approach means thinking differently about learning tasks. As Girod and Cavanaugh (2001) argue, "Rather than asking students to complete predetermined and well-defined tasks such as worksheets . . . and projects designed with a single goal in mind, teachers must embrace learning activities that are ill structured, ill defined and open-ended" (p. 1). Taking an inquiry approach to learning with technology that places less emphasis on *acquiring* information and more on *applying* it to solve problems and construct new knowledge can promote the development of analytical thinking, problem solving, decision making, collaborative learning, creativity, and productivity, as well as stimulating in students a positive attitude toward learning and a willingness to take more responsibility for their learning. Online activities that engage learners in authentic projects anchored in real-life contexts promote cognitive and social development when students are encouraged to interpret and think critically about information, construct arguments based on evidence, and represent their new understandings in multiple ways while working collaboratively and engaging in task-oriented dialogue with others.

 Technology Connection For more information on the benefits of integrating technology in the classroom, have a look at the report on a 10-year study entitled *Changing the Conversation about Teaching, Learning and Technology: A Report of 10 years of ACOT (Apple Classrooms of Tomorrow) Research*, available at http://www.apple.com/education/k12/leadership/acot/pdf/10yr.pdf.

Using Online Activities to Develop Higher-Level Thinking, Decision-Making, and Problem-Solving Skills

As we saw in Chapter 9, there are many ways to support students' research through the use of technology-based resources such as online encyclopedias, informational websites, virtual museums, and educational software. Here, we go beyond the subject of using the web to collect information, to exploring ways in which online technologies can be used to engage learners in *all* stages and dimensions of the inquiry process.

One of the most effective approaches to setting up online inquiry is by using a problem-based learning instructional model. Problem-based learning is guided by the belief that what is most important for students to know should be determined by a need to use information in authentic tasks. By situating the learning experience in the examination of authentic, real-life problems, students can be engaged in active problem solving that makes connections to their world while also helping them to acquire the targeted concepts and understandings. Using this approach, students can draw on others' perspectives as well as their own prior life experience to address a particular problem under investigation. The goal of problem-based learning is not to find a "right answer" to a problem, as there may be no single solution that everyone agrees on. Instead, the actual learning takes place through the *process* of solving a problem by thinking through the steps of an investigation, developing appropriate questions, researching various viewpoints, and producing a solution and/or plan of action, based on the evidence, to address the problem. The benefits of problem-based learning are that it promotes active student engagement with learning; it prepares self-directed learners, as students learn to make choices about how and what they learn; and it encourages collaborative learning.

A problem-based learning approach also offers teachers a useful starting point for initiating inquiry with students, using a structured method to help them build higher-level thinking and problem-solving skills. The rationale for using a structured inquiry approach at the K–12 level can be traced back to Bruner's cognitive development theory. For Bruner, the outcome of cognitive development was higher-level thinking. He argued, "Knowledge is a process, not a product" (Bruner, 1966, p. 72). Bruner's "discovery learning" and "inquiry teaching" methods envision the learners creating their knowledge by "rearranging or transforming evidence in such a way that one is enabled to go beyond the evidence so assembled to additional new insights" (Bruner, 1961, p. 22). Gaining insight requires an activity structure that scaffolds learners' experience so that they must move beyond simply finding information to using that information to think through and resolve a problem or issue.

Online activities that support problem-based learning, and thus enhance the development of higher-level thinking, include WebQuests, Web Inquiry Projects, interactive adventures, and virtual field trips. The following sections provide a discussion of the benefits of these activities, as well as useful examples accessible on the web.

WebQuests

When students are first introduced to online inquiry, they need to be taught the skills necessary for working in such environments. In the beginning, they will need more direction and scaffolding to guide them through the inquiry process and to support them at each stage of investigating a problem. At this point in students' learning process, a more structured type of online learning environment can be most beneficial in helping to develop the requisite skills. A WebQuest is one example of such a guided process.

WebQuests incorporate a problem-based learning approach that encourages students to apply critical thinking, problem-solving skills, and content knowledge to real-world problems and issues. A WebQuest is an inquiry-oriented activity in which most or all of the information used by learners is drawn from the web (Dodge, 1996). Students are provided with access to information sources such as online experts, current news sites, informational sites, and searchable databases. WebQuests are designed to efficiently make use of learners' time by focusing on *using* information rather than looking for it, and to support learners' thinking at the levels of analysis, synthesis, and evaluation (Dodge 1996). Through a WebQuest, students can actively explore issues, find answers, and reach moral and ethical decisions about real contemporary world problems. While engaged in inquiry using a WebQuest, students are constructing their own personal meaning about the problem/question under investigation. WebQuests can also enhance students' communication and social skills, as many activities involve working in cooperative groups and role taking.

A WebQuest usually consists of an introduction, a task, a process, resources, evaluation, and a conclusion. The introduction provides background information to the problem to be investigated, while the task and the process outline what is to be done and how to go about using the resources provided to address the task. The evaluation section typically provides information for students on how they will be assessed and often includes a rubric for providing feedback. The conclusion brings closure to the WebQuest by reviewing and summarizing the learning and often challenges learners to extend their learning in new ways.

WebQuests can be a powerful way for students to be immersed in historical events and to work with historical documents. For example, in the "Scrooge for Mayor" WebQuest (http://www.coollessons.org/Dickens.htm), students work in teams to develop a campaign proposal for Scrooge to use in his run for mayor of England based on information about labour, education, industrialization, and quality-of-life issues represented in Charles Dickens's novel *A Christmas Carol* (1843). Each campaign team is made up of a team manager, research analyst, public relations representative, and political strategist. Students are directed to focus on how Scrooge's viewpoint on daily life in London would need to change if he were to become mayor and what solutions to London's problems and programs he would need to address. Each person on a campaign team is responsible for writing a newspaper article describing what life was like in mid-nineteenth-century England, why change would be necessary, what changes the team proposed, and how those changes would improve things. Each team also has to write an editorial on the topic "Is the Industrial Revolution a good thing?" Finally, the teams are challenged to create a campaign poster, a pamphlet, and a PowerPoint presentation to communicate their ideas to Scrooge so that he can decide what to base his campaign for mayor on.

Another historically oriented WebQuest, "Pioneer Days in Canada," is provided by the Sir Wilfrid Laurier School Board (follow the link on the book's companion website). This resource provides students with the opportunity to study pioneers by being transported back through time to a pioneer village in order to report on life in early-nineteenth-century Canada.

The website http://www.iwebquest.com provides a number of WebQuests, including the "Ancient Egypt Webquest," which engages students in a series of missions to learn about King Tut, early Egyptian daily life, and the study of archeology. Also available is the "Medieval Storytelling Quest," in which students study the history of the Middle Ages and then create their own story to teach their peers what they have learned about this historical time period.

Some WebQuests encourage students to take on cooperative learning roles such as group leader, recorder, communicator, encourager, evaluator, to bring more efficiency to their group work. Other WebQuests require students to choose a specific aspect of the topic under study and then locate, analyze, and synthesize the information provided based on that focus. The "Travel Canada WebQuest" (http://olc.spsd.sk.ca/DE/webquests/TravelCanada), for example, has students complete the quest activity by focusing on a specific province or territory, as does the "Canada WebQuest" (follow the link provided on the book's companion website). "The Big Wide World WebQuest" on the Knowledge Network Explorer website (http://www.kn.pacbell.com/wired/bww) is an example of an activity that combines cooperative roles and focus topics to engage primary students in an investigation about the world.

The most authentic WebQuests engage students in perspective taking on a particular problem or issue. Students investigate the context and the issue from a particular individual's perspective in order to build a better understanding of the individual, the event, and the setting. The goal is for the children to use the information they collect to construct an argument based on evidence. They then share their findings with the rest of the class, and the class tries to arrive at a consensual resolution to the problem under investigation. An example of this type of WebQuest is the "Preserving, Understanding and Transmitting Canadian Culture WebQuest" (at http://schools.sd68.bc.ca/coal/pg/canada/welcome.html), which allows students to study the history of British Columbia from a Chinese, an Aboriginal, and a European perspective.

Investigating problems from a number of different cultural perspectives can help learners to better understand the wide diversity of views on any one issue, as well as the important cultural foundations of those views. Perspective taking can also encourage students to learn to respect and appreciate diversity. In the WebQuest "Does the Tiger Eat Its Cubs?" (http://www.kn.pacbell.com/wired/China/childquest.html), for example, students explore how children in orphanages in China have been treated. The question to be investigated is, What's the truth about how children are treated in China? Students are divided into three teams and directed to investigate the information from three differing perspectives on the question. One team reads international news reports, another reads responses from the Chinese people, and a third examines the government of China's position as stated in its one-child policy. The class then comes back together and discusses their findings, engaging with the challenge of making a consensus decision on the issue. In the culminating activity, students write a letter to the government or to a human rights organization in which they express their opinion about what they feel should be done about the situation.

CLASSROOM APPLICATION

There are numerous online WebQuest databases that have been prepared by educators to meet varying content requirements of social studies curricula. Choose a grade level and topic from your provincial or territorial social studies curriculum guide, and then peruse some of the WebQuests available on the sites below to find one that both meets the suggested criteria of your curriculum and fits your goals for the study of the particular topic. How might you adapt this WebQuest so that it works for your program?

- École Whitehorse Elementary WebQuests: www.yesnet.yk.ca/schools/wes/webquest_collection.html
- Canadian History WebQuests: http://www.accesscable.com/~hgunn/Webquests/chdhist.html
- Prairie Spirit School Division #206 WebQuests: www.spiritsd.ca/teacherresources/tr/quests/default.htm
- WebQuest Locator—Social Studies: www.gecdsb.on.ca/d&g/DP/locatorh.asp
- WebQuest.Org : http://webquest.org

You can also create your own WebQuest using templates that are available on the internet. One resource for templates is Bernie Dodge's WebQuest Page: http://webquest.sdsu.edu/LessonTemplate.html.

ACTIVE ENGAGEMENT

It is important to be aware that not all WebQuests are well designed. You will need to carefully examine the ones you find online—both in terms of content coverage and how effectively the activity is structured—before using them with a class. Effective WebQuests should have the following elements:

- an engaging opener
- a clear question/problem and task
- roles that match the issue/problem being investigated
- up-to-date and helpful resources
- evidence that higher-level thinking is required
- opportunities for students to receive feedback
- a conclusion that allows for the demonstration of students' learning, suggests how this learning could apply to other situations, and offers suggestions for further learning

You will also find rubrics online that can be used to determine the quality of WebQuests. For example, have a look at the BestWebQuests site (http://bestwebquests.com/bwq/matrix.asp) and the Rubric for Evaluating WebQuests web page (http://webquest.sdsu.edu/webquestrubric.html). Are there any criteria for effective WebQuests suggested at these sites that could be added to our list above?

Web Inquiry Projects

A WebQuest is a good starting point for develop problem-solving strategies by leading students through a structured and scaffolded inquiry experience. However, these activities usually provide limited opportunities for students to set their own direction and plan their investigation. Once their inquiry skills have been developed, students need to be given more control over their online learning experiences. Molebash (2004) notes that the support offered by the WebQuest can gradually be "faded" by (1) giving less specific guidance to students and gradually allowing more flexibility in how and what students are to produce; (2) providing fewer web links and expecting students to find their own resources; (3) gradually shifting scaffolding such as note taking, information organizing, and writing prompts from required to implicit; and (4) adding more extension ideas for students to explore further.

Web Inquiry Projects are one example of how to extend the WebQuest idea beyond structured inquiry to more open-ended inquiry by encouraging higher levels of thinking and student engagement. A Web Inquiry Project is a facilitated learning plan that promotes open-ended inquiry using online information by encouraging learners to actively pursue answers to interesting and relevant questions (Molebash, 2004). Web Inquiry Projects place more emphasis on having students determine their own task, define their own procedures, and play a role in finding appropriate online resources.

 Technology Connection Have a look at the examples of Web Inquiry Projects at the Web Inquiry Projects website: http://edweb.sdsu.edu/wip/examples.htm. How might you be able to use the approach shown at this site in your teaching with technology?

Interactive Online Adventures

Another type of web-based problem-solving activity is the interactive online adventure, in which students are involved in authentic tasks designed to help them better understand a particular phenomenon. Using technology in this way can make abstract content and complex ideas more accessible and comprehensible to students. There are a multitude of these adventure activities available online, but a description of some of the more effective ones is provided here.

The Canadian War Museum website offers the "Armoured Warrior" (http://www.warmuseum.ca/cwm/armwar/indexwareng.html), an online adventure based on real-life experiences of Canadian tank crews in World War Two. And at the same site, students can experience what life in the trenches in World War One might have been like in the "Over the Top" adventure (http://www.warmuseum.ca/cwm/overtop/teachers_e.html).

The Canadian Museum of Civilization's "An Adventure in New France" (www.civilization.ca/vmnf/boucher/index.html) is an interactive adventure that allows students to explore and keep a diary of their adventures as they travel along with pioneer Pierre Boucher. At the same website, the "Journey to Kitigaaryuk" adventure (http://www.civilization.ca/kids/kitigaaryuk) takes students on a trip to the Canadian Arctic with a young boy from England. And in the "Great Upper Canada Adventure" (http://sydenhamdiscovery.ca/english/game.asp), Grade 6 students can take on the role of settlers in early Upper Canada.

The British Broadcasting Corporation's (BBC's) "Walk Through Time" online adventure (http://www.bbc.co.uk/history/walk/games_index.shtml) transports students through a time tunnel to explore the concept of change over time as they investigate life during Roman, Viking, Tudor, and Victorian times. Also from the BBC, "Josie and Gleep in a Step Back in Time!" takes children back in time to the reign of Queen Victoria (http://www.bbc.co.uk/education/dynamo/history/stepback.htm).

At the Parks Canada Youth Zone website (www.pc.gc.ca/apprendre-learn/jeunes-youths/index_e.asp), the "Dress Canada's History" adventure teaches students about the origins of Canada's cultural diversity through an exploration of clothing worn during various historical time periods. Also at this site, students can access (among other adventures) the "Budding Explorer," an adventure about Samuel de Champlain, and the "Women in Canadian History" adventure.

Simulations are another example of online adventures that promote higher-level thinking and problem-solving skills. (For a review of the benefits of using simulations to support research in social studies, see Chapter 9). Edmonton: A City at War (www.cityatwar.ca) is one example of a simulation that allows users to take on the roles of two fictitious characters, both who lived in Edmonton during WWII, and engage in problem solving and making decisions about their daily lives as they deal with adversity.

Virtual Field Trips

Virtual field trips are another means of engaging students in online experiences. These field trips can allow students to travel through both time and space to places that would otherwise be out of reach, but unlike online adventures and simulation activities they do not require that students take on roles to solve problems or make decisions. Virtual field trips can also provide students with opportunities to make observations and actively engage in exploring suppositions, examining multiple perspectives, and tapping into expert resources. For example, to support the development of geographical and cultural understanding, Industry Canada's "Lessons from the Land: A Cultural Journey through the Northwest Territories" (www.lessonsfromtheland.ca) takes students on a journey through a series of locations to learn about the people and the land of the Northwest Territories. Another useful virtual tour, "Plate Tectonics: Our World in Motion" (http://www.uen.org/utahlink/tours/tourFames.cgi?tour_id=13380), helps students to grasp a difficult geographical concept—plate tectonics—as students are provided the opportunity to interact with and manipulate the information on the tour.

Virtual field trips often provide not only text describing the particular site being visited but also vivid images of it. For example, on the China Virtual Tours page of the China Vista site (http://www.chinavista.com/travel/virtualtours.html), students can view the Great Wall of China, the Emperor's Imperial Palace and other royal palaces, the Terracotta Soldiers, and Tiananmen Square, as well as images of the nation's cities and countryside and other geographical features. These visuals can offer children important contextual information to help to personalize their study of a country from afar. The Kids' World Geography website (http://www.northvalley.net/kids/cities.shtml) is another useful resource that offers numerous virtual field trips to other countries.

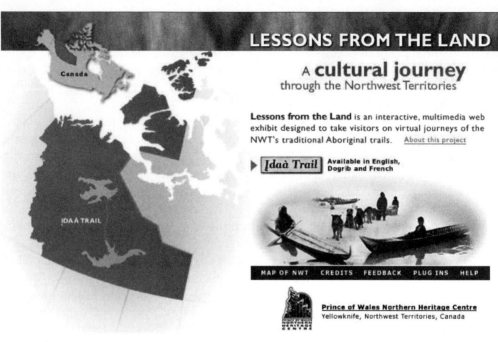

"Lessons from the Land: A Cultural Journey through the Northwest Territories"

Another example is the BBC's interactive 2 Cities site (http://www.bbc.co.uk/schools/twocities), where students can explore two capital cities—Belfast and Mexico City—from the perspectives of children who live there. Further, at the Journey into Amazonia site, hosted by PBS (http://www.pbs.org/journeyintoamazonia/teacher.html), students can explore the geography of the Amazon River in South America. PBS also offers students the opportunity to take a virtual tour of the Panama Canal (http://www.pancanal.com) as they learn about its history and construction.

w w w Technology Connection Websites can provide live virtual experiences through the use of web cameras (webcams), which are digital real-time cameras. The following sites offer these types of experiences:

- EarthCam: http://www.earthcam.com
- Australian Government Antarctic Division Webcams: http://www.aad.gov.au/default.asp?casid=27
- Africam.com (images of wild animals in Africa): http://www.africam.com
- Animal Planet Critter Cams: http://animal.discovery.com/cams/cams.html
- The Yukon Education Student Network list of animal webcam sites: http://www.yesnet.yk.ca/studentlounge/webcams

CLASSROOM APPLICATION

Mr. Ross wanted to teach his Grade 5 class about the Iditarod race in an integrated way as a part of his social studies unit on the geography of Canada and the Arctic. To motivate the students' interest in the topic and address some of the reading outcomes set by his province's ministry of education, he began by having them read the children's book *Stone Fox* by John Reynolds Taylor. While reading, the students generated a list of questions about the Iditarod to be addressed over the remainder of the unit. In groups, they completed Jill Olson and Molly Corbett's "Support Your Musher: An Iditarod WebQuest" (http://www.madison.k12.wi.us/jefferson/science/idit.htm), in which they learned about the race and the costs associated with participation as they prepared a presentation for a potential sponsor of a musher. Once the race began, the class regularly checked on the progress of the various mushers at the official Iditarod website (www.iditarod.com) and watched the finish line on the Iditarod webcam (http://www.iditarod.com/webcam). In math, they graphed statistics about the dog teams and their progress. Mr. Ross also arranged epals for his students with a school in Nome, Alaska, where the race ends, so they could talk with children who had direct experience with the race (see http://www.epals.com).

Using Online Activities to Develop Collaborative Skills

WebQuests and online adventures including virtual field trips are usually geared to groups of children or individuals within one classroom. Teachers also need to recognize that the classroom no longer confines learning, and that every classroom has the potential to be a global learning environment. Opportunities to investigate real-world issues through computer-based collaboration and sharing of knowledge and experiences can help to expand students' learning. Active participation in such collaborative activities with peers in classrooms around the world can help students to gain personal knowledge about other cultures and can promote understanding of multiple perspectives. Engaging in these online learning communities can help students to overcome their often limited views of the world and can contribute to their development as global citizens.

In addition to developing their critical thinking, creative thinking, and problem solving skills, engaging in online collaboration can also enhance the development of students' communication skills. Online conversations can prompt students to self-check and think more carefully about their ideas, to clarify inaccuracies, to reframe prior ideas, and to decide how best to articulate those ideas so that they are clear to others. The reflective time before responding that asynchronous technologies (i.e., those in which not everyone is online at the same time) allow can also result in more analytical and strategic responses from students. Some key online avenues for sharing and exchanging information are emails, blogs, discussion boards or forums, telecollaborative projects, webcasts, and videoconferencing. A discussion of the benefits of these activities is provided in the following sections.

Email Exchanges

Children tend to see information gathered through online collaborative activities as being more connected to authentic local, national, and global issues.

Students are fascinated by the possibilities of electronic communication for contacting other students and adults in different parts of the world for the purposes of exchanging ideas about topics of mutual interest. Students view information gathered in this fashion as more connected to "real" local, national, and global issues. Email is one of the most popular technologies for exchanging information. One-to-one communication through writing can be highly motivating for children, and web-based exchanges give students an opportunity to interact with a real audience and speak for themselves without having to face the intimidating context of a live classroom. And electronic communication can be particularly freeing for children with special needs—especially those who have difficulties with oral communication.

Some electronic information exchanges are between students and an expert. For example, at Odyssey World Treks (http://www.worldtrek.org/odyssey), students can engage with adventurers as they travel around the world. They can email questions to the adventurers and read daily updates on the website to keep in touch with the latest discoveries as the journeys unfold. The UPLIFTS (Unique Project Learning by Integrating Folk Tales and Stories) Project is an example of this type of exchange being carried out successfully. The website (http://projects.cbe.ab.ca/riverbend/uplifts) shows how a group of children studying about China worked with a Canadian writer, David Bouchard, to create folktales about what they learned.

www **Technology Connection** Students can visit the following websites to email experts in specific fields questions about their area of study:

- Ask an Expert: http://www.homeworkspot.com/reference/expert
- AllExperts: http://www.allexperts.com
- Electronic Emissary: http://emissary.wm.edu

Another effective way of doing these exchanges is between students. For example, students could engage in an exchange of information with another classroom somewhere else in Canada in order to gain knowledge about other geographic areas and to appreciate the diversity and vastness of Canada's lands and peoples.

 Technology Connection To locate potential email exchange partner schools in Canada, visit the book's companion website for links to the following websites:

- SchoolNet (provides a province-by-province online directory of schools connected to the internet)
- Exchanges Canada website
- The Connected Classroom website, hosted by the Quebec English School Network (also offers links to French-speaking partner schools)
- The Kids from Kanata organization website (offers partnerships with schools in Aboriginal communities)

International classroom exchanges can also be very powerful learning experiences. Through these types of exchanges, children can learn about the customs, traditions, and cultural similarities and differences of other countries. One way to start this type of exchange is by sending an electronic postcard such as those available at the Canadian Culture website: http://www .canadianculture.com/ecards. Children also need to be taught to be cautious when approaching someone online and when sharing information. See the Meeting Someone Online page on the GetNetWise website for guidelines: http://kids.getnetwise.org/safetyguide/danger/harm.php.

 Technology Connection Visit the following websites to find partners for international email exchanges between students:

- Epals Global Network: http://www.epals.com
- Keypals Club International: http://www.worldkids.net/clubs/kci
- Intercultural E-Mail Classroom Connections: http://www.iecc.org
- Kidlink: http://www.kidlink.org

Blogs

Blogs (an abbreviation of the term "web log") are another vehicle for sharing ideas online. Blogs are journals that allow for user commentary in an interactive format. Individuals can share their thoughts, experiences, and learning with other individuals or the whole class, and can engage in discussions about topics of study either publicly or privately. To read more about blogs as learning tools, refer back at Chapter 1, p. 12.

 Technology Connection You can find blogging partners at the ePALS SchoolBlog website (http://schoolblog.epals.com). It is important that children are warned about the potential dangers of engaging in blogging. See the ConnectSafely website (http://connectsafely.org) for suggestions on safe blogging and social networking practices.

Discussion Boards or Forums

Another online communication tool that provides opportunities for student exchange of information is the discussion board or online forum. These interactive discussion arenas allow children to view others' comments and ideas on a discussion topic and to add their own thoughts. Participating classrooms can contribute on their own schedule instead of all of the classes having to be online at the same time. Discussion boards or online forums are authentic environments for exchanging information, as students often interact with other children of the same age who have similar needs and interests. These environments also allow for the attaching of files to entries so that individuals and classrooms can share projects they are working on.

 Technology Connection The ForumUp website (http://www.forumup.com) explains how discussion boards and forums work and how to set up your own.

CLASSROOM APPLICATION

Ms. Craig's Grade 5 students were involved in the Canadian Information Exchange: Sharing Knowledge Across Canada project, which linked schools and students across Canada in order for them to study the similarities and differences between various Canadian communities and to get a broader picture of the Canadian experience. A forum was used to link three schools—one on the East Coast, one on the West Coast, and one in central Canada—to enable them to share information about their lives and about their community, and to reflect on their ideas about how the geography and history of their respective area has shaped how they live today. Schools were selected using the contact information for schools provided at the websites of the Ontario Ministry of Education (http://sbinfo.edu.gov.on.ca), Nova Scotia Department of Education (http://www.ednet.ns.ca), and British Columbia Ministry of Education (http://www.bced.gov.bc.ca/schools).

Telecollaborative Projects

Telecollaborative projects are undertakings in which groups of people in different locations work together to exchange information and/or solve a problem. These projects can range from an exchange of email between learners in different locations regarding a specific topic of study to the collection from various locations of original data related to a particular global problem or issue in order to develop and share new insights. An example is Statistics Canada's "Census at School" (http://www19.statcan.ca/r000_e.htm), an international classroom project for students aged 8 to

18 in which students complete a brief online survey, collect and analyze their class results using a spreadsheet, and compare themselves with students in Canada and other countries.

The Kidlink website also offers a number of ongoing telecollaborative projects for all age ranges, including "Who Am I?" (http://www.kidlink.org/kie/nls/english/response/), which engages primary-aged children in researching the origins of their names and then sharing their findings via email with other groups of children enrolled in the project. A similar project, "What Does My First Name Mean?" engages children in researching and sharing the meaning of their first names (follow the link on the book's companion website).

Another telecollaborative project, the "Square of Life Project: Studies in Local and Global Environments" (http://www.k12science.org/curriculum/squareproj) has students collect and exchange information about their local environment with other schools around the world in order to foster global awareness. In the "Global Grocery List Project" (http://www.landmark-project.com/ggl), students contribute to a worldwide database of information on the distribution, cost, and use of a variety of grocery items. And the "Friends and Flags" project (http://www.friendsandflags.org) promotes cultural awareness by having students make a personally relevant contribution to a global peace chain.

Other telecollaborative projects engage classrooms and students in problem-solving and action-taking projects. For example, the "Making Our World Better" project (www.kidlink.org/english/voice/index.html) has children contribute their ideas and read the comments of other children from around the world on topics such as recycling, racism, poverty, violence, and war. They can also ask questions of other collaborators, share their thoughts, and plan action projects in online chats. The Voices of Youth site from UNICEF (http://www.unicef.org/voy) also offers a number of ongoing discussions and opportunities for getting involved in a variety of action projects.

ACTIVE ENGAGEMENT

Here are some more examples of websites that provide suggestions for online projects:

- 2Learn Project Centre: http://www.2learn.ca/Projects/ProjectCentre/projintro.html
- Learn to Telecollaborate! page on the Learn Quebec website: http://www.learnquebec.ca/en/content/pedagogy/cil/telecollab
- The Connected Classroom's Registry of Telecollaborative Projects page on the Learn Quebec website:http://www.learnquebec.ca/en/content/pedagogy/cil/cc-registry
- Using Technology in the Classroom page on the Saskatoon Public Schools website: http://www.saskschools.ca/curr_content/techclass
- Harnessing the Power of the Web: A Tutorial for Collaborative Project-Based Learning: http://gsh.lightspan.com/web

Decide on a grade level and content focus, and then examine these sites to find a project that you think might be suitable.

Webcasts

Webcasts are a type of collaborative learning whose use is gaining momentum, particularly with older students. Webcast technology allows students to view real-time events as they are happening, or to access archived events at a later time. Indian and Northern Affairs Canada's "Connecting Youth in Canada" webcast series (http://www.ainc-inac.gc.ca/connex/wbcst10_e.html), for example, is a forum in which Aboriginal students initiate conversations with other Aboriginal and non-Aboriginal students using webcasts and email. Archived webcasts are also available at the website—in both video and transcript form. Some of the archived discussion topics include growing up Metis, exploring the richness of cultural diversity, and the challenges facing youth. Another example, "The Jason Project" from National Geographic (http://www.jason.org/public/home.aspx), involves students in exploring environmental issues using webcasts as well as other electronic tools. And National Geographic Live provides an archive of social studies–related webcasts (http://www.nationalgeographic.com/nglive/archives.html).

Videoconferencing

Videoconferencing is another means of extending the learning experiences of students beyond the confines of the classroom—by visually connecting people at two or more locations at the same time over a computer network. Using videoconferencing, students can interact with expert guests at numerous sites without having to travel. Students can also be connected through videoconferencing to students in other classrooms or to organizations and educational facilities across the country and around the world. Having the opportunity to see, hear, and interact with others in real time makes the learning experience more meaningful for students, while also enhancing their critical thinking, communication, and collaboration skills. Videoconferencing technology also allows collaborators to share computer applications such as web pages, documents, and software.

CLASSROOM APPLICATION

As a part of their "My Community" unit, Mrs. Wong's Grade 1 class was studying transportation needs and options in their community. To bring an authentic experience to her students, Mrs. Wong connected her class to the control tower at the local airport using Polycom videoconferencing equipment. Through the use of this technology, the students were able to meet the controller and ask questions about his job as well as see the equipment that he uses and view the runway from the tower.

In another classroom, Mr. Klausen's Grade 6 class was studying about environmental pollution as part of their social studies unit on resource sustainability. The class was able to videoconference with the federal minister of the environment to ask questions about the plans and policies that were in place to address some of the local issues that they had identified in their research. They also debated Canada's stance on the Kyoto Protocol.

Technology Connection For descriptions of the different types of equipment used in videoconferencing, and for more information on how to set up a videoconferencing project, see "What does videoconferencing look like in K–12 classrooms?" at the Videoconferencing: A Digital Handbook for Teachers and Students website (http://www.d261.k12.id.us/VCing/) and "Videoconferencing for Learning" at the Knowledge Network Explorer site (http://www.kn.pacbell.com/wired/vidconf/intro.html).

Using Technology-Based Presentation Activities to Encourage Students' Producing and Sharing of Knowledge

Computers are most effective in schools when students use them as productivity and creativity tools to apply new learning. Equally as important for enhancing students' learning is their sharing of new understandings with others. While up to this point in the chapter we have focused exclusively on online activities as a means of developing students' higher-level thinking and collaboration skills, children can also benefit from using a combination of online *and* offline computer tools to produce and share social studies knowledge.

Presentation software allows students to design their own multimedia experiences to share their research and learning with others. For example, through the use of a slide-show format, students can structure a presentation to highlight the key aspects of what they have learned through their investigations. By including images and graphics in their presentations, students can demonstrate their understanding visually, which is increasingly important in today's image-driven world. Prepared images such as those available through online clip art sites (e.g., http://classroomclipart.com) can be used, or students can create their own graphics using software

illustration programs such as CorelDRAW, PC Paint, and Adobe Illustrator, or multimedia software such as Kid Pix Studio Deluxe. Students can also use equipment such as digital cameras to create their own image collections to represent learning in a particular subject area.

Presentation software can also facilitate students' integration of visual information such as graphs, tables, and charts into their presentations, as well as their inclusion of graphics and sound and video clips. Including a

Allowing for student authoring, publishing, and presenting shifts students from being solely receivers of knowledge to being constructors of new knowledge.

variety of formats such as text, sounds, graphics, video clips, and web pages in their presentations is an excellent way for students to engage all of the differing learning preferences in the classroom. An added benefit of presentation software is that it can help to make students' presentations clearer, neater, and better organized.

The two most commonly used presentation software programs are Microsoft PowerPoint and HyperStudio. *HyperStudio 5* (from Sunburst Technology) is a CD-ROM–based program that allows students to experience a multisensory learning environment. Students using HyperStudio can control the rate and direction of their learning and can make use of graphics, video, animation, and sound to meet their differing learning needs. Students can also create their own interactive multimedia presentations using this software.

w w w **Technology Connection**

- For demonstrations and free trial downloads of HyperStudio products, visit the Software MacKiev Company website: http://www.mackiev.com/hyperstudio/index.html. Also visit the Building Learning with Technology website's Hyperstudio Tutorial page: www.education.umd.edu/blt/hyperstudio.

- For more information on using PowerPoint, visit Act Media's PowerPoint in the Classroom website: www.actden.com/pp.

Children can also create their own movies to demonstrate what they have learned, using a video editing tool such as Apple's iMovie (for a tutorial, see http://www.apple.com/support/imovie/tutorial). They can either use a digital video camera to shoot their own moving images or take clips off the internet; they then cut and paste them together and add background music, voiceovers, and a title and credits.

As creators of knowledge, students should also be given opportunities to learn to make their own websites so that they can publish their work. Such an exercise has the added benefit of showing students how easy it is to become a web author. (For tutorials on how to create web pages, see the Web Monkey for Kids website from Lycos Canada (www.webmonkey.com/kids).

Respectful, Responsible, and Critical Use of Technology

A final factor related to technology that needs to be addressed in your social studies program is the issue of its respectful, responsible, and critical use by students. Students need to be made aware not only of aspects of "netiquette" (etiquette on the net) but also of the various impacts of technology on society.

First, in learning to see themselves as good digital citizens, students should come to understand the importance of observing the rules of netiquette when they are online. This includes their recognizing the importance of not causing damage to others' sites or computers by hacking or distributing worms and viruses and of not creating websites that are demeaning or malicious. Students also need to learn how to be wise and safe users of the various online technologies.

Second, toward the goal of promoting digital citizenship, you will need to consider the question of what information about technology's role in society should be included in your social studies program. Computers have significantly changed our educational and social systems. In order to become more technologically literate, students need to be encouraged to think critically about the technologies they are using and about the relevance and appropriateness of their use. Issues for discussion could range from the displacement of handwriting skills by keyboarding, plagiarism from the internet, and cheating on exams using electronics to the loss of socialization skills caused by online gaming and the potential for loss of identity as a result of using avatars in digital environments.

Digital citizens also need to be informed about and be able to debate issues related to the socioeconomic and political ramifications of rampant, uncontrolled technology use. Students should be given opportunities to explore and critically discuss what happens as society creates and implements technologies, particularly as this relates to moral, ethical, and equity issues arising from development and changes in human communication; how the concept of community is changing; what effects technology has on cultural unity and diversity; and how information itself is changing. The very important issue of the effects of inequitable access to computer technologies could also be adapted into a relevant discussion topic for all age levels.

Chapter Summary

This chapter on integrating online technologies into your teaching of social studies began by identifying the benefits of online activities for supporting and enhancing teaching and learning. Emerging from this discussion was an acknowledgement of constructivism as an effective approach to framing learning experiences involving online technologies. We then examined WebQuests, Web Inquiry Projects, online adventures, virtual field trips, email exchanges, blogs, discussion boards or forums, telecollaborative projects, webcasts, and videoconferencing as activities that have the potential to effectively address constructivist learning principles as well as the development of the digital literacy skills of higher-level thinking, problem solving collaboration, and communication at the elementary level. Next, we looked at ways to encourage students to view themselves as knowledge constructors by having them apply and share the results of their research through designing their own web pages, movies, and other technology-based presentations. The chapter concluded with an emphasis on the importance of teaching students to be respectful, responsible, and critical users of technology.

In summary, to maximize the use of technology in your social studies program, computer use should support student-directed learning, active student engagement, and student control over decision making. Emphasis should be placed on real-world, authentic issues and questions of interest to students, on activities that require higher levels of thinking and understanding, and on cooperative learning, both within and beyond the classroom walls.

Part Five

How Should Children's Learning in Social Studies Be Assessed?

In this part of the book we turn to the question of how to assess children's growth and learning in social studies. Even though assessment is the last of the five key questions to be addressed, it is not meant to suggest that deciding on assessment strategies is the final thing you should do as a teacher when planning your social studies program. In fact, the most effective assessment practice is on going from the beginning of the learning experience through to the end so it should be one of the first things that you consider in planning your social studies program.

Chapter 13 addresses the sub-question, "What different approaches to assessment are there?" The chapter begins by examining two differing views of assessment—a knowledge acquisition approach and a constructivist approach—each representing different teaching goals and views of children's learning needs. Three purposes of assessment—diagnostic, formative, and summative—are then addressed with the remainder of the chapter providing a variety of assessment tools that focus on each of these purposes. The tools examined here include tests, demonstrations, portfolios, self-assessment, anecdotal records, and student conferencing. Program evaluation is also identified as an important part of any assessment plan. The chapter concludes with a suggested strategy for dealing with assessment as a part of your overall social studies program plan.

Chapter 13

What Different Approaches to Assessment Are There?

Another very important question that you will need to think about in planning your social studies program and one that should be considered early on in the planning process is how best to determine what your students are learning from their social studies experiences and what their learning journey is like for them. You always need to be aware that there can be a big difference between the curriculum as taught and the curriculum as experienced. Just because you thought a lesson went well you cannot assume that that all of your students understood it in the way you hoped. Rather, you should seek evidence of understanding through student performance. How you go about determining what that performance should look like will differ depending on your students' learning preferences, interests and developmental levels, and on your goals and beliefs about how children learn. Selecting an approach to assessment that matches your goals and addresses your students' learning needs is very important for ensuring the success of your social studies program.

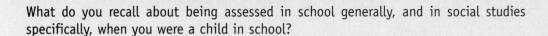

LOOKING BACK

What do you recall about being assessed in school generally, and in social studies specifically, when you were a child in school?

Distinguishing Assessment From Evaluation

When thinking about assessment, it is important to recognize that it is not the same as evaluation, although the terms are used often interchangeably. Assessment is the gathering of descriptive information throughout the learning process to guide both your students and you as the teacher in making decisions about how to help each child to progress. The process involves both the teacher and the students in observing, recording, and documenting the work the children do and how they do it. Evaluation is about making a judgment about the learner based on the teacher's interpretation of the assessment information collected. It is also a way of showing the students and their parents/guardians where their learning fits in relation to others at the same grade level in relation to the intended learning outcomes (Davies, 2000).

Teachers' Personal Professional Goals as Influences on Assessment Choices

As you might expect by now, there are alternative approaches to assessment reflecting different views of how to educate the good citizen and what kinds of growth are important to being and becoming that citizen. There are also different ideas about the purpose for assessment. In some assessment-related literature, a distinction is made between two ways of thinking about the purpose of assessment—assessment for learning and assessment of learning. Assessment of learning is about finding out what children know and can do in relation to the learning outcomes usually at the culmination of a unit of study. Assessment for learning is about assessment that is integrated into everyday instruction throughout the learning process to improve student learning (Stiggins & Chappuis, 2006).

w(w)w Technology Link

- A 2006 document from Manitoba Education, Citizenship, and Youth titled "Rethinking classroom assessment with purpose in mind" (http://www.edu.gov. mb.ca/k12/assess/wncp), identifies three purposes of assessment—assessment of learning, assessment for learning, and assessment as learning. In this model, assessment for learning is used by the teacher on an ongoing basis to gather information to assist in differentiating his/her teaching to improve learning, while assessment as learning focuses on the students and their metacognitive role in assessing their own learning. "It occurs when students monitor their own learning and use the feedback from this monitoring to make adjustments, adaptations, and even major changes in what they understand" (p. 13).

Here we will examine two contrasting approaches to assessment that show the difference between the purposes of assessment. These approaches are rooted in different beliefs about what is important knowledge, how best to determine student growth in relation to that knowledge, and the roles and responsibilities of teachers and students in assessment.

The Knowledge Acquisition Approach to Assessment

Teachers who take a more traditional knowledge acquisition approach to assessment believe that there is a universally agreed upon body of social studies content knowledge that all children need to accumulate. The teaching of that body of knowledge is considered

Teacher-to-individual student questioning is routine in the knowledge acquisition approach to assessment.

separate from the assessment of whether the child has learned it; thus, the teacher teaches and then tests. The focus of assessment from this view is on the amount of accurate knowledge that the children have acquired from the teacher and the textbook.

Knowledge acquisition assessment emphasizes a one-time approach to assessing knowledge based on a single set of data. Grading students is usually based on end products, on their memorization and recall skills, and on their ability to provide selected responses. The assessment tools used are teacher focused and reflect a one-way pattern of instruction from teacher to student.

The students' roles in the knowledge acquisition classroom are to respond to the teacher's questions, to focus on the memorization of facts, to complete the required teacher-directed work and to pass the test. Instruction is typically done in a didactic way with students listening to the teacher, responding to questions initiated by the teacher or the textbook and working independently. The emphasis is on low-level cognitive activities.

The most common tool used to assess student learning is the teacher-designed test. Testing is done typically at the end of a unit of study. These tests are made up generally of short answer, recall, and fill-in-the-blanks questions to which there is a selected response. The students are to give the right answers, uncritically. These tests are then used to produce scores that can be reported to parents and administrators. The scores rank students in comparison to each other. Competitiveness for the best marks is fostered. Motivation is extrinsic to the student and often includes reinforcement techniques such as stars on a perfect test paper or prizes for the highest marks. Because right-answer tests give teachers the power to distribute success and failure, making extensive use of these tests is one way to increase the teacher's power and control over students' learning.

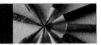
What goals and kinds of growth would be most important in this assessment approach? In your opinion, would the knowledge acquisition approach to assessment help you to achieve your goals as a social studies teacher?

A Constructivist Approach to Assessment

On the other end of the continuum is an approach to assessment based on constructivist learning theory. Constructivist theory maintains that students learn best when they are encouraged through inquiry to ask questions and to seek answers, when their ideas are invited and acknowledged as being important, and when they are given opportunities to examine their ideas and seek clarification through dialogue with the teacher and their peers.

A constructivist approach to assessment, therefore, focuses on the meaning that learners are co-constructing from their interactions with the world, while the learning is occurring. Knowledge about individual children and how they learn drives this approach. Through assessment, the teacher tries to reveal what the students know and understand and how those new understandings have developed. Rather than an expectation that all learners will arrive at the same place because of their learning experiences, this approach allows for the development, representation, and assessment of differing views. Assessment is varied and ongoing throughout the learning process.

Advocates of a constructivist approach to assessment envision learning as interactive, purposeful, and process oriented. Through the use of authentic problems and questions, students actively engage in learning tasks in which they need to work with their new knowledge by applying higher level thinking skills. Here, the teacher is more interested in the students' ability to use knowledge to create justifiable solutions to problems than in getting a "correct" answer. Such assessment fits the goals of teachers who want students to grow in their ability to do inquiry. Assessment is aimed at identifying and supporting that growth in understanding, rather than testing the recall of facts. The purpose of assessment is more likely to be to help students set goals for themselves and to help teachers work with students in planning what they need to work on.

Assessment that is constructivist is based on a set of criterion-referenced skills, not norms. Since the emphasis is on what the individual child can do, everyone has an equal chance and opportunity to succeed. In this way, cooperative learning is fostered. Students are compared to their own past performances and their personal goals for improvement are set based on where they have been, where they are going, and what they need to learn to get there. Students play a more active role in the assessment of their own learning by the use of things such as reflective exercises, self-assessments, and portfolios. Students typically view this type of assessment as being more relevant, respectful, confidential, fair, timely, and helpful. They are intrinsically motivated by a personal desire to better their own performance in relation to their learning goals.

Constructivist assessors are also concerned with authenticity or how closely the task or process being assessed replicates something that would be experienced outside of school. A teacher who assesses for authenticity would create natural or real-life settings and activities in order to document how learners think and behave over an extended period. The children would be assessed on a continuous basis on their academic achievement as well as on their personal and social growth. Rather than relying solely on a final product, the teacher would use multiple sources for gathering information that would give a more accurate picture of students' progress and emphasize the process of learning.

Table 13.1 summarizes the key differences between the two approaches to assessment.

TABLE 13.1 ■ Summary Chart Comparing the Two Approaches to Assessment

KNOWLEDGE ACQUISITION APPROACH TO ASSESSMENT	CONSTRUCTIVIST APPROACH TO ASSESSMENT
Assessment of learning	Assessment for learning
Happens at the end of a unit when learning is over	Ongoing throughout the unit; dynamic and integral part of the learning activities
Occurs in isolation	Intricately linked to learning and instruction
Teacher controlled	Encourages student accountability; student involvement in setting criteria and performance standards
Contrived context	Students assessed in the environment in which they are learning
Recall of information	Higher level application and assessment
Focused on what has been learned	Focused on the learner and the learning experience; performance based
Knowledge is objective	Knowledge is subjective
Norm referenced; results used to compare children to each other and to the norm	Criterion referenced; builds on students' strengths, used to give feedback and support learning

ACTIVE ENGAGEMENT

Examine the summary chart of the two approaches to assessment above (Table 13.1). What hidden curriculum is at work in each approach to assessment? How might each approach affect students' self-concepts and the way they see themselves as learners? How might the approach to assessment you choose influence the level of responsibility your students are willing to take for their learning?

Types of Assessment

Teachers who assess on an ongoing basis generally have three different purposes for assessing, namely diagnostic, formative, and summative.

Diagnostic Purposes

Diagnostic tools would be used to find out what students know at the beginning of the year, the unit, or the lesson in order to assist in determining students' strengths and weaknesses and in setting the direction for the instruction. Using diagnostic tools, teachers can find out where instruction needs to be differentiated based on students' needs, whether particular skills or content needs to be retaught or if certain content should be eliminated from the plan as it is already well known and understood by students. Diagnostic tools can also help students to test their own thinking and look for ways that their ideas are changing because of their learning experiences.

CLASSROOM APPLICATION

Here is an example of a diagnostic tool that Mr. Burns, a Grade 6 teacher, used to determine his students' beliefs about being a good citizen prior to beginning a unit on local government. What sort of information do you think he would have been able to collect from the use of this tool? How might he have used this information?

1. Being a good citizen means

voting in an election.	Agree	Disagree	Don't know
writing letters, sending an email or phoning members of the government.	Agree	Disagree	Don't know
writing letters to the newspapers.	Agree	Disagree	Don't know
signing petitions.	Agree	Disagree	Don't know
taking part in protests such as marches.	Agree	Disagree	Don't know
picketing.	Agree	Disagree	Don't know

2. A good citizen

obeys the law.	Agree	Disagree	Don't know
is always polite.	Agree	Disagree	Don't know
is loyal to his or her family.	Agree	Disagree	Don't know
works hard.	Agree	Disagree	Don't know
has good table manners.	Agree	Disagree	Don't know

studies hard in school.	Agree	Disagree	Don't know
pays his/her taxes regularly.	Agree	Disagree	Don't know
keeps up with what is happening in the world.	Agree	Disagree	Don't know
stands up when O Canada is played.	Agree	Disagree	Don't know
joins a political party.	Agree	Disagree	Don't know
tries to change things in the government.	Agree	Disagree	Don't know
3. a) If I wanted to, I could get someone in the city government to listen to what I want.	Agree	Disagree	Don't know
b) I believe that when I grow up I will have a fair chance of influencing people in government.	Agree	Disagree	Don't know
c) If a school rule was unfair I would do something to get it changed.	Agree	Disagree	Don't know

Other techniques for assessing children's preconceptions include KWLs or brainstorming, webbing, drawing a picture in response reading a story, completing a sentence such as "Peace is . . .," and role-playing.

Formative Purposes

A second purpose for assessment is the ongoing assessment that happens in the classroom on a daily basis. Both teachers and students engage in formative assessment. Teachers can use observation, one-on-one conversations, checklists, anecdotal records, and other tools to look at the progress that each individual student is making and to check for places that students need more scaffolding to extend their learning or where particular content or skills need to be retaught. Students can use journals, learning logs, self-assessment checklists, and questionnaires to do frequent checks into their learning journeys.

 **Technology Link**

- The Ontario Ministry of Education has provided sample assessment tasks for social studies and student samples of work for Grades 1 to 6. To view these samples go to http://www.edu.gov.on.ca/eng/curriculum/elementary and search for Social Studies and then the Ontario Curriculum Exemplars: Social Studies.

Summative Purposes

The third area of assessment occurs at the end of the unit to determine whether the teacher and students' goals and learning outcomes have been met.

Miss Harvey, a Grade 1 teacher, affixes a bare paper tree on the wall and attaches a package of cut out paper leaves. The children are asked to write down an idea about the topic they are going to be talking about in social studies on a leaf and add it to the tree (diagnostic). She encourages the children to keep adding new leaves whenever they feel like it throughout the unit (formative). At the end of the unit, she has the children look carefully at the ideas they have written on the topic tree and see if there are any that they would change or remove completely from the tree because of what they have learned (summative).

ACTIVE ENGAGEMENT

With a partner, discuss some ideas for tools that you could use for diagnostic, formative, and summative assessments.

Research on learning styles also suggests different methods of assessment, for example, an auditory learner would need to be able to show what he or she has learned in different ways than a visual or kinesthetic learner.

Children's Learning Needs as an Influence on Assessment Choices

We know a great deal about children's developmental needs and that knowledge can be used to help you decide on an approach to assessment in your social studies program. From the work on brain research, for example, we know that each child is unique and comes to any learning situation with concepts and patterns

266 PART FIVE How Should Children's Learning in Social Studies Be Assessed?

NEL

already established based on previous experiences. Assessment that uncovers these preconceptions and identifies how they are changed by engaging in new learning experiences is most beneficial. We also know that when children are actively and concretely involved in their learning, when they put what they have learned to immediate use, and when they can see real-world applications for it, they retain more knowledge. Student choice, initiative, and self-pacing encourage learning. Your assessment plan, therefore, would need to address diversity in the needs of each individual learner in your classroom and involve activities that are meaningful and useful for them.

w w w Technology Link

- While each learner learns in their own way and at their own pace there are some general learning milestones that can help in determining the age appropriateness of assessment activities. For example, see the Slatington Elementary website for grade level and subject area suggestions (http://schools.nlsd.org/sesnlsd/milestones.htm).

Another factor to consider regarding children's learning needs and assessment is the research on intelligence. According to Gardner's Multiple Intelligences Theory (2000), there are many ways of representing intelligence. Accordingly, children need flexibility in how they demonstrate what they have learned. Assessment in this case comes from finding out in what ways each individual is intelligent, not how intelligent she or he is. Such assessment is focused on outcomes, based on performance, and on students showing their new understandings in authentic and relevant ways.

Robert Sternberg in his Theory of Triarchic Intelligence (1985) argues that intelligence is not just one thing but also rather an interchange of three aspects—the analytical (the learner's ability to critique, compare/contrast, evaluate), the creative (the learner's ability to discover, imagine, predict, invent) and the practical (the learner's ability to apply the learning and put it into practice). Sternberg (1997) suggests that when we match instruction to students' abilities, achievement is improved, and that when we expand the range of abilities we "test" for, we also expand the range of students we identify as "smart." Gardner and Sternberg concur that the important thing about assessment is that intelligence is best defined in performance-based ways that are rooted in everyday activities rather than on traditional intelligence tests. Performance-based assessments also allow for cultural differences in determining what is considered intelligent (Sternberg, 1997/1999).

Thus, if assessment is intended to enhance students' learning and help them to grow as learners you as the teacher will need to consider carefully your students' learning needs in the approach to assessment that you choose for your social studies program.

REFLECTION POINT

What does this review of students' learning needs tell you about planning your assessment strategies for your social studies program?

Choosing Appropriate Assessment Tools

Once you have decided on an approach to assessment that matches your goals and your students' learning needs, you will need to select assessment tools that would best help to address those choices. In this section, you will have the opportunity to look at a variety of assessment tools. When examining each tool it is important to ask yourself some critical questions such as:

1. What purpose would the tool serve?
2. What information would the tool give you about your students and your program?
3. How and when should you use the tool?
4. Does the tool help you to assess knowledge, skills, and/or attitudinal outcomes?
5. Would the results of the tool adequately represent the student's performance and abilities?
6. Would use of the tool enable all students to demonstrate their attitudes, skills, and knowledge or does it unfairly disadvantage some students?
7. Would the tool adequately assess higher levels of understanding?

Testing as an Assessment Tool

LOOKING BACK

Think back on some of your own experiences with testing as a child in school. What do you remember? What experience, if any, have you had with standardized achievement and proficiency tests? What is your opinion of them? What hidden curriculum is at work in these approaches to testing?

Right-Answer Tests

Tests are the most commonly used assessment tool in social studies programs. Testing can have different purposes and formats depending on your goals and beliefs about student learning. One approach to testing is the right-answer test that is administered typically at the end of a unit of study to determine students' level of recall about important content that had been addressed over the duration of the unit. Typically these questions are lower level "who," "what," "where," "when," and "how" type questions.

Critics of this traditional approach to testing claim that the use of a single set of data such as "selected-response" testing does not provide a clear or accurate picture of what students can do with their knowledge. Learning is not a stand-alone occurrence. Right-answer tests tend to test isolated facts in an arbitrary order that confuses students and ignores the importance of holistic knowing and the integration of knowledge. Often what is learned to prepare for these tests is narrowly applicable and soon forgotten. The test often demonstrates only recall and, to some extent, comprehension of the content learned and shows only a narrowly defined view of what the student has learned. These tests rarely indicate whether students are able to interpret information for important purposes. As well, selected-response testing cannot assess students' ability to function as competent participants in society.

The other major concern with selected-response testing is that test scores continue to be used to classify children. There is little opportunity for the child to imagine himself or herself being successful at something if he or she continues to perform poorly on tests. All the motivation for learning is extrinsic to the learner as the teacher and the test score control how the child sees himself/herself as a learner.

When people assert that academic standards in the schools are declining, they think of scores on one-size-fits-all tests of information acquired and concepts understood. Standardized tests, for example, fit with many of the points raised about selected response tests. They are designed to perform an accountability role in education by providing an overall view of student achievement in the core subjects.

An entire industry has emerged around the formal testing mode of assessment.

Most standardized tests are norm referenced. They allow for comparisons between students' scores in schools, districts, and across the country. They do not diagnose students' work in a way that assists them because they don't show students where they went wrong. Students never see their corrected test papers. Even teachers have no idea where the students went wrong, nor do they usually play a part in test construction or scoring. As well, the questions are largely linguistic and the language of the test can be very difficult and confusing, especially for ESL students and students with poor reading skills. Test anxiety is another issue that arises from the use of standardized testing.

These tests also put pressure on teachers to narrow the curriculum and they often end up teaching to the test. They can also conflict with what the teacher believes about effective assessment. The challenge becomes finding a way to both address the important content in the curriculum and make it meaningful and developmentally appropriate for all of your students.

ACTIVE ENGAGEMENT

Find out if your province has standardized achievement tests for social studies at the elementary level. (See, for example, "Assessment practices of Canadian provinces" at http://www.education.gov.ab.ca as a starting point.) If there are such tests, find samples using the provincial ministry of education site for your province/territory (http://www.edu.gov.on.ca). Debate the value of these tests as assessment tools.

Open-ended Testing

An alternative to selected-response testing is open-ended testing. Open-ended test questions allow for different interpretations, generative responses, and higher level thinking. For example, a question like, "Should we strengthen our links with the United States? Support your answer with fully explained details" rather than "What links do we have to the United States" would allow students to explain their ideas and provide reasons for their response. Having these explanations can be very beneficial for the teacher in order to determine not only what the child is thinking but why.

When designing open-ended tests, you should consider which performances you want your students to be good at. In this way, tests can be designed to collect evidence of knowing. The content of these tests (the knowledge and skills assessed) would need to match both your proposed outcomes and the instructional emphasis. The test items would also need to represent the full range of knowledge and skills that are the primary targets of instruction.

Students can be involved in creating some of their own examination questions and in deciding what would constitute a good answer. In this way, expectations for student performance would be clear. To come up with their questions, students would need to reflect on what they have studied and make judgments about what would be considered to be the important things to test. Prior to the test, students could be encouraged to review the important learning together in study groups or by playing a review game. The actual test could even be set up as a game-like activity.

CLASSROOM APPLICATION

As review for an upcoming test, Mrs. Groves had her Grade 3 class come up with questions based on the content of a unit on Canada's geography they had just finished. She encouraged students to think beyond recall and one-answer type questions. She collected these questions and then chose ones that she felt best represented the content covered. The class was divided into five teams of four and each team was asked one of the questions. They worked as a team to come up with the answer. Play continued until all teams had the opportunity to answer several questions.

Students could also be given the opportunity to write an open-ended essay type exam that they could take home to work on. Allowing for this type of testing would better address the needs of second language learners and students with other special learning needs. Testing of students with learning challenges could also be conducted orally with the student responses being tape-recorded or scribed to allow them to look back and modify their answers.

Testing that is worthwhile is unobtrusive, allows ample time for students to respond, is free to extraneous factors that may confuse students, and can involve a group process.

Ms. Martin, a Grade 4 teacher, wanted to see how much her students learned about China as the unit came to a close. She gave the students a test that had one open-ended question: "Tell me everything that you have learned about China over the last few weeks in social studies. Try to include at least five new things that you now know about China. Use a new paragraph for each idea and provide specific evidence to support your claims." Students were awarded two points for each idea and the evidence provided for a total of 10. What do you think of this approach to testing?

Demonstrations of Learning as an Assessment Tool

While tests have an important place as summative assessment tools, they rarely allow for a thorough display of what is learned. Performance-based assessment is an alternative to testing that allows students to show what they have learned and how they can apply that knowledge. Some ways of engaging students in representing what they have learned include giving a talk on what has been learned about the topic, designing a mural about the key ideas and concepts from the topic, building a model to represent what was learned, doing a mind map showing key concepts and generalizations, writing a report, developing an interactive computer presentation, choreographing a dance related to the topic of study, designing a simulation, teaching or explaining to someone else what was learned, doing a photo essay about the topic, creating a song, summarizing with pictures related to something learned, engaging in a debate about an issue related to the topic, and creating a group project. Students could also be encouraged to design something of their own choosing to show what they have learned.

Using Rubrics

Rubrics can be a helpful tool for assessing students' demonstrations of their learning. A rubric usually contains a set of criteria that outline the skills and content to be developed along with a scale of performance ranging from acceptable to unacceptable (Figure 13.1). These criteria should help students to determine areas where their work still needs improvement.

Limiting the number of performance categories and amount of detail provided on the rubric is important to make it less confusing for students. Having samples of work that would show the quality of work at each level would also help with clarification. The rubric used to assess the learning should be made available to students prior to commencing the assessment activity so that the students can be guided by the requirements throughout the activity. Rubrics should also be seen as being flexible so that modifications can be made on an ongoing basis as the demonstrations of learning evolve. Involving the students in the creation of assessment rubrics is one way to help them both to take more ownership for the assignment and to understand better what is expected of them in terms of their performance and the demonstration of their learning.

FIGURE 13.1 ■ Sample Rubric for Assessing Student Written Work

4	3	2	1
— Ideas and reasons are organized, insightful and well developed with specific detail.	— Most ideas and reasons are organized, important, and clear with mostly specific detail.	— A few relevant ideas are evident and reasons have only a little elaboration; more general than specific.	— Ideas and development are unclear or irrelevant with mostly vague details; topic development is insufficient.
— Strong organizational strategy	— Generally strong organizational strategy	— Some evidence of organizational strategy	— Too brief to indicate organization
— Conventions of writing are accurate and effective in relation to purpose.	— Conventions of writing are generally accurate and effective in relation to purpose.	— Conventions of writing are generally accurate.	— Frequent or many mechanical errors may be distracting.

ACTIVE ENGAGEMENT

Examine the rubric provided in Figure 13.1 that was designed to assess a social studies project report. In your opinion, how useful would this rubric be for guiding students' work? What would you add to make it more helpful?

w(w)w **Technology Link** Visit the book's companion website for links to the web pages below. There are numerous websites containing teacher-designed rubrics that you may be able to adapt for your own use. See for example, sites such as:

- http://school.discovery.com/schrockguide/assess.html
- http://members.tripod.com/~ozpk/01rubric
- http://www.ncsu.edu/midlink/ho.html

You can also design your own rubrics using the following sites:

- Rubistar: http://rubistar.4teachers.org/index.php
- The Build Your Own Rubric activity at The 2Learn Project Centre: http://www.2learn.ca
- Rubrics.com: http://www.rubrics.com
- Teachnology: http://www.teach-nology.com

The Learning Portfolio as an Assessment Tool

Another alternative to the test that can provide a clearer picture of students' ongoing and overall learning is the learning portfolio. A learning portfolio is a purposeful collection of student work that exhibits to the student and to others the student's efforts, progress, or achievements. Learning portfolios are meant to be a celebration of a child's accomplishments because they focus on what the child knows and can do. Such a collection can assist teachers in monitoring and evaluating student performance and in diagnosing learners' strengths and weaknesses. Portfolios also illustrate student growth and learning over time.

ACTIVE ENGAGEMENT

Discuss in groups any experience you have in classrooms where portfolios were a part of the teacher's assessment plan. What ideas for the use of portfolios did you get from this experience? Why might you want to use portfolios as assessment tools in your social studies program?

Portfolios are a form of personal development because they promote student self-assessment and reflection on learning. Active involvement in the decision making about what to include in their portfolios to best represent their academic efforts is an excellent way to enhance students' learning. When deciding on pieces to include in their portfolios, students need to be encouraged to ask themselves why they are making the choices they are. They should reflect on their choices by completing sentence stems such as: "I chose this work because . . ." and "I think it shows my progress because . . ." Students develop new understandings of their thinking as they become accomplished at assessing their own work, thus promoting intellectual autonomy and self respect. As children express ideas and reveal their thinking, teachers can gain insights into how to design instruction to match students' demonstrated needs. See Figure 13.2.

FIGURE 13.2 ■ Things to Consider for Inclusion in a Learning Portfolio

- responses on KWLs or brainstorms at the beginning of a unit
- goal setting activity results
- sample research plans
- individual and team idea brainstorms
- progress reports
- completed retrieval charts and other data collection tools
- examples of work done throughout an investigation
- videotapes, audiotapes, photographs of the child engaged in activities
- reflections, journal entries, reactions, and feelings
- self assessments
- teacher comments and assessments
- photos of hands-on products created
- results of individual and group projects

Technology Link One possibility for creating portfolios is to create one electronically. Electronic portfolios are multimedia collections of students' work that can be made available on the web or by other media such as CD-ROMs. (For examples of how to create an online portfolio, see http://electronicportfolios.com.)

Self-Assessment as a Learning Tool

Another approach to assessment shifts control primarily to students by asking them to be self-assessors. Self-assessment places high priority on growth in independence, ownership, self-direction, and enhanced self-esteem. Students learn to take responsibility for their own learning by engaging at the outset in setting their own goals and making frequent checks to see how their learning relates to these goals. Such reflection helps children to establish links between previous knowledge and new knowledge because as students monitor their own thinking, they notice connections between what they used to know and what they now know. Not only does this connection-making help students to create meaning, but they also come to better understand the processes involved in learning and the strategies that help them to learn. They can then use this information to plan how to better approach future tasks and projects.

Journals or informal learning logs are useful tools for developing students' capacity to assess their own learning. Some examples of reflective questions to guide students' journaling are: "How is my thinking changing about . . . ?," "Why is this change important?," "How does this new learning fit with what I already know?," "What works best for me when I am trying to learn something new?," "How do I feel about what I have accomplished?," and, "What would I do differently the next time?"

Teachers also need to foster metacognition by teaching students how to think about their own thinking using probing questions such as: "What kind of thinking did you do in this lesson?," "How did you come to understand . . . ?," "What influenced your thinking about . . . ?"

Groups also need to be involved in assessing their success and overall group effort. After completing a particular group activity, group members could be asked to finish statements such as: "What we did as a group to cooperate with each other," "What cooperative skills we used," "What problems we encountered," "How we addressed these problems as a group," "What skills we got better at," and "What we would do differently the next time we work in groups." Opportunity should be provided for individuals to complete their responses to these sentence starters first and then to share with other group members and discuss their differing perceptions of the effectiveness of the group.

Students also need to be encouraged to examine their own personal contribution to the group by responding to such questions as: "How did I share my ideas in the group?," "Did I cooperate with the group members?," "Did I respect the ideas of others in my group?," "Did I share resources effectively with group members?," and "How well did I stay on task and complete my part of the group work?"

By using group and self-assessment, teachers can further determine students' personal and social growth and attitudinal development including their initiative, teamwork, leadership, independence, problem-solving and decision-making skills, and their respect for the ideas and contributions of others. Attitude objectives are often viewed as a difficult area to assess so taking opportunities such as this whenever they arise can be very beneficial for ensuring that all learning outcomes are being addressed in your social studies program.

REFLECTION POINT

What roles are students assigned when asked to self assess? What is the hidden curriculum? What conception of the good citizen does self-assessment suggest?

Anecdotal Records as Assessment Tools

Teacher-generated anecdotes about children's learning activities are valuable tools for both assessing children on their personal growth and development and for assisting the teacher with progress report writing. Observations of students both in and outside class help the teacher to notice the strengths and weaknesses of individual students. Watching students working alone, in small groups, and in large groups, at various times of day and under differing circumstances helps the teacher to develop a clearer understanding of students' existing attitudes, knowledge, and skills, and the areas in which they still need to grow. Anecdotes about students' work habits, cooperation, group skills, participation, creativity, on-task behaviour, enthusiasm, motivation, thinking skills, and knowledge of the content also provide relevant and useful information for future conferencing with parents and for reporting on student progress.

Anecdotes can be written based on information gathered by the use of teacher-designed and administered observation checklists or they can be written as informal point-form notes. An effective way of organizing these anecdotes is by preparing an alphabetized binder with a place for making dated entries for each of your students. The most comprehensive and effective way of maintaining these records is by keeping track of your observations and recording your thoughts on specific individuals on a daily basis.

REFLECTION POINT

Think about a child that you have had some experience with in a learning situation. Jot down some anecdotes about what you recall about that child. How might these anecdotes help you to plan to meet the child's needs?

Student Conferencing as an Assessment Tool

One other approach to assessment that advocates more student control is conferencing. Conferences enable teachers and students to share in the assessment process. Through the use of this tool, dialogue replaces assigning marks; the purpose for assessing shifts from ranking students to helping them set and reach personal goals. Conferencing can help students grow in their ability to be self-assessors through dialogical assessment, and to more realistically set learning goals for their next learning experiences. It is also an important strategy for uncovering student's thinking.

CLASSROOM APPLICATION

Conferences can range from informal conversations to more formal one-on-one interviews with children to talk about specific samples of their work. How might you use starters such as the following as assessment tools?

"I just wanted to talk to you about some of the things we have been learning about in class and to see what you think."

"What is the most important thing you have learned about in the unit we just finished?"

"Pretend you are teaching younger children about what you just learned. In your own words what would you share with them about the social studies topic we just finished?"

Tape recording these conferences and conversations and encouraging children to listen to them and then to reflect on their responses would add to the benefits for learning.

Caregiver/teacher/student conferencing is another important assessment strategy as it helps caregivers to take an active role in ensuring their children are performing to their capabilities and getting the most out of their schooling experiences. A partnership can develop between the caregivers and the child as they examine the child's work together, join in setting and attaining goals, and provide encouragement and support from home. Students can lead these conferences by sharing a prepared folder of materials such as a portfolio, and explaining the various pieces and the effort they put into them. Giving students control of the conference empowers them by making them more responsible and accountable for their own learning.

w(w)w **Technology Link** For more ideas on conferencing see the BC Ministry of Education document "Assessment Handbook Series: Student-centred conferences" (2000) at http://www.bced.gov .bc.ca/classroom_assessment/.

Look back to your response at the beginning of the chapter to how you were assessed as a student in school and reassess the effectiveness of that approach.

Program Evaluation as an Important Assessment Tool

While the assessing of students to determine growth in their knowledge, skills, and attitudes should be a major part of the overall assessment process, there is one critical component remaining. You will also need to think about how to assess your social studies program and the effectiveness of your goals, learning outcomes, resources, teaching strategies, and assessment strategies, both while they are in use and when you have completed a particular unit of instruction. These reflections can act as guides for future planning and for thinking about alternative ways to address the curriculum requirements.

While your personal reflections on each of these components will be important to future planning, it is also important to engage the children in your class in assessing the activities experienced to help you to improve your teaching. If you are going to meet the learning needs of your students, you need to find out what they think about the learning experiences you have designed for them.

CLASSROOM APPLICATION

Here are some examples of program assessment strategies that could help to uncover students' thoughts on their learning experiences.

1. You are a reporter for Activity Press. Make a tape recording of your review of a recent social studies activity. Briefly describe the activity. Rate the activity on a scale of 1 to 10 with 10 being great. State what you liked about the activity. Was it fun and if so why? What did you learn? Of what were you most proud? Did you dislike anything? If so, tell why. What suggestion do you have for improving the activity? Would you recommend this activity to a friend? Would you like to do this activity again? What would you like to learn more about? (Alternatively, you could have students interview each other using these questions.)

2. Student Interest Inventory on Social Studies Learning Centre Activities:

    Did you enjoy learning about . . . ?

    Do you think it is important to learn about . . . ? Give reasons for your answers.

    Did you enjoy working at the learning centre?

    (Continued)

What activities did you find most interesting?

Did you have difficulty reading the information at the centre?

Did you enjoy working in groups?

What did you learn that you didn't know before?

What did you not like about this centre?

3. Think/Pair/Share—First, ask individuals to complete these statements and then ask them to share their responses with a partner. Discuss the similarities and differences in their responses as a whole class and record their ideas on chart paper.

- The part I liked best about this social studies unit was _____ because . . .
- The part I liked least about this unit was _____ because . . .
- Six things that I learned while I was studying this unit were . . .
- Some questions I still have are . . .

It is important to build in opportunities for feedback throughout the teaching of a unit rather than just at the end. For example, a mid-point feedback form could be used to ask students to talk about what they are learning, what activities and resources they have been using, and which ones they feel have been the most and the least useful in helping them to learn. This ongoing program assessment could then be used to make changes to your plan at various points throughout the teaching of a unit in order to meet your students' needs better.

Designing an Overall Assessment Plan for Your Social Studies Program

Careful thought needs to be given to assessing your students in a way that works best both for you and for them. Decisions about assessment should come early in your social studies program planning process so that your goals match your content selection and the activities and resources used to address that content as well as how you determine students' learning in relation to your goals. Thinking about assessment early in your program planning will more likely result in continuity between your goals and how you determine if you have met those goals.

The following questions should help you to think about the place of assessment in your program plan. At the same time as you are deciding on the content that you might want to address, ask yourself:

On what should students be assessed in this unit? Why?

What will student understanding look like?

What would students need to demonstrate to reveal that they have a solid grasp of the essentials?

What learning outcomes should students be able to demonstrate?

What is the best way of collecting this information?

What tasks, activities, and products will be used to provide the student with the best possible opportunity to demonstrate the learning expected?

What type of tool and scoring criteria will be used to assess the performance and to determine student growth?

Are the tasks selected to measure a given learning assessment meaningful and worthwhile? Would the tasks selected motivate the students?

Is assessment oriented toward critical thinking and solving problems, not simply recall?

Will the assessment activities address the diverse needs of all learners in the classroom?

How will the results be used to improve students' learning?

ACTIVE ENGAGEMENT

Lorie Shepard (2005) argues that one of the most important things a teacher can do is to set up the classroom as a learning culture in which "classroom practices encourage peer assessment, regard errors as opportunities for learning and promote shared thinking . . . [and] both students and teachers focus on learning rather than grades" (p. 70). How does this quote help you to think about how to design an assessment plan for your social studies program?

Chapter Summary

In this chapter, you have been challenged to think about how to assess your students' learning in social studies as well as the effectiveness of your teaching and program planning. We began by looking at the differences between the terms assessment and evaluation, then at three different purposes of assessment—assessment for learning, assessment of learning, and assessment as learning. Two alternative ways to approaching assessment based on differing views of the purpose of assessment—a knowledge acquisition approach and a constructivist approach—were then examined with these varying purposes of assessment in mind. You were challenged to think about which alternative approach fits best with your personal professional goals and the learning needs of your students.

You also had the opportunity to look at a variety of assessment tools as alternatives to the standard testing approach most often used. These include rubrics, learning portfolios, questionnaires, self-assessment tools, anecdotal record-keeping, and conferencing for determining student learning and for reporting progress to caregivers. As well, both ongoing personal reflection and student feedback on your teaching is important to ensuring that you are doing everything you can to promote student growth and enjoyment of their social studies experiences. Here too your choice of tools will be dependent on different purposes of assessment and whether your goal is assessment for learning, assessment of learning, or assessment as learning.

Finally, you have been encouraged to see assessment as an ongoing part of your social studies program that should also be treated as a critical component of the planning process and one that should be considered early on in that process.

Closure

Connecting the Pieces of the Plan

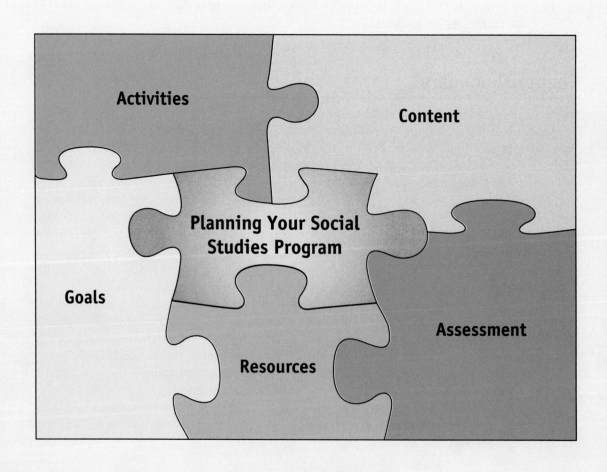

Activities

Content

Planning Your Social
Studies Program

Goals

Assessment

Resources

We have now completed our separate look at each of the five key questions related to planning your social studies program. It is time to see how these pieces of the planning puzzle fit together as a guide for your teaching of social studies. We have discovered that when planning for teaching you will need to decide on your personal professional goals, the curricular goals, and the learning outcomes (what your students should know and be able to do as a result of their learning experiences); to select the content to be covered (the overarching understandings, concepts, inquiry questions, skills and processes, attitudes and dispositions); to choose the resources to be used, both by you as the teacher and by your students; to determine what teaching activities and learning experiences will best help to achieve your goals; and to identify the assessment strategies that will help to show both your students and you what they are learning both during and as a result of their learning experiences. The order in which these five key components of planning have been addressed is an arbitrary one, and is not meant to suggest that planning should follow a particular lock-step sequence. At times, you may want to think about your assessment outcomes first or, when a new resource comes into your hands, you may want to examine it first and then think about and plan around it.

Planning for teaching can take many formats. It will take some experimenting with different ones to figure out what works best for you. The sample instructional plan in Chapter 14 models how the five components of planning can work together. This plan was designed by a teacher who wanted to incorporate a global education orientation using a constructivist approach in her teaching of social studies.

Chapter 14

Promoting Children's Understanding of Globalization through Social Studies: An Instructional Plan

ACTIVE ENGAGEMENT

While you are examining this sample plan, think about what you are learning both about the teaching of social studies content from a global education orientation and about the planning process. Notice how the assessment component of planning has been addressed in this instructional plan. Why do you think it has been threaded throughout the plan instead of being treated separately? Ask yourself if this plan demonstrates a social constructivist approach and how it develops students' global understanding? Is there anything in this unit that is potentially controversial in nature? What changes, if any, would you make to this unit if you were to try it in your classroom in the future? What other ideas could you add to extend the unit? See Figure 14.1 on the next page for an overview of the plan.

FIGURE 14.1 ■ Overview of Instructional Plan

LEARNING OUTCOMES	CONTENT	RESOURCES	ACTIVITIES	ASSESSMENT
— Understand concepts of over-consumption and consumerism — Name problems caused by over-consumption and consumerism — Recognize advertising as an example of how over-consumption is encouraged — Define the concept of globalization — Identify the problems arising from globalization — Understand issues facing developing countries due to globalization — Understand ecologically sustainable and just modes of consumption — Develop attitudes of empathy and caring for others — Apply skills of researching, conceptualizing, imagining, hypothesizing, synthesizing, cooperating, role playing, persuasive writing, presenting, debating, decision making, action taking, and reflecting	— Positive and negative effects of consumerism and over-consumption — Needs versus wants—effects of advertising — Advertising as affected by globalization — Pollution as a consequence of over-consumption — Defining globalization — Effects of globalization — Importance of rivers — Effects of globalization on rivers e.g., dams — Positive and negative impacts of globalization	a) Student Resources • "The Fisherman and His Wife" by the Grimm Brothers • Sample advertisements • Sample products from other countries • Pictures of Canadian-made products • Pictures of smog emissions from factories • "Understanding Globalization" Reader's Theatre • Pictures of dams • "Where Go the Boats?" Robert Louis Stevenson • Internet search sites b) Teacher Resources • Alternatives for a Different World http://www.alternatives.ca/ • Focus on the Global South http://www.focusweb.org/ • Global Exchange http://www.globalexchange.org/ • Global March Against Child Labour http://www.globalmarch.org/ • International Rivers Network http://www.irn.org/ • New Internationalist http://www.newint.org/ • OXFAM http://www.oxfam.org.uk • Third World Network http://www.twnside.org.sg • United Nations Development Program http://www.undp.org • UNESCO http://www.unesco.org • UNICEF Child Labour http://www.unicef.org/protection/index_childlabour.html • World Bank http://www.worldbank.org/ • World Social Forum 2004 http://www.rediff.com/news/wsf04news.htm • Advocacy Toolkit http://www.socialstudies.org/toolkit/educational/handouts/advertising_marketing/kids_advertising_rules.cfm • Media Awareness Network http://www.media-awareness.ca/english/resources/	• Think/Pair/Share • Group work • Storytelling • Shared reading • Create a product and advertisement • T-Chart synthesis • Discussion • Comparing and contrasting products • Role play • Investigation into factory pollution • List making • Action taking • Readers' theatre • Poetry analysis • Research • Forum debate • Group presentation	• Diagnostic: brainstorm ideas, identify key words • Formative: self-assessment, reflective journaling, peer feedback, group work effort, observation, anecdotal records • Summative: revisit initial ideas rubric

Brenda Basiga has been teaching elementary school for 25 years. She designed this unit for a Grade 6 class.

Goal Setting

Teacher Goals

I believe that each child in my classroom is unique and brings his or her own interests, feelings, talents, abilities, and needs to the learning environment. My goal is to build on my students' strengths by providing a range of activities and resources to try to meet their needs and respect the diverse backgrounds and learning preferences they bring to the classroom. In addition, since literacy is such an important aspect of schooling my goal is to provide literacy experiences in social studies through the activities I plan and the resources I select.

I believe that my students bring a wealth of knowledge and experience to the classroom. My goal is to find out what my students know when they come into my classroom and help them to grow from there. As well, I want to encourage ongoing assessment that involves my students and helps them to grow throughout their learning experiences.

I believe that children learn best when they play an active role in their education, especially when they have opportunities to work with others and share their ideas, but I also feel that they need some personal processing time while they are involved in learning activities. My goal is to build many opportunities for my students to both work together and to be reflective.

I feel that when children are interested in something and see its connection to their lives, they become more motivated and the learning stays with them. My goal is to involve my students in a social studies program that develops them as young citizens by engaging them in investigating issues of importance to them and by empowering them to try to make a difference in their world by becoming stewards of the earth and its peoples. I feel that global education as an orientation to social studies best fits with my goals. I want the children in my class to understand the impact of things happening around the globe on their lives as well as understanding that the way they live their lives impacts others around the world. Through my teaching of social studies, I hope to help them to see how they can begin to deal with global change as well as how they can help to make the world a more equitable and caring place for everyone.

Curricular Goals

- To develop students' understanding about Canada's links to the world through the examination of global communities.
- To acquire knowledge of key social studies concepts, including change, power, the dynamics of the marketplace, and the environment.
- To learn about Canada's role in an interdependent world, especially as it relates to trading relationships.
- To understand the importance of active citizenship and caring for others.
- To acquire the skills of inquiry, communication, and critical thinking to solve problems and make decisions on issues that are relevant to their lives.

- To relate and apply the knowledge acquired through their social studies experiences to the world outside the classroom (Ontario Ministry of Education, Social Studies, 2004).

Student Learning Outcomes

- Students will express understanding of the concepts of over-consumption and consumerism.
- Students will be able to name problems caused by over-consumption and consumerism.
- Students will be able to recognize advertising as an example of commercial and corporate control over peoples' lives by encouraging over-consumption and consumerism.
- Students will be able to define the concept globalization.
- Students will be able to identify the problems that can arise from globalization.
- Students will be able to demonstrate understanding of the issues facing third world countries because of globalization, including the destruction of local means of livelihood, natural resources, cultural identity, and community life.
- Students will be able to explain the importance of finding modes of consumption that bring about ecological sustainability, equity, and social justice.
- Students will develop attitudes of empathy for others and demonstrate how to take responsibility in caring for them.
- Students will be able to apply the skills of getting meaning from context, conceptualizing, imagining, hypothesizing, researching, synthesizing, cooperating, role-playing, persuasive writing, presenting, debating, decision making, action taking, and reflecting.

Content Selection

This unit has two focus areas—the effects of globalization, and consumerism and over-consumption. One aspect of learning to take a more global view of citizenship is to develop an understanding of what globalization entails and the possibilities and challenges that it brings to the world's citizens. One reason often given for cultural conflict is globalization, which pits one culture against another in the process of homogenization. Globalization is a process of the international integration of economies through restructuring of modes of production, distribution, and consumption of goods and services on a global scale. This restructuring is accomplished in part through the removal of trade restrictions and the opening of national borders to allow capital to flow freely between countries. Third world governments are attracted by globalization because of the development it promises to bring to poor countries. Institutions like the World Bank lend money to develop the economy of poor countries. Expectations are raised that globalization will create a more prosperous and egalitarian world as the term "development" suggests an increase in productivity and an improvement in the quality of people's lives. In reality, modernization often brings a larger economic disparity as poor countries become poorer, and rich countries become richer. High interest rates, free movement of capital in and out of the country through an open trade policy, and the conversion of vast farmlands to cash crops for export are often outcomes. Despite employment at the corporations' plants, often workers are paid poorly and health and safety standards are virtually non-existent. Environmental degradation occurs as forests and vast tracts of land are sacrificed, and water is polluted by factories' chemical and gas emissions. Consequently, global development creates much disparity so that massive poverty exists alongside unprecedented wealth. Over a billion people are unable to meet their basic needs amongst those whose consumption is not ecologically sustainable. Students need to be made aware of the disparity resulting from globalization and learn how they can help to address it.

Consumerism and over-consumption of wealthy countries are two of the main catalysts driving globalization. Multinational corporations advertise their products to make them look appealing and to influence consumer behaviour and attitudes. Obesity in the children of wealthier nations is on the rise, particularly in North America; while according to the World Watch Institute, there are 150 million (one in three) children in developing countries that are malnourished. Children need to be made aware of the link between consumerism and poverty. They should be helped to think critically about over-consumption and about how to change consumption patterns to decelerate ecological and environmental damage. Children also need to learn that we all have a responsibility to make it possible for the poor to have access to the basic necessities of life.

Resources

Student Resources

Visit the book's companion website for links to the web pages below.

Copies of "The Fisherman and His Wife" by the Grimm Brothers (available at http://www.fln.vcu.edu/grimm/fischer_e.html)

Samples of advertisements

Sample products from other countries

Pictures of Canadian-made products

Pictures of smog emissions from factories

Copies of Reader's Theatre script, "Understanding Globalization"

Pictures of dams

Overhead of poem "Where Go the Boats?" by Robert Louis Stevenson (available at http://www.darsie.net/library/kid_poems.html)

Internet search sites

Teacher Resources (also can be used for students' research)

Visit the book's companion website for links to the teacher resources.

Activities (30–45 minutes per activity)

Activity #1 Diagnostic Assessment

Working in partners, ask students to Think, Pair, Share in which they begin by individually writing down a list of things that they would like to have (wants) if they could have anything they wished. Have them share their lists and their reasons for their choices with a partner. Gather the lists and keep them for comparison later as an assessment activity to see if any changes in attitude have occurred after the lesson is taught. (Skills: reflecting and cooperating.)

Activity #2 Storytelling

Have students working in small groups share the reading of the story "The Fisherman and His Wife" and then ask them to reflect on the story as a group using questions like, Did you like this story? What did you like about it? Why? Which part did you not like? Why?

Hold a large group discussion to develop comparing/contrasting, getting meaning from context, and empathizing skills. Questions for discussion could include, If you were to choose, which character would you like to be? Why? What kind of person was the fisherman's wife? What makes you think that? Why do you think the fish did not grant the wife's last wish? In what way might we be similar to the fisherman's wife? Why do you say so? What is good about wanting so many things? What is bad about wanting things even if we do not need them? What happens when we keep wishing and getting many things? (We're no longer happy and content with what we have and what we get, nothing satisfies us, we want more.) Do you think your parents/guardians would like you to have all of the things that you wished? Do you think other children get as many things as you do? What about children in poorer countries where there often isn't enough food and many families are homeless? Observe students' cooperativeness and attentiveness and make anecdotal notes.

Activity #3 Understanding Advertising

Talk about how students know what things to wish for (i.e. from TV, flyers, friends). Begin to develop students' understanding about the power of advertising and the techniques used in advertisements to persuade and sell. (See the Media Awareness Network's Rules for Advertising to Children at http://www.media-awareness.ca.) Do you believe everything that you see on TV? What do commercials do to entice you to buy their products?

Have the children work in pairs to come up with a product to advertise. Challenge them to prepare a commercial for the product by creating a visual aide and a slogan that would encourage people to buy their product. Ask the children to present their advertisements. While each pair is presenting, encourage the audience to reflect on what they are watching by thinking about questions such as, Would people want to buy this product? Why? What else about commercials makes you want to buy the product? How does it make you feel when you see other people with the product after you buy it? Does it make you feel special to be part of a group that has the same product? How might people who don't have this same product feel? Assess the creativity of the posters and the level of effort and higher level thinking evident.

Activity #4 Comparing and Contrasting

Assemble various products manufactured in other countries with tags showing cost. Two or more products should be similar, one of which is manufactured in Canada and the other made in another country, for example, a shirt made in China costs $4.00 and a similar shirt made in Canada costs $10.00. Show the children the various products made in both Canada and other countries. Have the students come up with the name of the product, where it was made, and the cost by looking at the labels. Look particularly at two similar products, one made in Canada and the other made in another country. Ask how they are similar and how they are different. Ask the students to decide if Shirt A is cheaper than Shirt B and which shirt they would buy and why. Why do they think that the shirt from China is so much cheaper? (Answers will vary but try to elicit the idea that the cost to make a shirt in China is lower than it is to make the same shirt in Canada because shirt workers are paid more in Canada than in China.) Compare the cost of other products in a similar fashion.

To promote critical thinking, discuss the differences between the products by using questions such as, Why are there products in Canada that are made in other countries? Why do we allow products that are made in other countries into our country when the same things are made here? Is it okay to have these outside products here? Why? Do you think products made in Canada are also sold in other countries? What makes you think that way? Do you think these foreign products are also sold in countries other than Canada? What makes you think that way? Should we be buying products that are made only in our country? Why?

Show pictures of some other products from Canada that are sold in other parts of the world, e.g., oil, wheat, natural gas, meat, lumber, paper, as well as other examples of foreign products that are sold here. Ask the class if we can make all of the products that we need in our country and not have to buy from other countries. Why?

To help students to get meaning from context and develop generalizing and conceptualizing skills ask them to hypothesize: If our products are sold here and in other countries, while products made in other countries are sold in their home countries and other places, what is happening when all these countries are buying each other's products? (They are trading with each other.) Explain that when countries trade (buy and sell products) with each other, they actually depend on each other for products and other things. This is part of globalization. Ask students if they think globalization is a good thing in this case and have them give examples in their answers.

To develop predicting and synthesizing skills ask, What would happen if all of the products from other countries cost cheaper than similar products made in our country? What would happen to the products made in our country? What about the workers? Would this be good for Canada? Why? Explain that sometimes this happens in globalization. Is globalization good in this case? Why?

Explain that some countries are famous for certain things they manufacture and sell to the rest of the world or for famous people that live in those countries or for some other reasons. Give an example such as, Japan and Korea are famous for manufacturing electronics. (Be sensitive about racial profiling.) Have students give their own examples.

After everybody has had a turn, ask the class to think about the following question: What would it be like if the country that is famous for manufacturing something(s) is the only one allowed to make those particular products? Is this fair? Why? Keep anecdotal notes on both the students' willingness to contribute to the discussion and the thoughtfulness of their responses.

Activity #5 Role-play

Have students work in groups of three. One takes the role of the buyer, while the other two are selling similar products that are priced differently and made in different countries. The group should decide on the product and the countries to be represented. The vendors will try to outdo each other in convincing the buyer to take their product over the other. They can talk about the price, the quality, material used, and other features of the product. Before the end of the role-play the buyer has to choose the product to buy and explain the reasons for the choice. Using an observation checklist, assess the students on their teamwork and creativity. Have students complete a group assessment of their efforts.

Debrief the role-play by asking questions such as the following: Which product was chosen? Why? How did you feel about your roles? What did the vendors do or say to convince the buyer to take their product? How did the vendor feel when his or her product was not picked? Why? What about the buyer, what was it like choosing which product to buy? Why? What made the buyer decide which one to buy?

Activity #6 Investigation

Show a picture of a factory spewing smoke and ask students to describe what they see. Say to the class: Let's imagine that this is one of the factories that makes the products that we wish to have. Imagine what the activity both inside and outside the factory might be like and describe it. Where do factories like this get the raw materials they need to make things? What might happen to these materials, e.g., wood, water, plants, animals, and minerals as consumers continue to buy more of these products? (These questions are raised to link demand for products to degradation of ecology and the environment.)

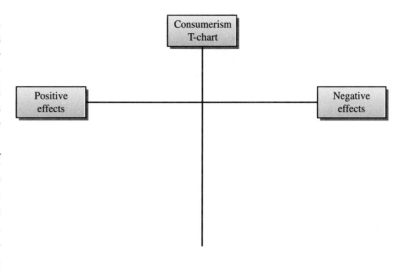

Investigate the issue of local pollution. If there is a factory in the area, have students write a letter to the management of the factory to inquire what they are doing to ensure that their factory doesn't pollute the air. Examine these letters to determine students' level of understanding about the issue.

Activity #7 Synthesis

Have students recall the positive and negative effects of consumerism by filling in a T-Chart.

Synthesize the learning by helping students to come up with generalizations such as, "Consumerism and over-consumption perpetuate poverty, inequity, and the depletion of the earth's limited natural resources," and "Everyone should share in the responsibility of saving the earth."

Ask the class: Should we feel responsible for the ill effects of over-consumption and consumerism? Why? What can we do to help control consumerism and over-consumption? List the ideas on chart paper. Turn these ideas into a commitment to action plan and revisit it often to see how the class is doing. Items might include minimizing wants, recycling, and making good use of supplies at school and at home to avoid buying unnecessary items.

Activity #8 Assessment

Go back to the lists of wants from Activity #1 and have students re-examine their choices and remove any that they feel they no longer need in light of what they have learned about consumerism. Use this as an assessment tool to determine how the students' ideas may have changed. Have students reflect on their learning and their effort in their journals.

The Effects of Globalization

Activity #1 Diagnostic Assessment

Write the word "globalization" on the board. Challenge the students to write down as many key words, sentences, phrases, or sketch drawings of things associated with the word "globalization" that they learned from the activities on consumerism. Use this diagnostic activity to gather information on what the students know about the topic before it is discussed. This activity also develops the skill of hypothesizing. Collect the students' initial ideas to use as an assessment tool for comparison at the end of the series of lessons.

As a pre-planning activity, have students generate questions about globalization. Record these questions and keep them in a visible place so that they can be addressed throughout the remainder of the unit.

Activity #2 Reader's Theatre

Explain to the class that they will be engaging in a Reader's Theatre drama that should help them to understand the possible effects of globalization. Using the prepared script, go through the characters and ask for role players. (You can add other characters or duplicate the roles to ensure that every student is involved.) Those who do not take speaking parts can make or move props or make labels for each of the characters. Each character should be identified by a label pinned to his or her shirt. The characters are grouped according to the speaking order to show in a simple way the "domino" effect of globalization.

Distribute copies of the script and have students silently read their character's lines. Once the students are familiar with their parts, have them work together in groups by reading their parts to each other. Move all the furniture to the sides of the room. Have the students form a circle around the cleared area by sitting each group together around the room so that all the groups are facing into the centre of the circle. One group at a time, each group stands and reads their lines. As each group finishes reading their lines, it returns to its place in the circle. This applies to all the groups except Group 1 who is sitting at a table and Group 5 who is seated around a table during Part II. After Part I is read, have all students stand up and walk around the circle clockwise to stretch their legs until all the groups are back to their original spots in the circle. Continue reading Part II. Observe students' cooperativeness and level of on-task behaviour.

Reader's Theatre Script, "Understanding Globalization"

Cast of Characters:

Group 1—A Global Trade Organization (GTO) representative, a Bank of the World representative, the president of the Republic of _____ (create a name for the third world country) and the vice president of the Republic of _____.

Group 2 —Four presidents of four different transnational corporations (Big D's Restaurants, Food Xporters Inc., The Miners, and Electronix Store).

Group 3—Three presidents of three different local businesses (clothing, handicraft, and furniture).

Group 4—A local rice farmer, a vegetable farmer, two factory workers, and a restaurant worker.

Group 5—A dad, a mom, a son, and a daughter.

Part I

Group 1

(The Global Trade Organization (GTO) representative and the Bank of the World (BW) representative are seated beside each other on one side of a desk. On the opposite side of them are seated the president and the vice president of the Republic of _____. Every one is smiling at each other, appreciative of each other's presence.)

Bank of the World representative: Good morning/good afternoon Ms./Mr. _____ and to you, too Mr./Ms. _____ (Everybody shakes hands.) I'm glad that you have eventually decided to borrow money from our bank. We understand your situation and we will definitely help your country. We are here for you.

GTO representative: Yes, it is certainly nice to see both of you here and we are pleased to be of service to you.

President: We would like to borrow some money so that we can modernize our country. We would like to be competitive with the rest of the world.

Vice president: With the money you lend us we will be able to build roads to the countryside, start up new businesses, develop our farms, and create new jobs for our people.

GTO representative: Oh, you don't worry about jobs for your people. We will bring you the jobs. Countries all over the world will want to come here and build factories, industries, farm your lands, develop your natural resources, especially if you build roads to the countryside to make it easier to transport products.

President: You are very generous and we appreciate you very much.

Vice president: Our people are so poor and need employment. We are excited and we look forward to the jobs that your businesses will offer.

Bank of the World representative: You understand, of course, that there are conditions that you have to meet when borrowing money from us, just like in other transactions. Everybody has to meet with those conditions, like the Philippines, Brazil, India; no one is an exception.

Vice president: What sorts of conditions are there?

Bank of the World representative: For example, you will have to pay interest on your loan. To make sure that you will be able to pay for your loan, we have to approve some of the policies of how you run your country. Not all of them, this is still your country. You can run it the way you want. We're only interested in some of them.

GTO representative: For example, it would be nice if you do not let foreign businesses that come to your country pay taxes because other countries will let you do the same if you bring business over there. You can come and go. Your money is free to go in and out of other countries too and it's good for everybody. This is called free trade.

President: Okay, we agree. Thank you for your help.

Group 2

Big D's representative: Great! We'll open restaurants all over the Republic of _____. Many tourists come for their beautiful beaches so we'll make sure that we put Big D's restaurants along the beach line. The local people will enjoy our food as soon as they try it, especially our French fries.

Food Xporters Inc. president: Oh yeah, another market to introduce many of our products too. Our fruits and juices are excellent. Once the locals try them, they won't want to eat their local produce any more, including their vegetables. Our clothing fashion will really click here. Teenagers will look so fashionable in our western style clothes and shoes. Their parents will want to wear them too.

The Miners president: The labour cost here is so cheap because people have no jobs. Once we open our mining operation, everybody will want to get a job with us. They won't even care about the pollution and dangers the mining operation will create. They'll all want a job.

Electronix Store president: Are you kidding? The people here are into electronics. Everybody wants to own a TV set for sure. I can just imagine the demand for our product, now that we can make them here. So many will want a job with us, that even if we pay them peanuts, they have no choice but to take it. After all, we will still have to train them. But that's easy enough because they're smart and they'll be interested in the job. Too many people here are unemployed. It's their loss if they don't take what we offer. We can always move and set up shop in another country.

Group 3

President of local clothing company: I can't believe it! I have a chance to sell the clothes we make in foreign markets. This is a wonderful opportunity to be able to export them to other countries. Tourists from Canada buy my clothing because they like the details and the embroidery we put on it.

President of local furniture company: I have always dreamed of expanding my business to other countries. With free trade I will show the world the finest furniture anyone can ever own. I have been very successful here in my country, but now is the time to try it elsewhere and make more of a profit.

President of local handicraft company: Other markets will like the handicrafts I make out of seashells. The shell lamps and chandeliers look very pretty. The shell soap dish is quite exquisite. I can show the world my products by opening my business in another country. Free trade will help me do this.

Group 4

Rice farmer: At long last, we are able to get some help from the government. The roads to be built will make transporting our harvest to the market easier. Perhaps farmers don't have to go very far because our farms will be accessible to buyers. They'll just come here and we can do business right at my farm.

Vegetable farmer: Good, buyers usually buy my entire produce of the season. With the paved roads, they can come to see my harvest and I don't have to seek them out. Foreign businesses might also want to export my vegetables to their country because they use my produce over there too. Things seem promising.

Restaurant worker: Big D's is opening restaurants here in our country! That's fantastic. I'm going to apply for a job there. I hear that they are hiring college graduates for their restaurants. It's about time that I am able to make use of my college education.

Factory worker 1: I have an opportunity to find a job at Electronix Store. I went to trade school and I learned how to put a radio together. But that was a long time ago.

Factory worker 2: You can only try, although they are looking for younger workers. Putting the circuits and tiny wires together require good eyesight. My cousin applied at the Electronix Store last week and he was told that sometimes a worker might have to look under the microscope to be able to connect wires. He did not get a job because he is older. Other factories are opening up, so we can apply there.

Factory worker 1: I heard that a clothing factory is looking for workers. Maybe we can try our luck over there.

Group 5

Dad: How has your day been today?

Son, daughter, mom: Good, just fine.

Dad: You know what, on my way home I noticed that a new building is being built on the main street not too far away from here. The sign says, "Big D's is coming soon."

Daughter: Wow, that would be nice. Could we go there, please?

Dad: It's not even up yet.

Mom: I was at the market today and I noticed a different kind of fruit on the fruit stand. For a while I thought they were guavas. They looked very similar to guavas, but the fruit vendor told me they were pears. I bought a couple just to try.

Son: Could we try them now, please?

Mom: Okay.

(Everybody quietly stands as soon as soft music is played. The characters walk around the circle and stop when they reach their original positions. The activity continues on with Group 1 having a conversation on the same set.)

Part II—One Year Later

Group 1

Bank of the World representative: I'm sorry Mr./Ms. President that I have to demand payment on your loan. You have not paid for it for almost a year now. The interest alone is piling up and I'm afraid you won't be able to repay it at all.

President: We have been trying very hard, but it has been difficult to save dollars to pay for it because the transnational corporations are all sending their profits back to their country. They are not spending them here in our country. They should be helping us because they are making money because of us, from our people working and buying, and from using our natural resources.

Bank of the World representative: They can do whatever they want to do with their money. It's theirs, not yours.

Global Trade Organization representative: Free trade allows them to do that. Their money can move in and out of the country. You can do the same thing too with your own money.

Vice president: You know we have no money otherwise we would be able to pay off our loan. Meanwhile, our rain forests are denuded, flooding our villages and towns. The mining operations have turned our land upside down, polluting our rivers.

GTO representative: That's free trade. Why doesn't your country do the same things in other countries? You're allowed.

BW representative: I'll give you a little break. Here's what you can do. For the meantime, you can just pay for the interest of your loan until you can afford to pay for the main loan.

President: We don't have the money even just to pay for the interest. We would if the transnational corporations would buy our local products. But they don't. It's unfair.

BW representative: Here is another plan that might work for you. You can borrow more money to pay for your loan and the interest.

Vice president: But that's making our loan even bigger. We'll never be able to get out of debt.

BW representative: I'm sorry, but those are your choices.

President: Okay, we'll pay the interest and the main loan by borrowing more money from you.

GTO representative: That sounds good.

Group 2

The Miners president: I think we have to pull out of this country. I would have wanted to stay because our labour cost is lower than in any other country.

Big D's president: Why are you moving out? We're staying. We're doing very well here. We're opening restaurants in every major city in this country.

The Miners president: We too have made a lot of money, but the workers are complaining so much about the danger of their work and the pollution we're creating. They're asking for compensation for their injuries. Besides, we have taken out most of the minerals in the pits.

Food Xporters president: That's too bad. We don't allow our employees to form unions so they can't hurt us. We're importing more and more products into the country. We're even competing with local products and the local businesses can't win because our products are subsidized and are cheaper. Who would want to buy a more expensive product when there is a cheaper one of the same kind?

Electronix Store president: We'll stay put too. There are lots of good workers in the country; we can afford to be choosy with them. As soon as we notice that a worker's skill and or vision are failing, we lay him or her off right away so we don't have to pay for their health insurance or pension.

Group 3

President of furniture company: Did you guys try exporting your products to foreign markets?

President of clothing company: I did, but I did not do well. There were so many conditions being imposed on my business. My products had to pass many standards and I had to pay for several licences to be able to operate overseas. The cost of transporting my goods was too high. So I pulled out of there before I went bankrupt. I'm still trying to recoup my expenses. What about you?

President of furniture company: I was doing okay until the rainforest where I was getting my lumber from was taken over by transnational corporations. I couldn't get any more wood for my furniture. I'm upset because I was so careful not to overlog the rain forest. Today I hear that the commercial loggers have denuded the rain forest causing lots of flooding in the area.

President of handicraft company: None of us can compete with the big foreign corporations. Their money can go in and out of countries without penalty or taxation. They are big businesses; they can afford to lose money for a while because they have lots of it. Then when the market is better, they are able to get back what they lose. We only have so much. If we don't do well even just for a little while, we lose because our money will only go so far.

Group 4

Restaurant worker: I got a job at Big D's restaurant and have been working there for about a year now. I have to find another job, though because I don't get enough hours of work. They only give me so many hours so they don't have to pay for any benefits. They don't give me enough hours to make me a full-time worker either. My pay is not enough to feed my family. I must say I'm glad I have a job, better than nothing, I guess. What about you?

Factory worker 1: I used to work for Electronix Store, but I've been out of a job now since I hurt my hand trying to solder wires together. The soldering rod overheated on my hand and I burned it. I went to the hospital for a while and the company paid for my hospitalization. When I got better, I was not allowed to return to work. I tried to get paid for my injury, but they said that I was careless with my work. I did not get anything from the company. I have saved some money. I hope I can live off it until the next job. How about you? (Referring to factory worker 2.)

Factory worker 2: You and I have been so unlucky. I got a job from the clothing factory and I worked there until last month. I became very sick. You see the factory had very poor ventilation. The fluff from the clothing materials stayed around our work area. There was no way to get rid of it. When I first started there, I kept sneezing and I just ignored it. After a while, I started to cough. Not wanting to lose my job, I tried to get rid of it by taking some cough syrup that I bought over the counter. It went away for a while. But when it came back I had a coughing fit and I could not breathe. I ran to the washroom and drank a lot of water. I felt better. The next day, I had a coughing fit again and I was gasping for breath. I had to be rushed to the hospital. The doctor advised me not to go back to work at the factory. Besides, I was so scared of another attack so I did not go back to work there. The doctor gave me a letter that said that the fluff made me sick, but the company did not pay me. I'm hopeful I'll find another job in one of the other factories. Do you know of any one looking for workers?

Rice farmer: No, sorry. If I found one I'd take the job myself. I used to be able to live off my rice farm. Not any more. So much rice from other countries such as the U.S., Thailand, China, Vietnam is now being imported to our country. The rice from these countries is subsidized so it is cheaper and of course, people will want to buy it instead of my rice. I cannot compete with their prices because our government doesn't give me any help. My cost is too high because I have to buy fertilizer and pesticide, and pay for irrigation, which are all expensive. I might have to find another means of livelihood. I'm sad because my ancestors have been farmers and I think I am a good farmer.

Vegetable farmer: We're in the same boat, my friend. Imported vegetables are killing my livelihood. Like rice, vegetables coming from other countries are also subsidized and I cannot compete with their prices. Besides I might sell my land and move to the city. There is a big company trying to buy all the villagers' land so it can build a commercial vegetable farm. How can we small farmers survive?

Group 5

(Family is gathered around the dinner table, except for the son.)

Daughter: This again? I'm so sick of this food. We have this almost every day! Why can't we go to Big D's?

Mom: Eat what we have. Before Big D's came, you never complained about our food. What's wrong with it now?

Daughter: All my friends eat there, why can't I go there too? They're cool and I'm not.

Dad: Just eat your food; sometime we'll go to Big D's. Where is your brother by the way? We hardly see him these days and we can't talk to him.

Daughter: He's in his room, talking to his friend on his cell phone.

Mom: Son, time for dinner. Get off that phone.

(No reply is heard. The classroom lights are turned off.)

Activity #3 Debrief

In their journals, have the children write a synthesis of their experience with and their feelings about the role play. As a group, orally reflect on the dramatization by asking questions such as: What have you learned from the drama? What is globalization? What are the effects of globalization? Are they good? Why? Are the effects bad? Why? Who benefits the most from globalization? Why do you say so? Can we ever get rid of globalization? Why? How can we make it work for most of a country's citizens? What is the role of local government? Note students' level of understanding about the issues raised in the role-play.

Activity #4 Poetry Analysis

Put a copy of the poem "Where Go the Boats?" by Robert Louis Stevenson on the overhead and have the class do a choral reading of the poem.

"Where Go The Boats?"
Dark brown is the river,
Golden is the sand.
It flows along forever,
With trees on either hand.
Green leaves a-floating,
Castles of the foam,
Boats of mine a-boating—
Where will all come home?
On goes the river
And out past the mill,
Away down the valley,
Away down the hill.
Away down the river,
A hundred miles or more,
Other little children
Shall bring my boats ashore.

Next, read the poem to the class and ask the students to keep their eyes closed as the poem is being read so that they can imagine the things being described in the poem. Have them pay close attention to words that help them picture the events.

To facilitate discussion about the poem, use questions such as, What images did you see? Paint the picture in words. What words stuck out as the poem was being read? Did the author write it as a young person or as an adult? What makes you think that way? What is the author trying to tell us? How did you feel as the poem was being read? How do you think the author feels about rivers? About boats? About children?

To develop hypothesizing, critical thinking, and reflecting skills, ask the following questions: What do you think about rivers? How would you feel if you lived by a river? Describe some of the things you would do. Why are rivers important? What do rivers do for us? Who lives in the river?

Activity #5 Research

Explain to the class that one outcome of globalization often is the damming of rivers to provide the necessary electricity and water supply to operate factories. Ask the class what they know about dams using questions such as: What are some of the ways that dams can help us? Can dams also harm us? How?

Show pictures of dams. Have students describe what they see. Ask students to research about the uses and benefits of dams as well as the dangers and harm they pose to people and aquatic species by using the Internet. Review proper searching techniques, i.e., narrowing searches using "and"—dams and benefits, dams and danger.

Have students share their information with the class by asking them to respond to the following questions: What are dams? Why are they built? How are they used? What benefits do we get from them? Do other species benefit from them? Why? What harm do they bring to

humans, animals, and aquatic species? How do they help the environment? How can they contribute to the destruction of the environment?

Activity #6 Forum

Present the issue: While dams can make our lives easier due to the benefits we get from them such as electricity, water supply, flood control, and others, they also bring harm to us, to other species, and to the environment. Our government has proposed the construction of a dam about 300 km from here. In a panel discussion, let us hear your views about the proposal. Would you agree to build a dam about 300 km from here? An open forum is scheduled today.

Have the students pick a particular stakeholder group to join such as the government group composed of the local member of Parliament, mayor, premier; a group of

contractors and workers on the dam; the residents of the area where the dam is to be built; the director and executives of an electric company; Indigenous peoples in the area; human rights activists and environmentalists; and others. Ask each group to get together and plan their arguments. Have them choose a spokesperson for each group. Act as moderator so the activity does not become a one-sided debate and everyone is heard. After sufficient time is given for research and for preparing arguments, start the open forum. All stakeholders in the decision-making process for dam construction should be allowed to voice their opinions and be given mutual respect.

Stop the open forum when no new arguments are being offered. Debrief by asking the following questions: What did you think about the exercise? Did you get your point across? Why do you say so? Do you feel you were in the appropriate group? What makes you think so? How could you have improved your representation of your stakeholder? What did you learn from this exercise? Help students to synthesize their learning, e.g., dams are both advantageous and disadvantageous to people; and dams can destroy the environment by altering eco-systems.

Assess students' contributions, effort, willingness to express opinions, and offer of evidence to support ideas.

Activity #7 Checking for Understanding

Have students prepare a group talk on the impact of dams on the planet using either PowerPoint, Inspiration, a three-dimensional model, or another method of their choice to support the key points in their presentation. Ask each group to include at least three points to support any claims. Compare the students' ideas expressed in this essay to their initial ideas about dams in order to determine any learning that has taken place. Observe how well they function as a group. Have each group assess their effectiveness as a group. Ask the class to provide feedback to their peers by answering the questions: What did you learn from this presentation, what was your favourite part, and what would you suggest for improvement?

Activity #8 Synthesis and Commitment to Action

Help students to synthesize their learning about the effects of globalization by arriving at generalizations such as: globalization impacts us in both positive and negative ways; globalization makes countries become interdependent on each other; globalization can cause environmental degradation if unregulated; governments and citizens must work together to regulate the activities of transnational corporations so that the effects of globalization can be more beneficial rather than detrimental.

Brainstorm a list of ways that the students can commit to action such as by buying products that are made in Canada to help with our country's economy or cutting down on their purchases altogether, by sharing their feelings about globalization with government officials; by putting up a poster around the school listing ways for others to minimize consumption of water and electricity in school and at home, etc. Post this list and revisit it frequently to see how students are doing in their action taking. (See the Advocacy Toolkit at http://www.socialstudies.org/toolkit/.)

Activity #9 Summative Assessment

Have students write a position paper about the positive and negative impacts of globalization on their lives. Begin by reviewing how to write a position paper and examining the rubric to be used for assessment (Figure 14.2). Make sure that students understand what each level of work identified on the rubric might look like. Ask for at least three points in the discussion. Compare the completed work to the key word responses given in Activity #1. Look for growth in students' understanding about the meaning of globalization and its effects.

The Importance of Planning Ahead

Planning will be a very important part of your social studies program because not only can it help you to stay organized and prepared, it can also ensure that you are making the best use of the time allotted to social studies. Planning ahead can also help you to think about when

FIGURE 14.2 ■ **Assessment Rubric**

EXCELLENT	GOOD	FAIR	UNSATISFAC-TORY
• Introduces and outlines the issue	• Introduces the issue but does not outline the issue	• Does not introduce or outline the issue	• Assignment not completed
• Gives opinion on issue	• Gives opinion on issue	• Gives only an opinion on issue	
• Backs up opinion with reasons/explanations	• Backs up most opinion with reasons/explanations	• Opinion is not backed up with reasons or explanations	
• Uses facts to support opinions	• Attempts to use facts to back up opinion	• Does not attempt to use any facts to support opinion	
• Flows smoothly; ideas are grouped together in a coherent way	• Good flow, some trouble putting ideas together	• Ideas do not flow smoothly	
• States final stance on issue as part of conclusion	• Has a conclusion, but final stance not stated	• Does not state final stance	
• Shows very clear understanding of issue	• Shows good understanding of issue	• Shows difficulty understanding issue	
• Good copy, neatly done	• Good copy, neatly done	• Not good copy or has problem with neatness	

and how to use a wide range of learning and assessment experiences in order to meet all of the learning preferences in your classroom. Planning can help you to incorporate the use of a range of resources and can act as a reminder to book these resources ahead of time to ensure they are available when you need them. This is particularly important if you are in a school that has more than one of each grade and you have to share resources or if you plan on bringing in outside resources such as videos, kits, field sites, books, or guest speakers. Finally planning can also help you to identify places in your program where you can integrate other subject areas into your teaching of social studies or to make cross-curricular connections.

Planning can take many formats. You have seen one example of how to organize an instructional plan here but you should examine other organizational strategies to find one that works best for you.

www Technology Link Most ministries of education and provincial teachers' associations have sample social studies plans on their websites. Follow the links provided on the book's companion website. See for example:

- Saskatchewan Ministry of Education social studies plans: http://www.sasked.gov.sk.ca/docs/elemsoc/elemsoc.html
- Manitoba Social Science Teachers' Association: http://www.mssta.mb.ca/plan_k-5.html and http://www.mssta.mb.ca/plan_6-8.html

Here are some other websites that also have examples of plans for teaching social studies:

- The Canadian Teacher: http://www.thecanadianteacher.com/lessonsearch.htm
- About Canada Online social studies lesson plans: http://canadaonline.about.com/od/socialstudies
- Units4teachers: http://www.units4teachers.com
- Lesson plans for K–2 social studies: http://lessonplanz.com/Lesson_Plans/Social_Studies/__Grades_K-2/index.shtml
- Educational resources in social studies: http://www.cln.org/subjects/socials.html
- Centre for Technology and Teacher Education social studies instructional resources: http://www.teacherlink.org/content/social/instructional

Chapter Summary

In this final chapter, I have attempted to show how each of the five aspects of planning that we have been examining throughout this text can be pieced together to design an instructional program for your teaching of social studies. As you have seen, the teacher's personal professional goals based on her beliefs about teaching and learning and her preferred approach to citizenship education through global education as well as the curricular goals and the student learning outcomes all helped to shape the content, activities, resource, and assessments strategies selected throughout the unit. Students were engaged in a variety of activities including individual and group work as well as reflective time for personal processing. A number of activities involved the development of students' reading, writing, viewing, communicating, and listening skills as well as technological literacy. Assessment was ongoing throughout the unit and combined diagnostic, formative, and summative assessment to help the teacher determine where the individual child needed some assistance and to help the child set personal goals for growth.

Now the challenge for you as a future teacher of social studies is to try designing an instructional plan for yourself. A good place to begin the design process is to look back at your own beliefs about teaching and learning and your views on the purpose of social studies and of citizenship education.

EPILOGUE

The constructivist-oriented approach taken in this book is based on a model of teacher preparation that promotes reflective practice. Through the readings and activities you have been challenged to examine your own personal goals for your social studies program as you began to uncover and reflect on your current beliefs about what is most important for your students to learn in social studies, as well as the best way for students to learn, and your role and your students' roles in that learning. As part of this reflection, you have been encouraged to think about how your beliefs have been shaped by your experiences prior to entering your education program, especially in relation to what those experiences have caused you to believe and value about your roles and responsibilities as an educator. These beliefs act as powerful filters through which everything you experience as a teacher will be sifted.

Now it is time to revisit your earlier goal choices. First, mark the continua in Table E.1 to reflect your current goals for social studies, and then compare these responses to your choices in Table 1.1 in Chapter 1.

TABLE E.1 ■ Determining Your Social Studies Goals

MY SOCIAL STUDIES GOALS	STRONGLY DISAGREE	DISAGREE	UNSURE	AGREE	STRONGLY AGREE
Social studies should assist the learner in the search for "self."					
Social studies should focus on issues of globalization.					
Students should learn the basic obligations and responsibilities of good citizenship from their social studies teachers.					
Learning facts and concepts should be the primary objective of a good social studies program.					
Actively involving children in community projects is the best way to learn about being a good citizen.					
Social studies ought to be concerned primarily with history and geography.					

(Continued)

MY SOCIAL STUDIES GOALS	STRONGLY DISAGREE	DISAGREE	UNSURE	AGREE	STRONGLY AGREE
Elementary-age children can understand how to bring about change.					
Developing attitudes is the least important aspect of social studies.					
The most important resource for classroom learning is a good textbook.					
Building an active citizen self-concept requires doing something about the problems and issues studied.					
Learning to become a thoughtful problem solver and decision maker is an important part of social studies.					
Social studies should teach students to take pride in their cultural and ethnic heritage.					
Map skills are probably the most important skills in the social studies curriculum.					
It is most important that students investigate to find answers to their own questions in social studies.					
Students need to develop the ability to question their own cultural conditioning.					
Social studies teachers should use reflection to help students clarify their thinking about issues that concern them.					
Students should learn about cultural universals* in social studies.					
Students should learn methods of inquiry and analytical skills.					

*Cultural universals are those things that are common to a group of people and that are passed on to succeeding generations—i.e., family roles, belief systems, communication, education, food and clothing preferences, etc.

Have you changed your priorities? What values are revealed in your current choices? What ideas for the good citizen do your choices indicate? What are the implications for student and teacher roles and hidden curriculum suggested by your preferences? What new insights and awareness do you have? How can you now translate these goals into decisions about content, resources, activities, and assessment? What does this tell you about your possible goals for your social studies program?

As your learning-to-teach journey continues, you will need to reflect constantly on the goals that you believe in, as they will help to shape your future social studies program in your classroom. The way you decide on your own highest priority goals for teaching social studies will play a key role in what kind of student growth you look for when deciding "what works." As you continue to reflect on your practice, you will need to commit strongly to thinking about how well your activities are achieving the kinds of long-term growth you seek in your students.

A central purpose of this book is to help you to become a better decision-maker about priorities of student learning and growth, and then use those high priority goals to choose content, materials, activities, and assessments that best contribute to those goals. My hope is that you now feel better prepared to make those important decisions about your social studies program; however, this is not the end of the journey.

Learning to teach in a way that supports and encourages student learning in social studies is a life-long journey. Therefore, it is important that you stay abreast of the latest research and suggestions for best practice throughout your teaching career. There are a number of excellent organizations that can help you in this endeavour. Each province has a social studies council as a part of their teacher federation that you can join to meet other colleagues and share ideas. *Canadian Social Studies* is a scholarly journal with articles on the latest trends. The National Council for the Social Studies in the United States also has a number of publications, including *Social Education, Theory and Research in Social Education* and *Social Studies and the Young Learner*. A number of chat rooms and teacher discussion boards have been provided throughout the text that you can join in as well. All of these options are excellent ways to continue your pursuit to be the best social studies teacher you can be.

And so the journey continues . . .

REFERENCES

Adler, D. (1993). *A picture book of Anne Frank.* New York: Holiday House.

Adler, S. (1994). Reflective practice and teacher education. In W. Ross (Ed.), *Reflective practice in social studies,* Bulletin 88. Washington, DC: National Council for Social Studies.

Alberta School Boards Association. (2001). *Shaping young people into good citizens.* Available online at http://www.asba.ab.ca/news_and_views/downloads/pdf/asba_public_consult_full.pdf.

Allen, Rodney F. (2000). Civic education and the decision-making process, *Social Studies, 91*(1), 5–8.

Alter, G., Monson, J., Larson, B., & Morgan, J. (2000). *Social studies content for the elementary school teacher.* Upper Saddle River, NJ: Prentice Hall.

Anderson, L., & Krathwohl, D. (Eds.). (2001). *A taxonomy for learning, teaching, and assessing: A revision of Bloom's Taxonomy of Educational Objectives.* New York: Longman.

Banks, J., & Banks, C. (2007). *Multicultural education: Issues and perspectives.* Hoboken, NJ: John Wiley & Sons.

Bannatyne-Cugnet, J. (2000). *From far and wide: A Canadian citizenship scrapbook.* Toronto: Tundra Books.

Barell, J. (1991). *Teaching for thoughtfulness. Classroom strategies to enhance intellectual development.* New York: Longman.

Barr, R. J., Barth, J., & Shermis, S. (1977). *Defining the social studies,* Bulletin 51. Washington, D.C.: National Council for the Social Studies.

Barton, K. (1997a). History—It *can* be elementary: An overview of elementary students' understanding of history. *Social Education, 61*(1), 13–16.

Barton, K. (1997b). "Bossed around by the Queen": Elementary students' understanding of individuals and institutions in history. *Journal of Curriculum and Supervision, 12*(4), 290–314.

Barton, K. (2005). Primary sources in history: Breaking through the myths. *Phi Delta Kappan,* June, 745–753.

Barton, K., & Levstik, L. (1996). "Back when God was around and everything": The development of elementary children's understanding of historical time. *American Educational Research Journal, 33,* 419–454.

Bernard-Powers, J. (1996). Engendering social studies: Perspectives, texts, and teaching. *Theory and Research in Social Education, 24*(1), 2–7.

Bickmore, K. (1999). What passes for citizenship? Conflict and feminist challenges to the social studies. ERIC Document #438212.

Bickmore, K. (2004). Educating for peace-building citizenship. In A. Sears & I. Wright (Eds.), *Challenges and prospects for Canadian social studies* (pp. 150–163). Vancouver: Pacific Educational Press.

Bilson, G. (1981). *Goodbye Sarah.* Toronto: Kids Can Press.

Blades, A. (2001). *Mary of mile 18.* Montreal: Tundra Books.

Blair, T. (2003). *New teacher's performance-based guide to culturally diverse classrooms.* Boston: Allyn and Bacon.

Bloom B. S. (Ed.) (1956). *Taxonomy of educational objectives. Handbook I: The cognitive domain.* New York: David McKay.

Bloom, L., & Ochoa, A. (1996). Responding to gender equity in the social studies program. In B. Massialas & R. Allen (Eds.), *Critical issues in teaching social studies K–12,* Albany, NY: Wadsworth Publishing Company.

Bognar, C., Cassidy, E., & Clarke, P. (1997). *Social studies in British Columbia; Results of the 1996 provincial learning assessment.* Victoria, BC: Ministry of Education, Skills and Training.

Bouchard, D. (1997). *The elders are watching.* Vancouver BC: Raincoast Books.

Bouchard, D. (1999). *If you're not from the prairie.* Vancouver BC: Raincoast Books.

Bouchard, D. (2002). *The song within my heart.* Vancouver BC : Raincoast Books.

Bransford, J., Brown, A., & Cocking, R. (Eds.) (2000). *How people learn.* Washington, DC: National Academy Press.

Brett, J. (1994). *Town mouse, country mouse.* New York: Putnam.

Brooks, G., & Brooks, M. (1993). *In search of understanding: The case for constructivist classrooms.* Alexandria, VA: Association for Supervision and Curriculum Development.

Brooks. J., & Brooks, M. (1999). *In search of understanding: The case for constructivist classrooms.* Alexandria, VA: Association for Supervision and Curriculum Development.

Brophy, J., & Alleman, J. (2002). Primary-grade students' knowledge and thinking about the economics of meeting families' shelter needs. *American Educational Research Journal, 39*(2), 423–468.

Brooks. J., & Brooks, M. (1999). *In search of understanding: The case for constructivist classrooms.* Alexandria, VA: Association for Supervision and Curriculum Development.

Brown, J. (1996). *Flat Stanley.* New York: HarperTrophy.

Brownridge, W. (1995). *The moccasin goalie.* Victoria, BC: OrcaBook Publishers.

Bruner, J. (1960). *The process of education.* Cambridge: Harvard University Press.

Bruner, J. (1961). The act of discovery. *Harvard Educational Review, 31,* 21–32.

Bruner, J. (1965). *Man: A course of study.* Occasional Paper No. 3. ERIC Document #ED178390.

Bruner, J. (1966). *Toward a theory of instruction.* Cambridge, MA: Belknap.

Bruner, J. (1986). *Actual minds, possible worlds.* Cambridge, MA: Harvard University Press.

Butler, G. (1995). *The Killick: A Newfoundland story.* Plattsburgh, N.Y.: Tundra Books.

Caine, G., Caine, R., McClintic, C., & Klimek, K. (2004). *12 brain/mind principles in action.* Corwin Press.

Caine, R., Caine, G., McClintic, C., & Klimek, K. (2005). *12 brain/mind learning principles in action.* Thousand Oaks, CA: Corwin Press.

Caplan, G. (March 30, 1998). *Good schools, good citizens: A discussion.* Third National Forum on Education, St. John's, Newfoundland. Council of Ministers of Education, Canada. Available online at http://www.cmec.ca/nafored/ctf.en.stm.

Carbone. E. L. (1998). *Stealing freedom.* New York: Knopf.

Carrier, R. (1984). *The hockey sweater.* Montreal: Tundra Books.

Carrier, R. (2004). *The flying canoe.* Toronto: Livres Toundra.

Castle, C. (2000). *For every child: The UN Convention on the Rights of the Child in words and pictures.* London: Hutchinson.

Chan, G. (2004). *An ocean apart: The Gold Mountain diary of Chin Mei-Ling* Markham, ON: Scholastic Canada.

Chamberlin, C. (1992). What vision of democracy should guide citizenship education? *Canadian Social Studies, 27*(1), 30.

Chiodo, J., & Byford, J. (Spring 2004). Do they really dislike social studies? A study of middle school and high school students. *Journal of Social Studies Research.* Available online at http://www.findarticles.com/p/articles/mi_qa3823/is_200404/ai_n9406032.

Citizenship and Immigration Canada. (2005). *A look at Canada.* Available online at http://www.cic.gc.ca/english/pdf/pub/look.pdf

Clark, P., & Case, R. (1997). Four purposes of citizenship education. In R. Case & P. Clark (Eds.), *The Canadian anthology of social studies.* Burnaby, BC: Simon Fraser University.

Clements, A. (2002). *Delores and the big fire: A true story.* New York: Aladdin.

Coerr, E. (1981). *Sadako and the thousand paper cranes.* Sydney: Hodder & Stoughton.

Cooper, A. (2006). *The hanging of Angelique: The untold story of Canadian slavery and the burning of Old Montreal.* Toronto: HarperCollins.

Craighead George, J. (1972). *Julie of the wolves.* New York: Harper & Row.

Crocco, M. (1997). Making time for women's history . . . when your survey course is already filled to overflowing. *Social Education, 61*(1), 32–37.

Dabcovich, L. (1997). *The polar bear son: An Inuit tale.* New York: Clarion Books.

David, L. (2003). *Horace Splattly, the cupcaked crusader.* New York: Dutton Children's Books.

Davies, A. (2000). *Making classroom assessment work.* Courtney, BC: Building Connections Publishing Inc.

Davis, J. (Ed.). (1983). *Planning a social studies program.* Boulder, CO: Social Science Education Consortium.

Deir, E. (1997). The place of geography within social studies. In P. Wright & A. Sears (Eds.), *Trends and issues in Canadian social studies* (pp. 130–146). Vancouver: Pacific Educational Press.

Dewey, J. (1916). *Democracy and education: an introduction to the philosophy of education.* New York: Macmillan Company.

Dewey, J. (1933). *How we think.* Boston: D.C. Health & Co.

Diamond, M., &. Hopson, J. (1998). *Magic trees of the mind.* New York: Dutton Books, Penguin-Putnam Group.

Dodge, B. (August 20, 1996). Active learning on the Web (K–12 Version). A Presentation to the Faculty of La Jolla Country Day School, La Jolla, CA. Retrieved from http://edweb.sdsu.edu/people/bdodge/active/ActiveLearningk-12.html.

Downie, M. (1980). *A proper Acadian*. Toronto: Kids Can Press.

Downey, M. (1994, April). After the dinosaurs: Elementary children's chronological thinking. Paper presented at the annual meeting of the American Educational Research Association, New Orleans.

Edinger, M. (2001). Time travel with primary sources. *Instructor, 111,* 18–20.

Egan, K. (1986). *Teaching as story telling*. London, ON: The Althouse Press.

Egan, K. (2006). *Teaching literacy: Engaging the imagination of new readers and writers*. Thousand Oaks, CA: Corwin Press.

Egan, K. (1991). John Dewey and the social studies curriculum. *Theory and Research in Social Education, 8,* 37.

Egan, K. (1997). Story forms and romantic perspectives: Alternative frameworks for planning in social studies. In R. Case & P. Clark (Eds.), *The Canadian anthology of social studies* (pp. 309–318). Burnaby, BC: Simon Fraser University.

Egan, K. (2006). *Teaching literacy: Engaging the imagination of new readers and writers*. Thousand Oaks, CA: Corwin Press.

Ehlers, M. (1999), "No picture in my head": The uses of literature in the development of historical thinking. *OAH Magazine of History, 13*(2), 5–9.

Eisner, E. (1979). *The educational imagination*. New York: Macmillan.

Elwin, R. (1990). *Asha's mums*. Toronto: Women's Press.

Evans, M., & Reynolds, C. (2004). *Educating for global citizenship in a changing world*. Toronto: Ontario Institute for Studies in Education. Available online at http://cide.oise.utoronto.ca/globalcitizenship.php.

Florian, D. (1999). *Winter eyes*. New York: Greenwillow Books.

Freire, P. (1970). *Pedagogy of the oppressed*. New York: Seabury Press.

Fulwiler B., & McGuire, M. (1997). Storypath: Powerful social studies instruction in the primary grades. *Social Studies and the Young Learner, 9*(3), 4–7.

Gardner, H. (1983). *Frames of mind: The theory of multiple intelligences*. New York: Basic Books.

Gardner, H. (1999). *Intelligence reframed. Multiple intelligences for the 21st century*. New York: Basic Books.

Gardner, H. (2000). *Intelligence reframed. Multiple intelligences for the 21st century*. New York: Basic Books.

Gardner, J. (1980). *Stone fox*. New York: Harper Collins.

Gay, G. (2000). *Culturally responsive teaching: Theory, research and practice*. New York: Teachers College Press.

Girod, M., & Cavanaugh, S. (2001). Technology as an agent of change in teacher practice. *Technological Horizons in Education (T.H.E.) Journal, 28*(9). Available online at http://www.thejournal.com/magazine/vault/A3429B.cfm?kw=0&gw.

Glassford, L. (1992). Ten reasons for questioning the activist citizen model of elementary social studies, *Canadian Social Studies, 27*(1), 28–29.

Goodlad, J. (1984). *A place called school.* New York: McGraw-Hill.

Goto, H. (2002). *The water of possibility.* Regina: Coteau Books.

Gouvernement de Québec. (2001). Quebec Education Program: Preschool Education, Elementary Education. Available online at http://www.mels.gouv.qc.ca/DGFJ/dp/programme_de_formation/primaire/educprg2001h.htm.

Granatstein, J. (2000). *How we teach history matters most.* Available online at http://www.greatquestions.com/e/q6_granatstein_2.html.

Greenwood. B. (1998). *The last safe house: A story of the Underground Railroad.* Toronto: Kids Can Press.

Grossman, V. (1991). *Ten little rabbits.* San Francisco: Chronicle Books.

Groth, J., &. Albert, M. (1997). Arts alive in the development of historical thinking. *Social Education, 61*(1), 42–44.

Grumet, M. (1996). The curriculum: What are the basics and are we teaching them? In J. Kincheloe & S. Steinberg (Eds.) *Thirteen questions: Reframing education's conversations* (pp. 15–22). New York: Peter Lang.

Guild, P. (1994). The culture/learning style connection. *Educational Leadership, 51*(8), 16–21.

Guild, P. (1997). Where do the learning theories overlap? *Educational Leadership, 55*(1), 30–31.

Hamanaka, S. (1995). *Peace crane.* New York: Morrow Junior Books.

Hampton, M. (2001). *The cat from Kosovo.* Halifax: Nimbus.

Harrison, T. (1992). *O Canada,* Toronto: Kids Can Press.

Hartzler-Miller, C. (2001). Making sense of "best practice" in teaching history. *Theory and Research in Social Education, 29*(4), 672–695.

Haskins, J. (1993). *Get on board: The story of the Underground Railroad.* New York: Scholastic.

Healy, J. (1990). *Endangered minds: Why our children can't think.* New York: Simon and Schuster.

Heidbreder, R. (1996). *Eenie, meenie Manitoba: Playful poems and rollicking rhymes.* Toronto: Kids Can Press.

Hicks, D., Doolittle, P., & Lee, J. (2004). Social studies teachers' use of classroom-based and web-based historical primary sources. *Theory and Research in Social Education, 32,* 213–247.

Hirsch, E. (1987). *Cultural literacy: What every American needs to know.* Boston: Houghton Mifflin Company.

Hodgetts, A. B. (1968). *What culture? What heritage?* Toronto: Ontario Institute for Studies in Education.

Hootstein, E. (1995). Motivational strategies of middle school social studies teachers. *Social Education, 59*(1), 23–26.

Hoover, W. (1996). The practice implications of constructivism. *SEDL Newsletter, 9*(3). Available online at http://www.sedl.org/pubs/sedletter/v09n03/practice.html.

Hope, A. (1996). It's time to transform social studies teaching. *The Social Studies,* July/August, 149–151.

Hughes, A., & Sears, A. (1996). Macro and micro level aspects of a program of citizenship education research. *Canadian and International Education, 25*(2), 17–30.

Hurren, W. (2004). School geography and academic geography. In A. Sears & I. Wright (Eds.), *Challenges and Prospects for Canadian Social Studies* (pp. 118–125). Vancouver: Pacific Educational Press.

Hutchins, H. (1995). *Tess.* Toronto: Annick Press.

Ignatieff, M. (2000). *Does history matter?* Available at http://www.greatquestions.com/e/q6_ignatieff_2.html.

Jackson, L. (2005). Blogging: "It's elementary my dear Watson." Available online at http://www.educationworld.com/a_tech/tech/tech217.shtml.

Jackson, P. (1968). *Life in classrooms.* New York: Holt, Rinehart and Winston.

Janzen, R. (1995) The social studies conceptual dilemma: Six contemporary approaches. *The Social Studies,* May/June, 134–140.

Jensen, E. (1998). *Teaching with the brain in mind.* Alexandria, VA: Association for Supervision and Curriculum Development.

Jensen, E. (2000). *Brain-based learning.* San Diego: Brain Store Incorporated.

Johnson, A. (1983). *The value of facing a challenge: The story of Terry Fox.* La Jolla, CA: Value Communications.

Katz, L., & Chard, S. (2000). *Engaging children's minds: The project approach* (2nd ed). Stamford, CT: Ablex.

Kee, K. (2004). Towards a new world history and citizenship course in Quebec. *Canadian Social Studies, 38*(2). Available online at http://www.quasar.ualberta.ca/css.

Kielburger, C. (1998). *Free the children.* Toronto: McClelland & Stewart.

Khan, R. (1999). *Muslim child: A collection of short stories and poems.* Toronto: Napoleon.

Kogawa, J. (2005). *Naomi's road.* Markham, ON: Fitzhenry & Whiteside.

Krull, K. (2001). *Supermarket.* New York: Holiday House.

Kusugak, M. (1992). *Hide and sneak.* Toronto: Annick Press.

Kusugak, M. (2001). *My Arctic 1, 2, 3.* Willowdale: Annick Press.

Kymlicka, W. (1992). *Recent work in citizenship theory.* A report prepared for Multiculturalism and Citizenship Canada, Ottawa, Ontario.

Laird, E. (1991). *Kiss the dust.* New York: Penguin.

Layden, J. (1998). *Against the odds.* New York: Scholastic.

Lee, P. (1998). Making sense of historical accounts. *Canadian Social Studies, 32*(2), 52–54.

Lenhoff, R., & Huber, L. (2000). Young children make maps. *Young Children, 55*(5), 6–12.

Lento, E., O'Neill, K., & Gomez, L. (1998). Integrating Internet services into school communities. In C. Dede (Ed.) *Learning with technology* (pp. 141–169). Alexandra, VA: Association for Supervision and Curriculum Development.

Levine, D. (1998). *Remote control childhood? Combating the hazards of media culture.* Washington, DC: National Association for the Education of Young Children.

Levine, K. (2002). *Hana's suitcase: A true story.* Toronto: Second Story Press.

Levine, M. (2002). *A mind at a time.* New York: Simon & Schuster.

Levstik, L. (1996). NCSS and the teaching of history. In O. L. Davis Jr. (Ed.), *NCSS in retrospect,* Bulletin 92 (pp. 21–34). Washington, DC: National Council for the Social Studies.

Levstik, L., & Barton, K. (2001). *Doing history: Investigating with children in elementary and middle schools.* Mahwah, NJ: Lawrence Erlbaum Associates.

Levstik, L., & Barton, K. (2005). *Doing history: Investigating with children in elementary and middle schools.* Mahwah, NJ: Lawrence Erlbaum Associates.

London, J. (1995). *The sugaring off party.* New York: Dutton Children's Books.

Lowry, L. (1989). *Number the stars.* Boston: Houghton Mifflin.

Lowry, L. (1993). *The giver.* Boston: Houghton Mifflin.

Manitoba Education. (2003). *Kindergarten to Grade 8 social studies: Manitoba curriculum framework of outcomes.* Available online at http://www.edu.gov.mb.ca/ks4/cur/socstud/framework/k-8framework.pdf.

Manitoba Education, Citizenship, and Youth (2006). *Rethinking classroom assessment with purpose in mind, Kindergarten to Grade 12.* Available at http://www.edu.gov.mb.ca/k12/assess /wncp.

Martin, B. (1987). *Knots on a counting rope.* New York: Holt.

Matas, C. (2002). *Sparks fly upward.* New York: Clarion Books.

McBee, R. (1995). Can controversial issues be taught in the early grades? The answer is yes! *Social Education, 60*(1), 38–41.

McCall, A. (July 2006). Supporting exemplary social studies teaching in elementary schools. *The Social Studies.* Available online at http://www.accessmylibrary.com/coms2/summary_0286-24375275_ITM.

McCarty, T. (1995). What's wrong with "Ten Little Rabbits"? *New Advocate, 8*(2), 97–98.

McCully, E. (2006). *Marvelous Mattie: How Elizabeth E. Knight became an inventor.* New York: Farrar, Straus and Giroux.

McDermott, G. (1993). *Raven: A trickster's tale from the Pacific Northwest.* San Diego, CA: Harcourt.

McGugan, J. (1994). *Josepha: A prairie boy's story.* Red Deer, AB: Red Deer College Press.

McKay, R., & Gibson, S. (2004). *Social studies for the 21st century: A review of current literature and research.* Lewiston, NY: Edwin Mellen Press.

McKeown, M., & Beck, I. (1990). The assessment and characterization of young learners' knowledge of a topic in history. *American Educational Research Journal, 27,* 688–726.

Mercredi, M. (1997). *Fort Chipewyan homecoming: A journey to Native Canada.* Minneapolis, MN: Lerner Publications.

Mezirow, J. (1990). *Fostering critical reflection in adulthood.* San Francisco: Jossey-Bass.

Mezirow, J. (2000). *Learning as transformation: Critical perspectives on a theory in progress.* San Francisco, CA; Jossey-Bass.

Molebash, P. (2004). Web historical inquiry projects. *Social Education, 68*(3), 226–229.

Mowat, F. (1956). *Lost in the barrens.* Boston: Little, Brown.

Mowat, F. (1961). *Owls in the family.* Toronto: McClelland & Stewart.

Munsch, R. (1995). *From far away.* Toronto: Annick Press.

Murray, B. (2004). *Thomas and the Metis sash.* Winnipeg: Pemmican.

Nakagawa, M., & Ookda Pang, V. (1997). Cooperative pluralism: Moving from "me" to "we." In M. Haas & M. Laughlin (Eds.), *Meeting the standards* (pp. 115–117). Washington, DC: National Council for the Social Studies.

Neatby, H. (1953). *So little for the mind.* Toronto: Clarke, Irwin.

Nickle, J. (1999). *The ant bully.* New York: Scholastic.

Noddings, N. (1992). Social studies and feminism. *Theory and Research in Social Education, 20*(3), 230–241.

Novak, J., & Gowin, D. (1984). *Learning how to learn.* New York: Cambridge University Press.

O'Dell, S. (1960). *Island of the blue dolphins.* Boston: Houghton Mifflin.

Ogle, D. (1986). K-W-L group instructional strategy. In A. S. Palincsar, D. S. Ogle, B. F. Jones, & E. G. Carr (Eds.), *Teaching reading as thinking* (pp. 11–17). Alexandria, VA: Association for Supervision and Curriculum Development.

Olsen, S. (2004). *Catching spring.* Victoria, BC: Orca Book Publishers.

Ontario Ministry of Education. (2004). *Social studies curriculum: Grades 1 to 6.* Available at http://www.edu.gov.on.ca/eng/curriculum/elementary/sstudies18curr.pdf.

Ontario Ministry of Education. (2004a). *Literacy for learning: The report of the expert panel on literacy in Grades 4 to 6 in Ontario.* Available online at http://www.edu.gov.on.ca/eng/document/reports/literacy/panel/literacy.pdf.

Ontario Ministry of Education. (2004b). *The Ontario curriculum: Social studies Grades 1 to 6.* Available online at http://www.edu.gov.on.ca/eng/curriculum/elementary/sstudies18curr.pdf.

Osborne, K. (1997). Citizenship education and social studies. In I. Wright & A. Sears (Eds.), *Trends and issues in Canadian social studies* (pp. 39–67). Vancouver: Pacific Educational Press.

Pages, J. (2007). Newspaper activities support children's learning in many ways. Available online at http://kidbibs.com/learningtips/lt40.htm.

Pai, Y. (1990). *Cultural foundations of education.* New York: Merrill/Macmillan.

Palmer, J., Smith, B., & Grace, C. (1993). A developmental approach to teaching geography in the primary grades. *Journal of Geography, 92*(3), 125–128.

Patrick, J. (Nov. 2000). Political socialization of youth: Reconsideration of research on the civic development of elementary and secondary school students in the United States and abroad. Presentation at National Council for the Social Studies conference, San Antonio, TX.

Paulsen, G. (1987). *Hatchet.* New York: Bradbury Press.

Peace Child International. (2001). *Stand up, speak out: A book about children's rights written by young people around the world.* London: Two-Can.

Pearson, K. (2000). *The sky is falling.* New York: Morrow.

Perkyns, D. (2003). *Last days in Africville.* Vancouver, BC: Beach Holme Pub.

Poulin, S. (1987). *Can you catch Josephine?* Montreal: Livres Toundra.

Robb, L. (2003). *Teaching reading in social studies, science and math. Practical ways to weave comprehension strategies into your content area teaching.* Toronto: Scholastic.

Robert, N. (2002). *The swirling hijab.* London: Mantra.

Robinson, F. (1970). *SQ3R: Effective study* (4th ed). New York: Harper & Row.

Rodgers, C. (2002). Defining reflection: Another look at John Dewey and reflective thinking. *Teachers College Record, 104*(4), 842–866.

Sadler, R. (2003). *The kid's book of black Canadian history.* Toronto: Kids Can Press.

Schnur, S. (2002). *Winter: An alphabet acrostic.* New York: Clarion Books.

Schug, M., Todd, R., & Beery, R. (1984). Why kids don't like social studies. *Social Education,* May, 382–387.

Sears, A. (1996). What research tells us about citizenship education in English Canada. *Canadian Social Studies, 30*(3), 121–127.

Sears, A. (1996). Something different to everyone: Conceptions of citizenship and citizenship education. *Canadian and International Education, 25*(2), 1–16.

Sears, A. (2004). In search of good citizens: Citizenship education and social studies in Canada. In A. Sears & I. Wright (Eds.), *Challenges and prospects for Canadian social studies* (pp. 90–106). Vancouver: Pacific Educational Press.

Segall, A. (1999). Critical history: Implications for democratic citizenship. *Theory and Research in Social Education, 27*(3), 358–374.

Seixas, P. (1993). Historical understanding among adolescents in a multicultural setting. *Curriculum Inquiry, 23*(3), 301–327.

Seixas, P. (1999). Beyond content and pedagogy in search of a way to talk about history education. *Journal of Curriculum Studies, 31*(3), 317–337.

Seixas, P., & Peck, C. (2004). Teaching historical thinking. In. A. Sears & I. Wright (Eds.), *Challenges and prospects for Canadian social studies* (pp. 109–117). Vancouver: Pacific Educational Press.

Dr. Seuss (1971). *The Lorax.* New York: Random House.

Sherman, A. (1994). Democratic experiences for early-years students. In A. Sears & I. Wright (Eds.), *Challenges and prospects for Canadian social studies* (pp. 274–279). Vancouver: Pacific Educational Press.

Shulman, L. (1986). Those who understand: Knowledge growth in teaching. *Educational Researcher, 15*(2), 4–14.

Shulman, L. (1987). Knowledge and teaching: Foundations of the new reform. *Harvard Educational Review, 57,* 1–22.

Silver, H., R. Strong, & Perini, M. (1997). Integrating learning styles and multiple intelligences. *Educational Leadership, 55*(1), 22–27.

Silverstein, S. (1974). *Where the sidewalk ends.* New York: Harper Collins.

Silverstein, S. (1976). *The missing piece.* New York: Harper & Row.

Silverstein, S. (1981). *A light in the attic.* New York, NY: Harper & Row.

Silverstein, S. (1981). *The missing piece meets the big O.* New York: Harper & Row.

Singer, D., & Revenson, T. (1996). *A Piaget primer: How a child thinks*, revised edition. New York: Penguin Books.

Skeel, D. (1996). An issues-centred elementary curriculum. In R. Evans & D. Saxe (Eds.), *Handbook on Teaching Social Issues*, Bulletin 93 (pp. 230–236). Washington, DC: National Council for the Social Studies.

Smith, D. (2002). *If the world were a village: A book about the world's people.* Toronto: Kids Can Press.

Smits, H. (1997). Citizenship education in postmodern times—Posing some questions for reflection. *Canadian Social Studies, 31*(3), 126–130.

Smucker, B. (1978). *Underground to Canada.* Toronto: Puffin Books.

Soley, M. (1995). If it's controversial, why teach it? *Social Education, 60*(1), 9–14.

Sowden, S., Stea, D., Blades, M. Spencer, C., & Blaut, J. (1996). Mapping abilities of four-year-old children in York, England. *Journal of Geography, 95*(3), 107–111.

Spears, E. (1983). *Sign of the beaver.* Boston: Houghton Mifflin.

Spier, P. (1980). *People.* Garden City, NY: Doubleday Books.

Strong-Boag, V. (1998). No longer dull: The feminist renewal of Canadian history. *Canadian Social Studies, 32*(2), 55–57.

Sylwester, R. (2003). *A biological brain in a cultural classroom: Enhancing cognitive and social development through collaborative classroom management.* Thousand Oaks, CA: Corwin Press Incorporated.

Takashima, S. (1971). *A child in prison camp.* Montreal: Tundra Books.

Tanner, J. (1987). *Niki's walk.* Philadelphia, PA: Philadelphia Book Co.

Thornton, S. (2004). *Teaching social studies that matters: Curriculum for active learning.* New York: Teachers College Press.

Thornton, S. (2005). *Teaching social studies that matters.* New York: Teachers College Press.

Trottier, M. (1998). *Prairie willow.* Toronto: Stoddart Kids.

Valentine, J. (1994). *One dad, two dads, brown dad, blue dads.* Los Angeles, CA: Alyson Wonderland.

VanAllsburg, C. (1990) *Just a dream.* Boston: Houghton Mifflin.

Van Draanen, W. (2004). *Shredderman: Secret identity.* New York: Knopf.

Varma-Joshi, M. (2004). Understanding multiculturalism in the social studies classroom. In A. Sears & I. Wright (Eds.), *Challenges and prospects for Canadian social studies* (pp. 150–163). Vancouver: Pacific Educational Press.

Vinson, K. (1998). The "traditions" revisited: Instructional approach and high school social studies teachers. *Theory and Research in Social Education, 26*(1), 50–82.

Vos, I. (1995). *Anna is still here.* New York: Puffin.

Vygotsky, L. (1978). *Mind in society.* Cambridge, MA: Harvard University Press.

Vygotsky, L. (1986). *Thought and language: Revised edition.* Cambridge: Massachusetts Institute of Technology.

Wallace, I. (1975). *The sandwich.* Toronto Kids Can Press.

Walsh, A. (1994). *Shabash!* Victoria, BC : Beach Holme.

Walters, E. (2003). *Run.* Toronto: Viking Canada.

Waterton, B. (1980). *Pettranella.* Vancouver, BC : Douglas & McIntyre.

Werner, W. (1993). Considering new guidelines for multicultural curricula. *Canadian Social Studies, 27*(4), 154–155.

Whiteside, K. (2000). Building geography skills and community understanding with constructivist teaching methods. ERIC Document #ED442733.

Wiegand, P., & Stiell, B. (1996). Children's estimations of the sizes of the continents. *Educational Studies, 22*(1), 57–68.

Wiggins, G. (1989). The futility of trying to teach everything of importance. *Educational Leadership,* November, 44–59.

Wineburg, S. (2001). *Historical thinking and other unnatural acts: Charting the future of teaching the past.* Philadelphia: Temple University Press.

Wolfe, P. (2001). *Brain matters: Translating research into classroom practice.* Alexandria, VA: Association for Supervision and Curriculum Development.

Wright, I. (1997). Getting involved in the landscape: Making geography come alive. In R. Case and P. Clark (Eds.), *The Canadian anthology of social studies,* 41–49. Burnaby, BC: Simon Fraser University.

Yee, P. (1996). *Ghost train.* Vancouver, BC: Douglas & McIntyre.

Zhao, Y., & Hoge, J. (September 2005). What elementary students and teachers say about social studies. *The Social Studies.* Available online at http://www.accessmylibrary.com/coms2/summary_0286-12092886_ITM.

CREDITS

This page constitutes an extension of the copyright page. We have made every effort to trace the ownership of all copyrighted material and to secure permission from copyright holders. In the event of any question arising as to the use of any material, we will be pleased to make the necessary corrections in future printings. Thanks are due to the following authors, publishers, and agents for permission to use the material indicated.

Chapter 1. 5: © NorthGeorgiaMedia/Shutterstock, Inc. **6:** © Jaimie Duplass/Shutterstock, Inc. **12:** © Leah-Anne Thompson/Shutterstock, Inc.

Chapter 2. 24: © iStockphoto.com/Thomas Gordon **30:** © Nadejda Ivanova/Shutterstock, Inc. **33:** Courtesy of Inspiration Software, Inc. **35:** © Ariel Skelley/Digital Railroad

Chapter 3. 41: © 2008 JupiterImages and its Licensors. All Rights Reserved. **42:** © iStockphoto .com/Ronnie Comeau **44:** © Mark Aplet/Shutterstock, Inc.

Chapter 4. 63: © iStockphoto.com/Bonnie Jacobs **65:** © Michael Chamberlin/Shutterstock, Inc. **73:** © iStockphoto.com/Bonnie Jacobs

Chapter 5. 82: © Netea Mircea Valentin/Shutterstock, Inc. **103:** © Patrick J. Endres/Alaska PhotoGraphics **107:** © iStockphoto.com/Yvonne Chamberlain

Chapter 6. 114: © iStockphoto.com/Leigh Schindler **115:** © 2008 JupiterImages and its Licensors. All Rights Reserved. **123:** © Jay Dickman/CORBIS

Chapter 7. 139: left, © Collins Bartholomew **139:** right, © Collins Bartholomew **141:** © Photo Create/Shutterstock, Inc. **150:** © 2008 JupiterImages and its Licensors. All Rights Reserved. **154:** left, Library & Archives Canada/C-085854 **154:** middle, Library & Archives Canada/C-126302 **154:** right, Library & Archives Canada/C-095320 **155:** © 2008 JupiterImages and its Licensors. All Rights Reserved.

Chapter 8. 158: © NorthGeorgiaMedia/Shutterstock, Inc. **161:** © iStockphoto.com/Eileen Hart **167:** © ZoomTeam/Shutterstock, Inc. **171:** "Cold" from WINTER: An Alphabet Acrostic by Steven Schnur. Text copyright © 2002 by Steven Schnur. Reprinted by permission of Clarion Books, an imprint of Houghton Mifflin Company. All rights reserved.

Chapter 9. 174: © 2008 JupiterImages and its Licensors. All Rights Reserved. **183:** © North GeorgiaMedia/Shutterstock, Inc. **188:** Courtesy of Riverdeep Inc., A Limited Liability Company. **189:** top, Courtesy of Riverdeep Inc., A Limited Liability Company. **189:** bottom, Explore Canada/ Explorer le Canada is a production of TVLT New Media Language Training Inc. Production information is available at http:www.newlanguage.ca. The CD-ROM has been licensed by the Ontario Ministry of Education for use in provincial schools. **190:** © Terrie L. Zeller/Shutterstock, Inc.

INDEX

Resource selection *(contd.)*
    student needs as influence on, 142–146
    teachers and students as resources, 156
    textbooks, 149–151
    See also Children's literature; Electronic resources
Respect, as resource selection criteria, 149
Reynolds, Cecilia, 74
Riel, Louis, 140
Right-answer tests, 268–269
Riverdeep Inc./The Learning Company, 188
Robert, Na'ima Bint, 166
Rodgers, Carol, 12
Role play, 233, 290
Rosie's Walk (Hutchins), 109
Rubrics, 271–272, 272f, 303f
Run (Walters), 163

S
Sadako and the Thousand Paper Cranes (Coerr), 171
Sadler, Rosemary, 162
Safety, internet, 182, 249, 254
The Sandwich (Wallace), 165
Saskatchewan, 47
Scaffolding, 25, 29
Schnur, Steven, 170
Schug, Mark, 6
Scope, of content, 128–129
"Scrooge for Mayor" WebQuest, 241
Search engines, 184–185
Searching, internet, 178–180, 184–185
Sears, Alan, 6
Selected-response testing, 268–269
Self-assessment, 274–275
Senses
    classroom activity for engaging, 120
    learning style and, 142, 143f
Sequence, of content, 129
Service learning, 65–66
Seuss, Dr., 171
Shabash! (Walsh), 163
Shared direction classrooms, 201–206

Shared direction inquiry, 220–222
Shephard, Lorie, 279
Shredderman (Van Draanen), 166
Shulman, Lee, 117
Sign of the Beaver (Spears), 166
Silverstein, Shel, 164, 171
SimCity (software), 188
Simulation-based software, 187–191, 245
Simulation (drama), 234–235
Sir Wilfrid Laurier School Board, 241–242
Skills, 82, 83
Skinner, B. F., 24
The Sky is Falling (Pearson), 165
Slavery, 161–162
Smith, David J., 167, 190
Smucker, Barbara, 161
Social action, 65
Social constructivism
    learning theory based on, 28–39
    principles of, 30–37, 30f, 212–213
Social context, learning influenced by, 35
Social Education (journal), 307
Social sciences
    Active Engagement, 111
    citizenship education and, 60–61
    in social studies content, 91, 102–111
    as social studies in Quebec, 45–47
Social studies
    citizenship education and, 49–77
    curricular definitions of, 45–49
    goals for, 17–18t, 305–306f, 307
    social sciences and, 91
    student attitudes about, 5–7, 24, 28, 40–41, 114, 218
    teacher attitudes about, 41–42
    teacher candidate attitudes about, 43–45
Social Studies and the Young Learner (journal), 307
Social studies councils, 307
Sociology, 111
Software. *See* Computer software
So Little for the Mind (Neatby), 58

The Song within My Heart (Bouchard), 166
Sparks Fly Upward (Matas), 163
Spears, Elizabeth George, 166
Spier, Peter, 167
Spiral approach to content sequence, 130
Spreadsheet programs, 192
SQ3R reading strategy, 159
"Square of Life Project," 251
Standardized tests, 269
Stand Up, Speak Out (Peace Child International), 158
Statistics Canada, 177–178, 250
Stealing Freedom (Carbone), 161
Stereotypes, 149, 166–167
Sternberg, Robert, 267
Stevenson, Robert Louis, 299
Stone Fox (Taylor), 247
Story, learning activities based on, 235–236
Storyline strategy, 236
Structured inquiry approach, 240
Structure-of-the-disciplines movement, 59
Student conferencing, 276
Student-directed classrooms, 206–210
Student-directed inquiry, 223
Students
    attitudes of, about social studies, 5–7, 24, 28, 40–41, 114, 218
    goal setting for, 19
    internet research by, 177–187
    as reflective learners, 12–13, 36–37, 207–208
    as resources, 156
The Sugaring Off Party (London), 165
Summative assessment, 266
Supermarket (Krull), 158
"Support Your Musher" WebQuest, 247
The Swirling Hijab (Robert), 166

T
Tableau, 233
Takashima, Shizuye, 162
Tanner, Jane, 161
Taylor, John Reynolds, 247
Teacher candidates' attitudes about social studies, 43–45